AF572169

PAINTING WATER IN WATERCOLOUR

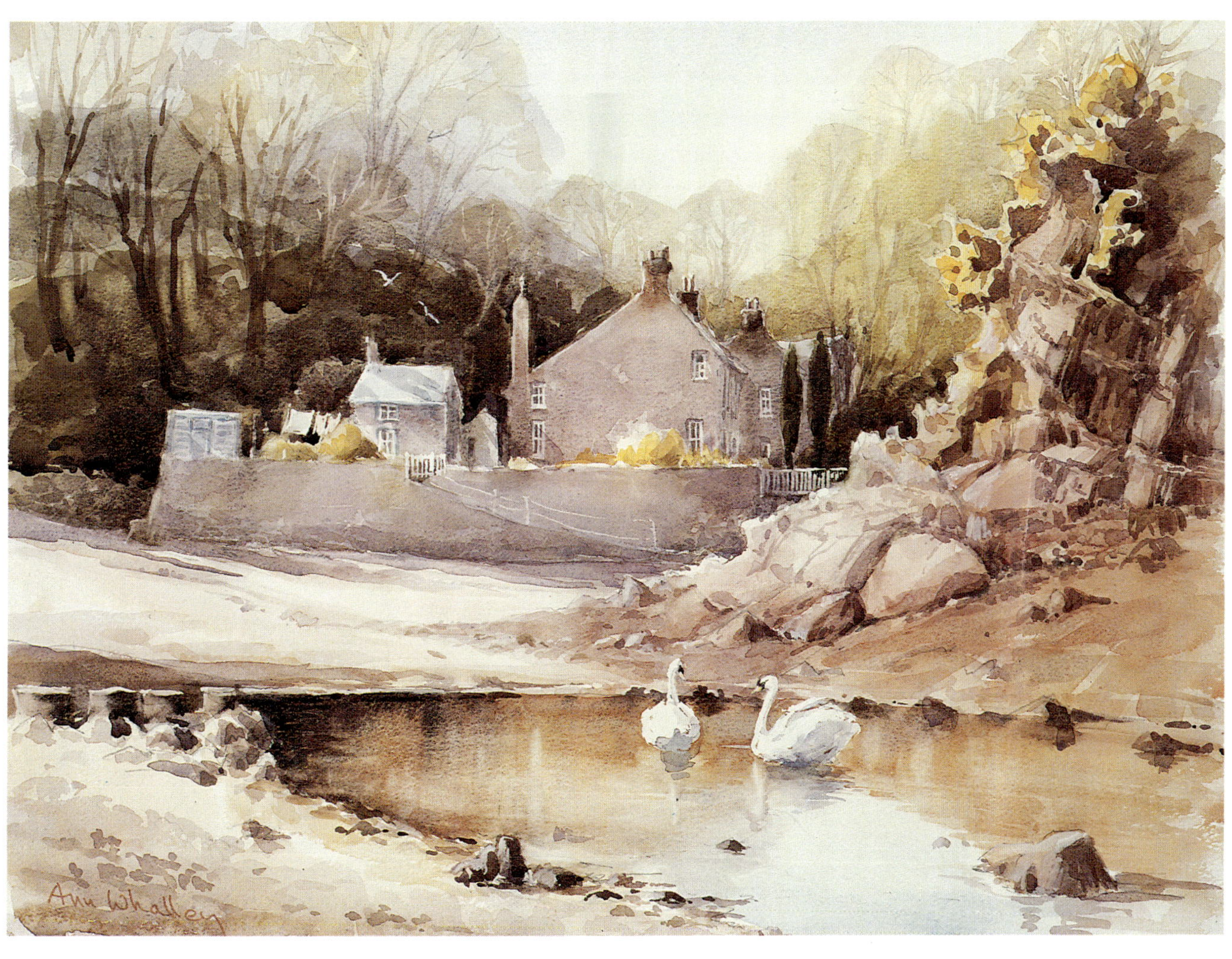

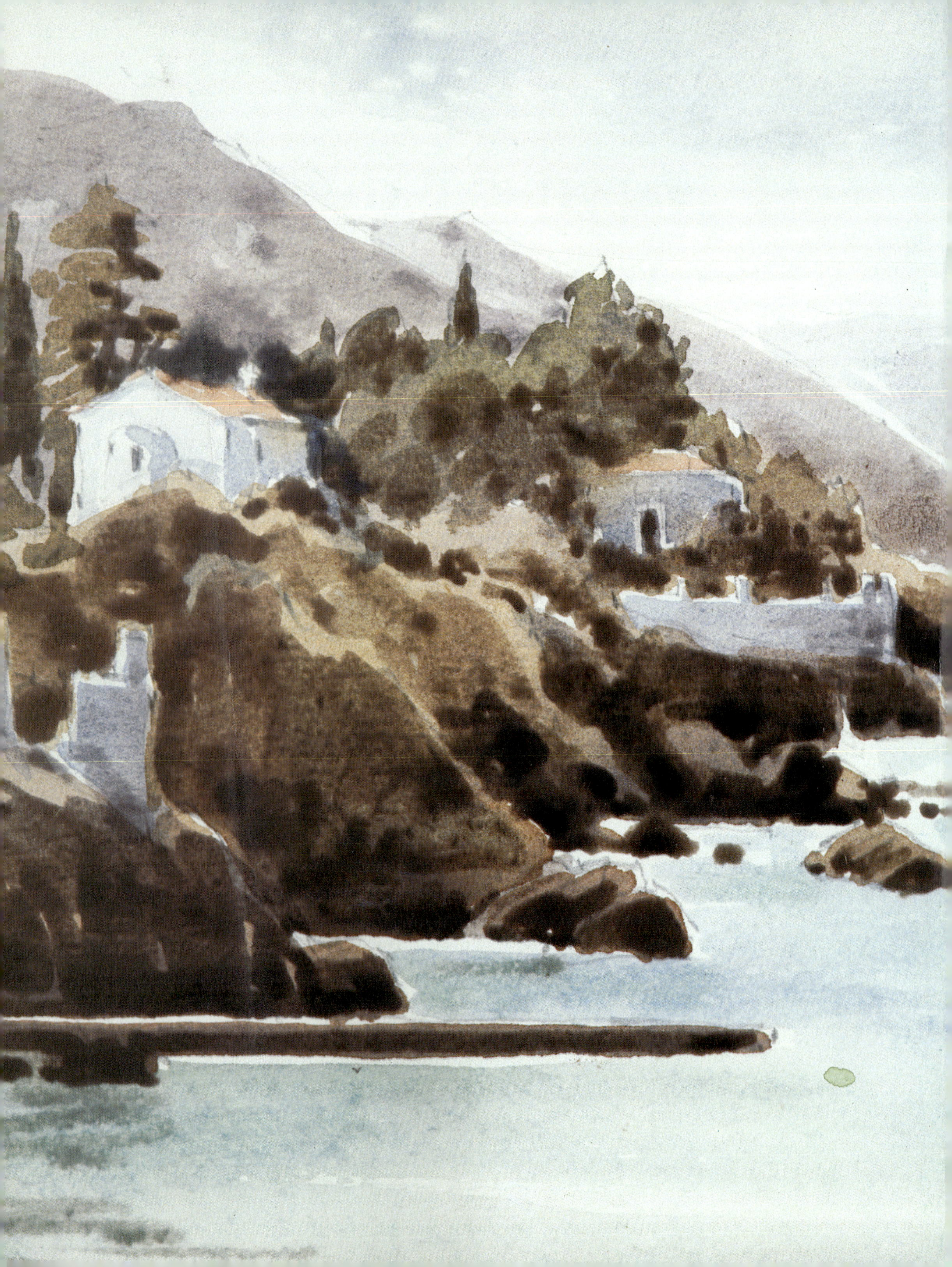

PAINTING WATER IN WATERCOLOUR

Ann Whalley

B.T. Batsford Ltd, London

Ann Whalley

First published 1993

Typeset by Keyspools Limited, Golborne, Lancashire and printed in Hong Kong

Published by B.T. Batsford Ltd
4 Fitzhardinge Street
London W1H 0AH

A catalogue record for this book is available from the British Library.

ISBN 0 7134 6969 2

I dedicate this book to Theo, my husband and greatest friend, for gallantly resisting the urge to interfere for the whole year it took to write this book, and then for his generous, expert and totally necessary help with its presentation; not to mention his constant support, understanding and love for this very prickly painter.

(Page 1) **Sandy Haven.**

(Pages 2–3) **Daybreak, Hydra.**

(Below) **North Yorkshire Coast.**

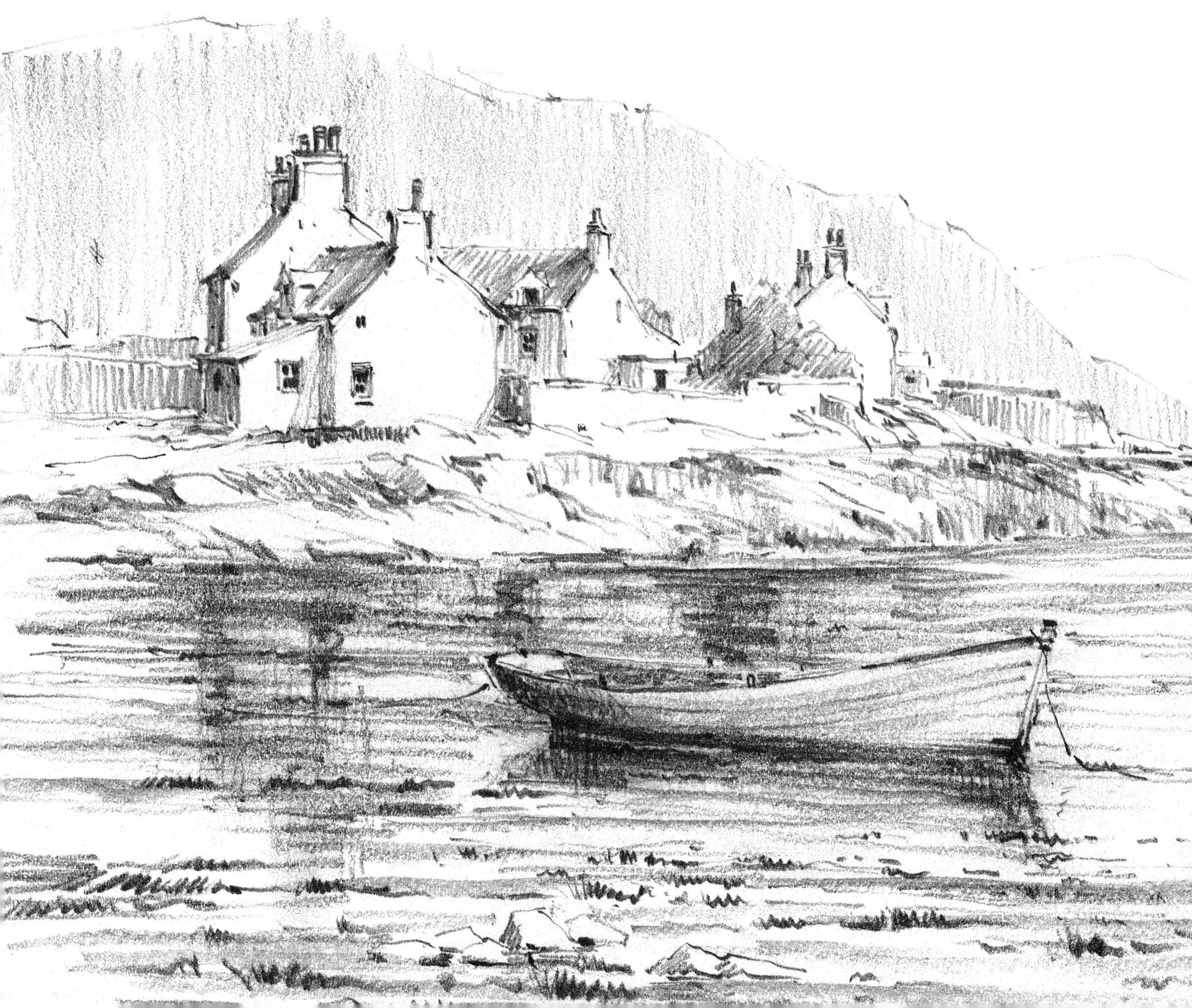

CONTENTS

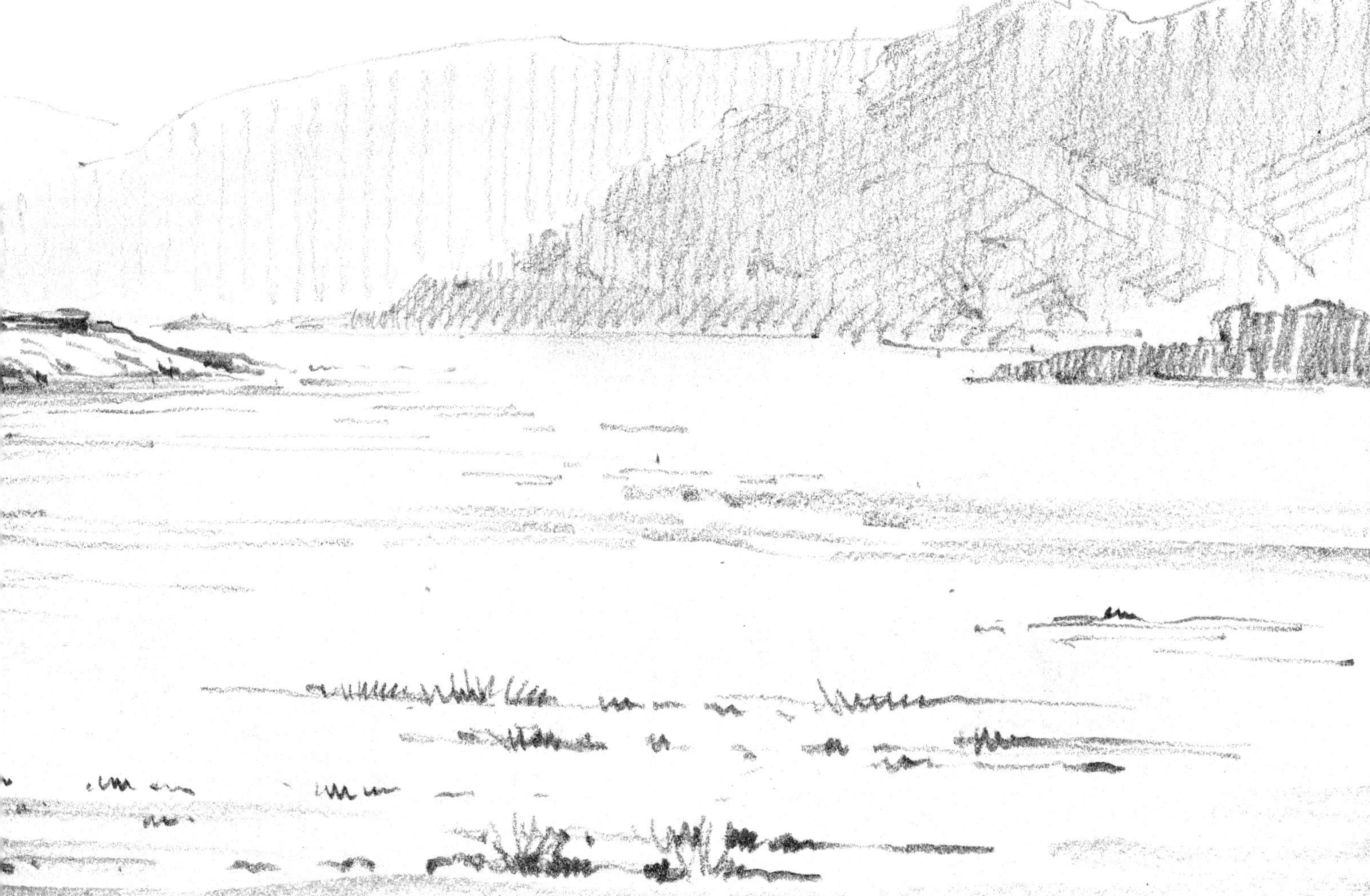

PREFACE

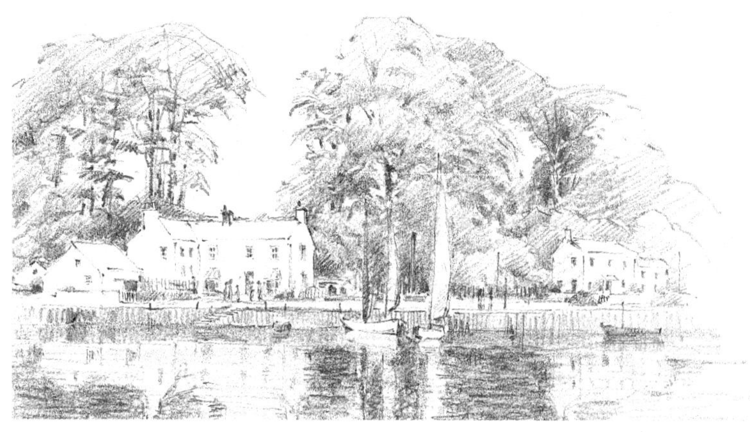

When I was invited to write a book on how to paint water, I have to confess that my immediate reaction was one of panic. Like most artists, I tend to think visually; words are not my natural means of expression or communication. And what on earth could I write on the subject that hadn't been said before by people far better qualified than I? Trained as a sculptor, and for eighteen years a working potter, what did I know?

I began my life as a painter about ten years ago, when rheumatism forced me to give up working as a potter. Having had no formal training, I suppose my initial approach was somewhat unorthodox. My efforts to record what I saw around me and to say something of what I felt were rarely crowned by success – and much of my painting was truly awful. I knew, however, that the problems I was experiencing were no different from those encountered by all painters; and I came to understand that it is the solutions which are important, turning the problems into a positive learning process.

A training in sculpture concentrates on an essential skill: the ability to draw, and above all, to draw the human form. Hours spent in the life room are of incalculable value in developing all the disciplines any artist must have, whatever his means of expression: analysis, selection, logic, accuracy and interpretation.

There is no fudging a life drawing – any indecision or muddled thinking is immediately detected. I was taught that it didn't matter how many or how few marks I made on the paper, as long as every mark was in the right place and conveyed information. This search for honesty still motivates all my work, and makes each new painting a voyage of discovery.

Most professional artists are fairly ruthless characters with a single fixation – their work – with almost everyone and everything else coming a rather poor second. If you are to master even the most basic problems of painting in watercolour you will need total dedication: blood, sweat and tears, no less!

Painting can, on rare occasions, bring moments of almost unimaginable joy, but anyone who has tried will know that it also has a dark side, full of frustration and grief. Every success demands that you strive for even higher goals; every failure that you pick up the pieces, take a deep breath and start all over again.

If you truly care about your work, it is unthinkable that you could settle for anything less than

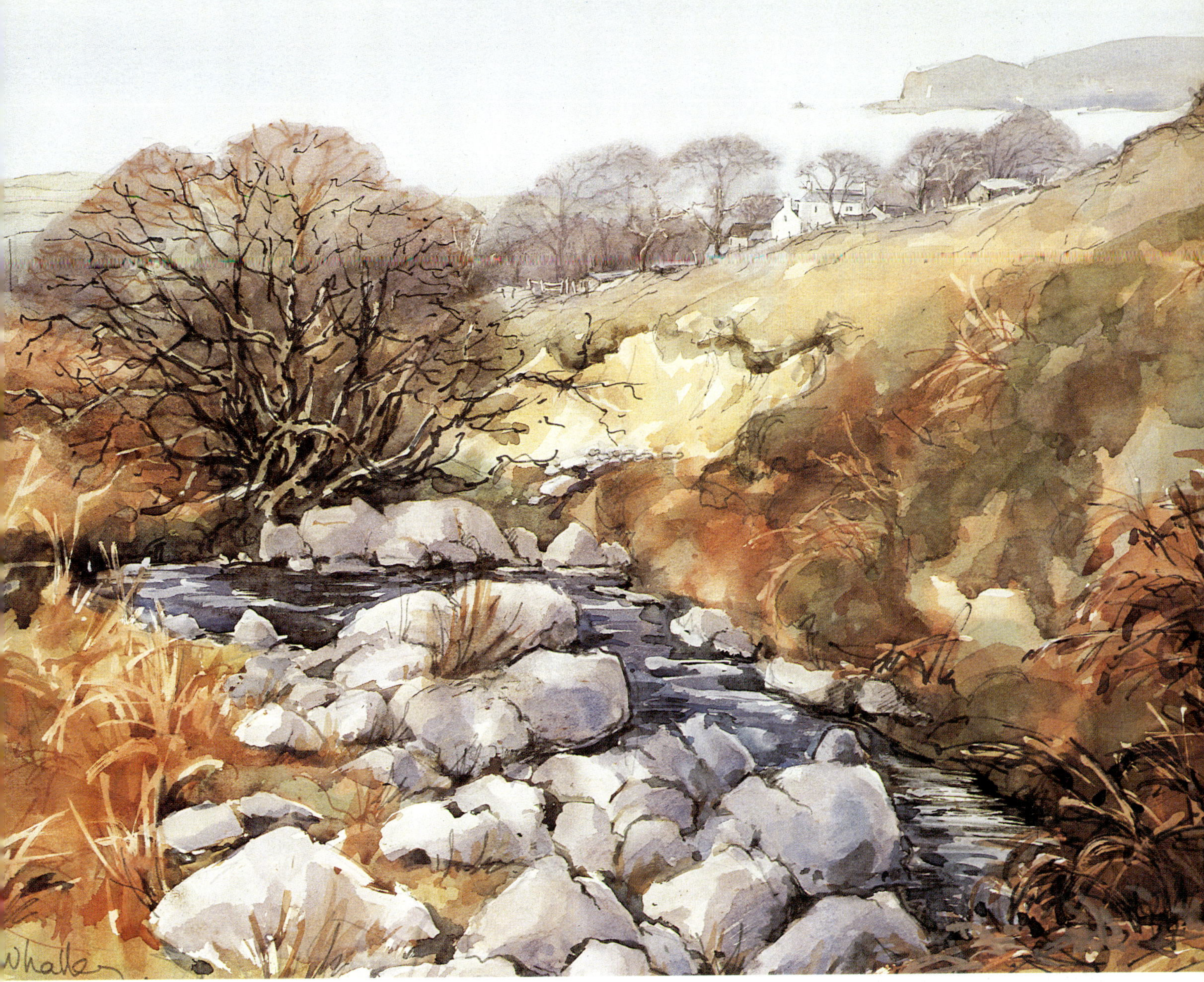

your best. Aim low and that is just where you will stay; aim for the stars and it is astounding what you may achieve.

The ideas and suggestions in the following pages arise from my own learning experience. Some of these may suit you and relate immediately to your thinking, others may not; but even so, be encouraged to apply as many as you can to your own work. It frequently happens that a new method or way of looking at things will act as a spur to set you free from some of the tired old concepts to which we are all guilty of clinging from time to time.

I am sometimes asked what makes a good artist. There is no easy answer to that question, but I think it has a lot to do with attitude of mind. In-born talent can only be as great as what one makes of it, and is so often thrown away and wasted. We all have some talent, but not everyone has the grit and determination to battle on and extend it to the full.

And the great painting – how does that come about? It certainly isn't the subject matter, or even

Above Newport Bay. *This is a winter painting with snow melt bubbling down between the boulders. Notice how the dead bracken and grasses lend colour.*

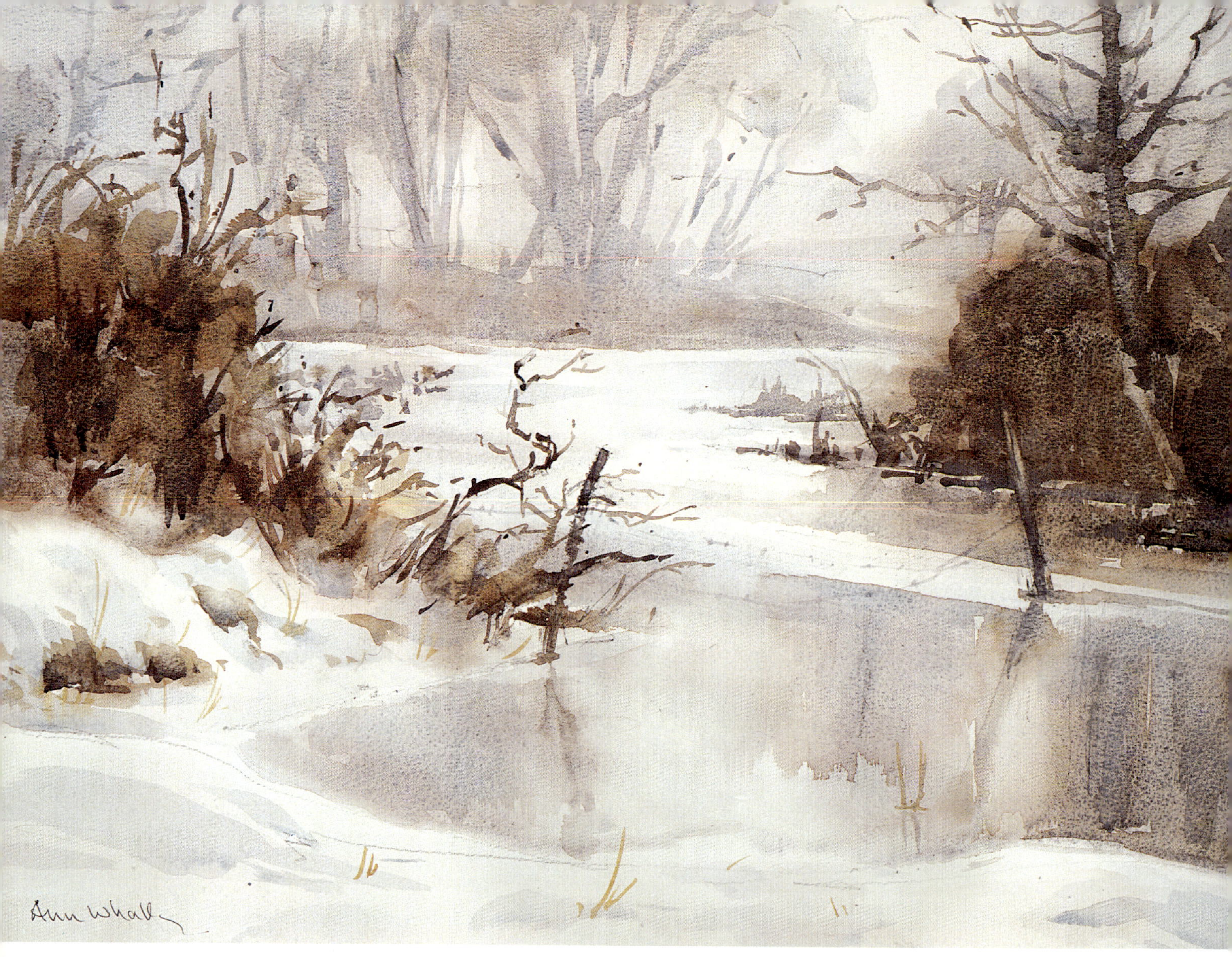

the artist's technical skill (valuable though this may be) that brings it into being. I think it stems from a personal awareness of life, a spark of visionary insight which can transform the ordinary into the extraordinary and convey it to others. This must be what our work as artists is all about, and, with this aim, each and every one of us is capable of imparting something of unique importance.

Ann Whalley

In the grip of winter. *The close tonal range and muted colours accentuate the feeling of relentless cold.*

INTRODUCTION

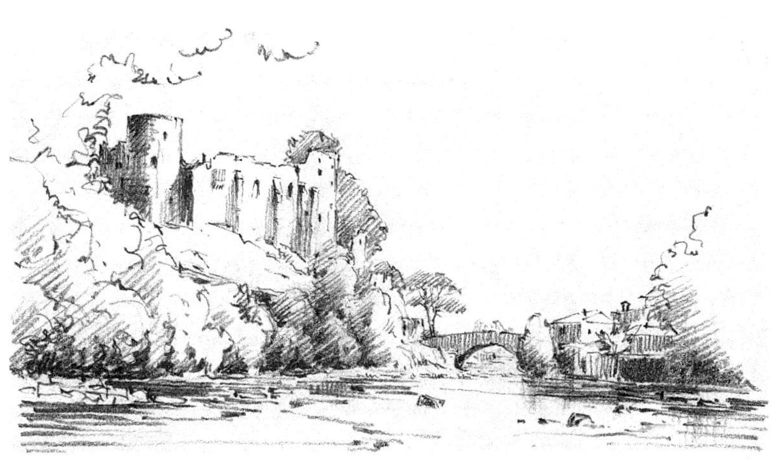

Water, the essential element, covers more than three-quarters of the earth's surface, and without it, life would not exist. For those who, like me, live near both a large river and the sea, it cannot fail to be a dominating influence. Sometimes gentle and benign, and at others powerfully destructive, I am always aware of its presence.

Few of my paintings are without a watery theme, and my quests for subject matter seem always to lead towards sea or river like a magnet. I find endless fascination in all its moods and the way it responds to every vagary of light – the very stuff of magic and illusion. How could anyone not be enchanted by this elusive beauty and excitement?

While accepting the strong emotional involvement which close proximity to water evokes, emotion alone will not produce good paintings. To paint water well, it is necessary to have an understanding of the way it behaves, and why. There are certain natural laws which govern the way it moves, how it responds to light and its ability to reflect, which must be recognized and understood. Only then will water start to *look* like water, and not like newly laid concrete or a corrugated-iron roof.

These complex matters will be dealt with in detail in subsequent chapters. For the moment, it is enough to say that the endless diversity of water demands of the artist an ability to observe with intense accuracy and analytical understanding, and, having so observed, to select and simplify in order to convey an impression with skill and fluency.

Water is of itself an inert substance, colourless and transparent. It receives movement from the wind, from the passage of objects across its surface, or from the slope of the land, and it draws colour from everything around it. It can only respond to external forces, and it is gravity which causes it always to find its own level.

Any aspiring painter of water must be made of stern stuff, and be prepared to endure physical discomfort in the pursuit of his or her subject. Direct observation being the only way forward, one can find oneself in some fairly inaccessible places from time to time. There have been occasions when I have felt that there must be easier ways to follow my calling than by clinging to a cliff in a force-ten gale while struggling with a soggy and rapidly disintegrating scrap of paper; or even sweltering on a foreign shore as the sweat drips off my nose and my glasses steam up! Of course, painting is not always like this,

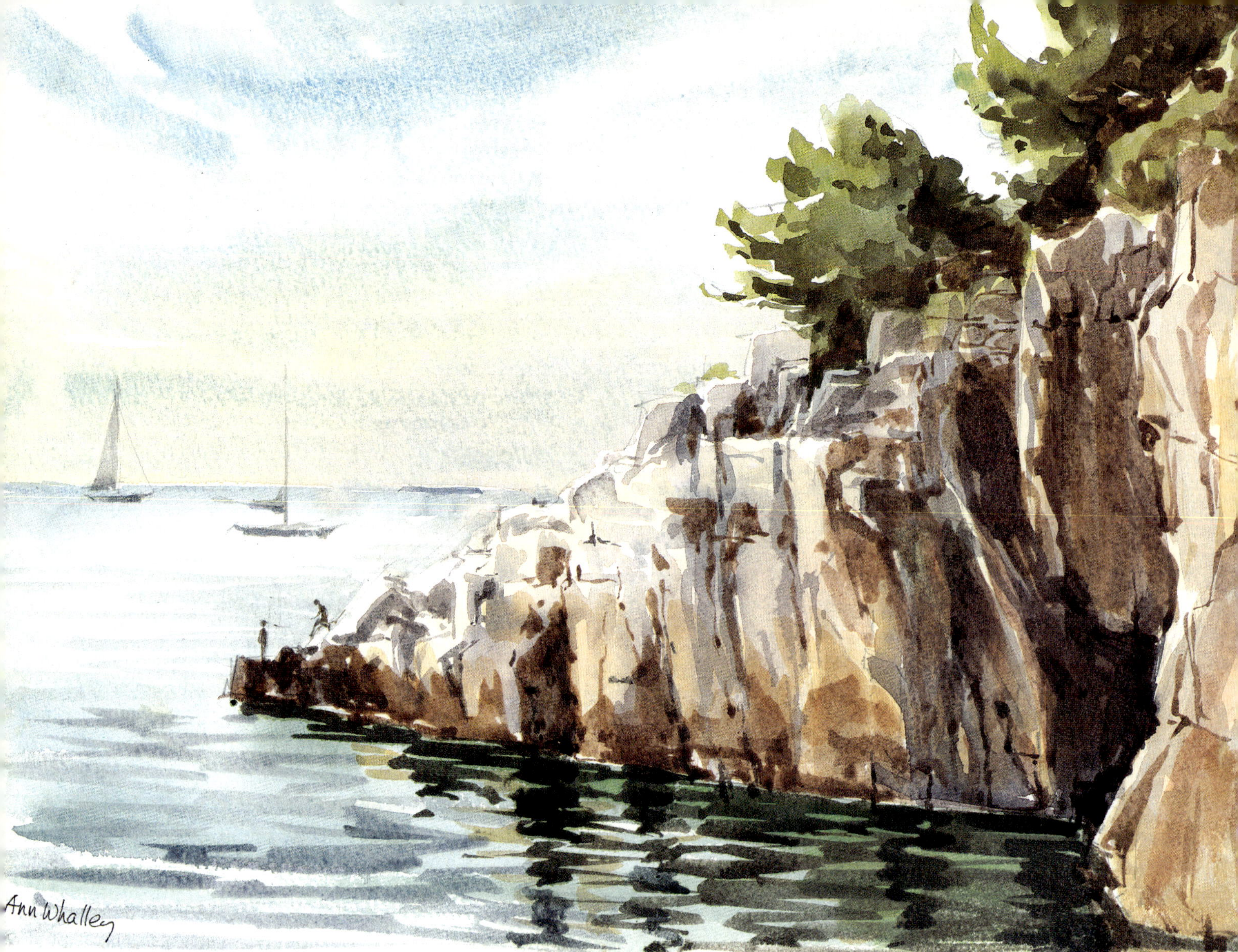

and on a fine summer day there can be few greater pleasures than to sit by a sparkling stream with the sun on your back and a prospect of exquisite loveliness inviting your attention.

The study of water cannot be isolated from the study of the whole world. It involves skies, cliffs, shores, mountains and meadows, buildings and boats, and every place where water flows, falls or collects. The part played by weather conditions, light, the time of day and the march of the seasons must be observed, as must all the rich evidence of life at the water's edge, whether human, plant or animal. It is, in fact, a study of all life, for without water, life cannot exist.

It may appear perverse that I should have chosen watercolour, arguably the most difficult and demanding medium there is, in which to paint. I think I started in happy ignorance of what I was letting myself in for, and then – being a pretty stubborn character – refused to give up. I love the sensuous way in which the colours move and flow into each other, and delight in exerting control at precisely the right moment. Transparent water-colour swirled on to white paper has a wonderful luminosity and freshness, and, when it works, has no equal. No other medium can give the same subtle delicacy or richness and depth, yet still retain the essential quality of spontaneity.

My paintings obviously do not succeed every time, and I throw away far more than I keep. No-one ever said that watercolour was easy, but for me that is part of its

Rovinj coastline.

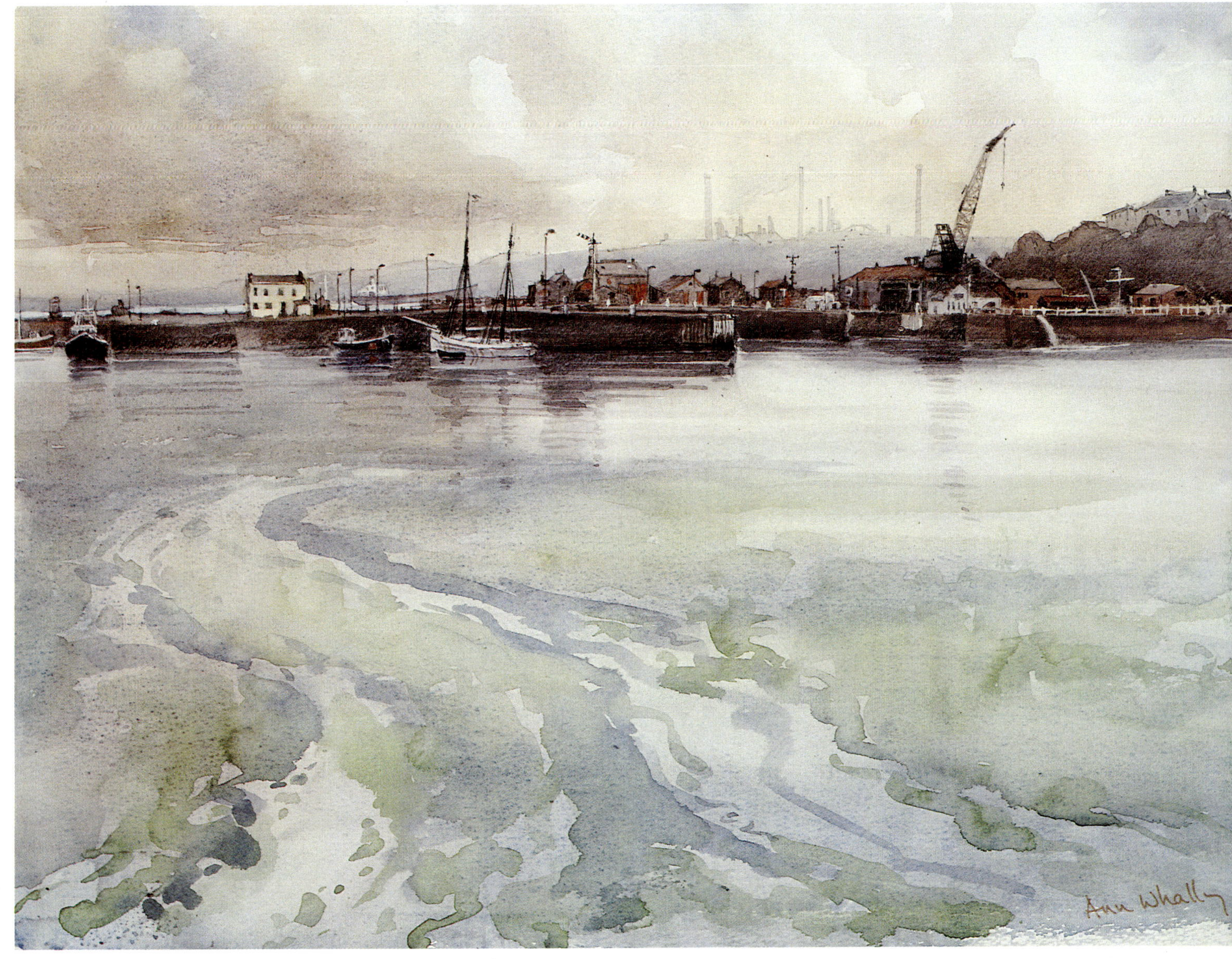

fascination and makes success all the sweeter. The speed and fluidity of working needed with watercolour come only with practice and confidence, and any uncertainty or corrections will be mercilessly revealed.

The single most important factor in producing a good watercolour is planning. That magical and seemingly effortless work that you so admire is undoubtedly the result of long hours of information-gathering, technical experiment, design work, colour and atmospheric observation, many practice runs and innumerable failures – I speak from experience! The dedicated watercolourist is a resilient and determined being not easily discouraged. Whatever today brings in the way of triumphs or disasters, the only thing that really matters is the *next* painting, and the undying conviction that it *will* be better than the last.

Milford Docks.

CHAPTER ONE

MATERIALS AND EQUIPMENT

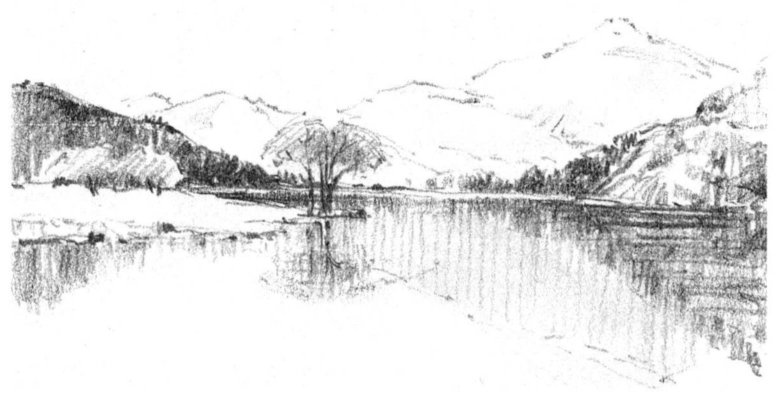

This chapter is intended to throw light upon some of the practical aspects which you will need to consider in order to make pictures.

Much has been written by people with greater formal training than I on the subject of artists' materials. My small nuggets of wisdom and advice were born in ignorance and developed through bitter experience and low cunning. The result is a personal collection of paints, inks, brushes and papers which works for me, and which I pass on with the caution that they may not all work for you. The paints and papers you use will have a profound influence on the character and quality of the finished work, and choice is always a very subjective process.

One thing is certain, and that is that watercolour demands the best: the best pigments, the best brushes and the best papers. Settling for anything less not only makes the job a great deal more difficult, but also seriously jeopardizes the chance of success. I watch despairingly as students scrub desperately at rock-hard cakes of inferior paint (ruining, incidentally, a perfectly good brush), knowing that however hard they scrub, the colours will always be dull, opaque and chalky.

PIGMENTS

Student's-grade paints, under whatever euphemism they come, are cheaper than artist's-grade paints for a very good reason: they contain less pigment, less glycerine and lots of chalk filler. Always choose the very best artist's-grade pigments, even if this means that you can afford fewer colours. This is probably no bad thing, anyway, and it is only by doing this that you will achieve the rich and transparent effects for which you are looking.

Most practising artists develop a range of colours which suits their own expressive needs. Over the past ten years I have experimented with everything that has come my way, often with very bizarre results.

There are certain colours which I use all the time – though not all in the same painting, I hasten to add – colours which I know will give me the particular effects I want. Although I would rarely use more than four different pigments in any one painting, I need a good number of possibilities to cope with the demands made by wide-ranging subjects and moods.

Blues

I do much of my painting either in far-west Wales or on the shores of the Mediterranean, and for this

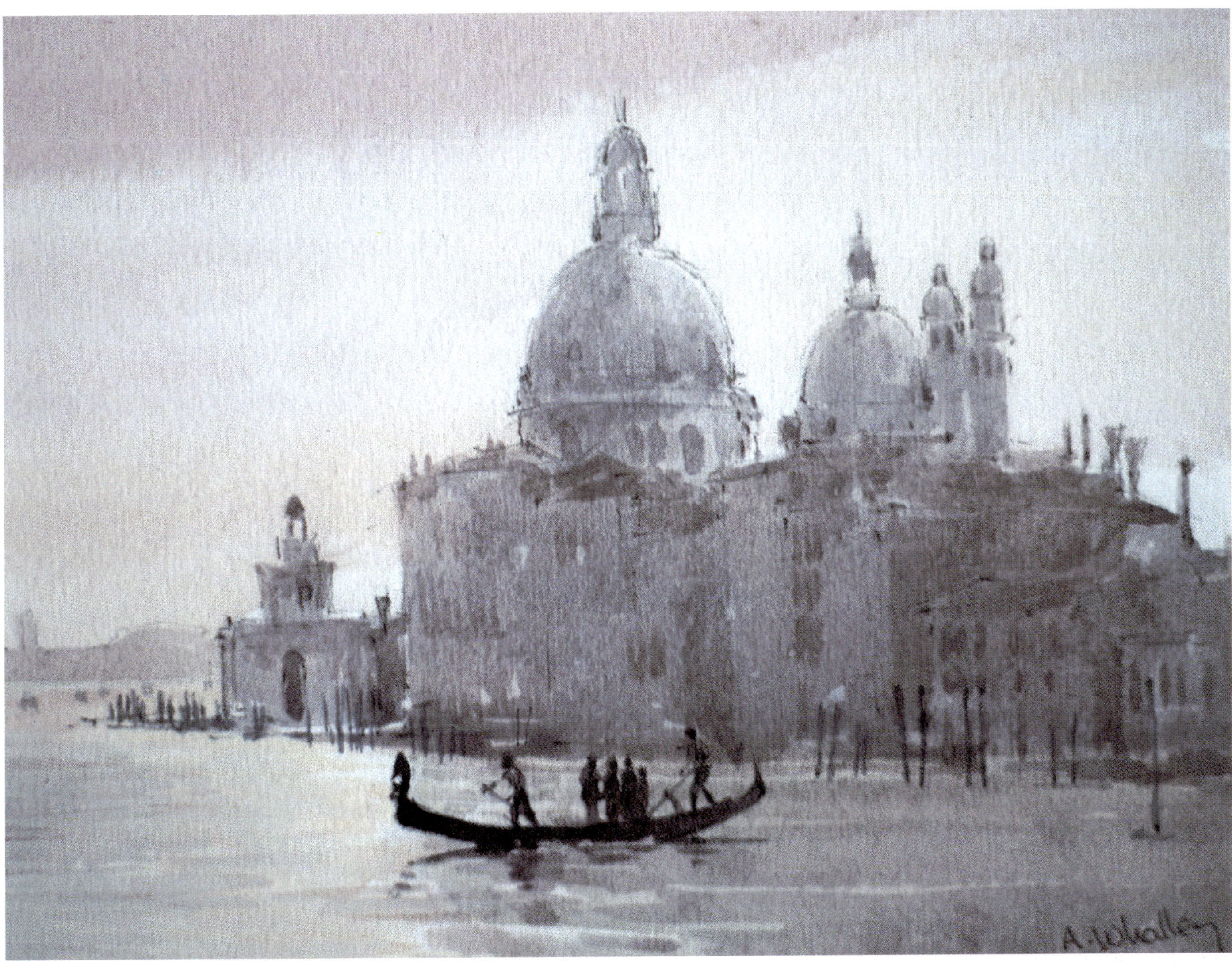

Santa Maria della Salute. *Venice in the early morning is spellbinding.*

reason I like to have a wide range of blues. Some of these tend towards the reds (such as ultramarine) and make lovely, pure lavenders and mauves; some edge towards green (such as Winsor and Prussian blue) and lend themselves to subtle foliage hues when mixed with earth colours.

Cobalt is perhaps the nearest we can get to a pure blue in pigment; and cerulean, while having a tendency to become opaque, gives exciting milky, smoky browns. Never under-estimate the value of indigo, especially in the creation of deep, luminous darks, or for toning down an over-bright blue sky without having to resort to the deadening effect of black.

Do please forget all about Payne's gray: it is not a pigment, but merely black mixed with ultramarine, and can be relied upon to create completely lifeless shadows.

Reds

Of the reds, I find both alizarin and cadmium useful. Good in themselves, they give startlingly different colours when mixed. Alizarin is a blue-red, very transparent and a lovely mixer.

Cadmium, a metallic oxide, is more of an orange-red. If used fairly dry it tends to be opaque and rather heavy, but it is a good pigment in small doses. When mixed with blues it produces an interesting brown-lavender, but is at its best with yellows and greens for autumn foliage.

Light red is more of a terracotta colour and works well with blues for tackling clouds. Rose madder and permanent rose have a wonderful transparency and seductive quality that I find hard to resist.

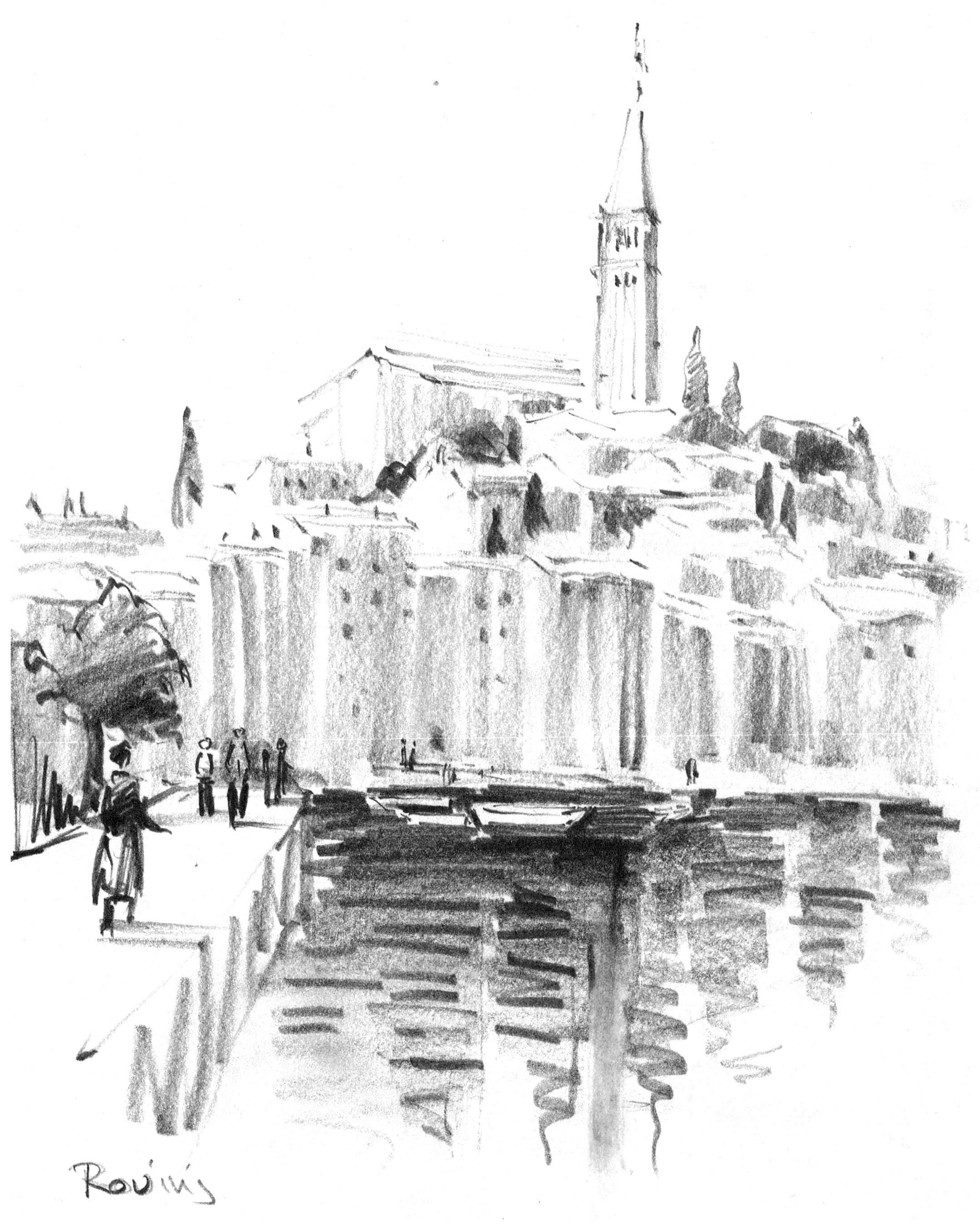
Rovinj

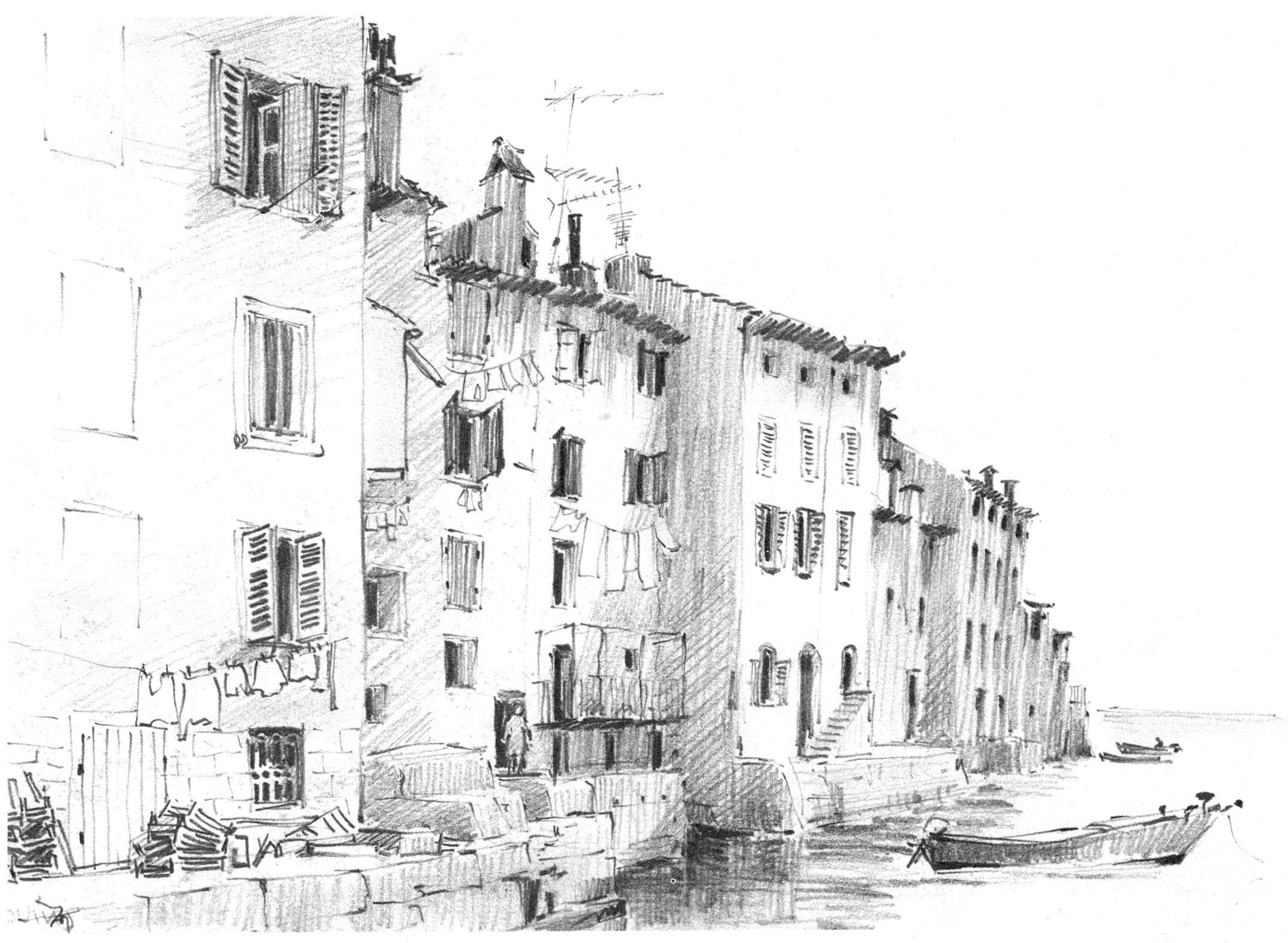

Rovinj waterfront.

Yellows

I use aureolin and gamboge yellows as they are pure, strong colours and retain their transparency well, and lemon yellow for cool, fresh touches. I find cadmium yellow a little crude and opaque.

Greens

There exists a school of thought which forbids the use of green pigments. I agree that the subtlest suggestion of green is best mixed from primary colours, but there are times when vibrant sap green or Hooker's green mixed with the siennas is the only way to achieve richness and depth, as well as transparency.

I believe that rules are merely guidelines and should frequently be broken, in watercolour as in many other aspects of life. It is very dangerous, as well as inhibiting, to work only by the 'rules', and I feel strongly that the end justifies the means. In other words, if it works, do it.

Earth colours

Naturally, you cannot do without all the earth colours (with the exception of yellow ochre, which I find opaque and insipid – raw sienna does the job far better).

Burnt sienna finds its way into most of my paintings, and is a natural enricher.

Raw umber is a quiet, greeny brown, while burnt umber is a hot, dark brown. All these earth colours mix well with other pigments.

Rovinj.

Narrowing this list down to the bare essentials, I would recommend:

- **cobalt**
- **ultramarine**
- **alizarin or rose madder**
- **aureolin**
- **lemon**
- **raw sienna**
- **burnt sienna**
- **burnt umber**

With these few colours you will find that you can obtain a huge variety of colours, tints and hues. A good exercise is to take each pigment in your box and mix it one at a time with every other pigment you have, noting how you obtained each colour. You will have quite a few surprises, and find that you have built up a whole new repertoire of colours in the process.

All the colours listed above have an invaluable asset in that they granulate readily – even on smooth paper – and therefore bring an important textural aspect to your washes. For this reason I would recommend that you curb your impatience and resist the use of a hairdryer to speed the drying process, as the granulation will fade away as you watch.

As you come to experiment with colour more freely, you may find a few more pigments which I have not mentioned and which

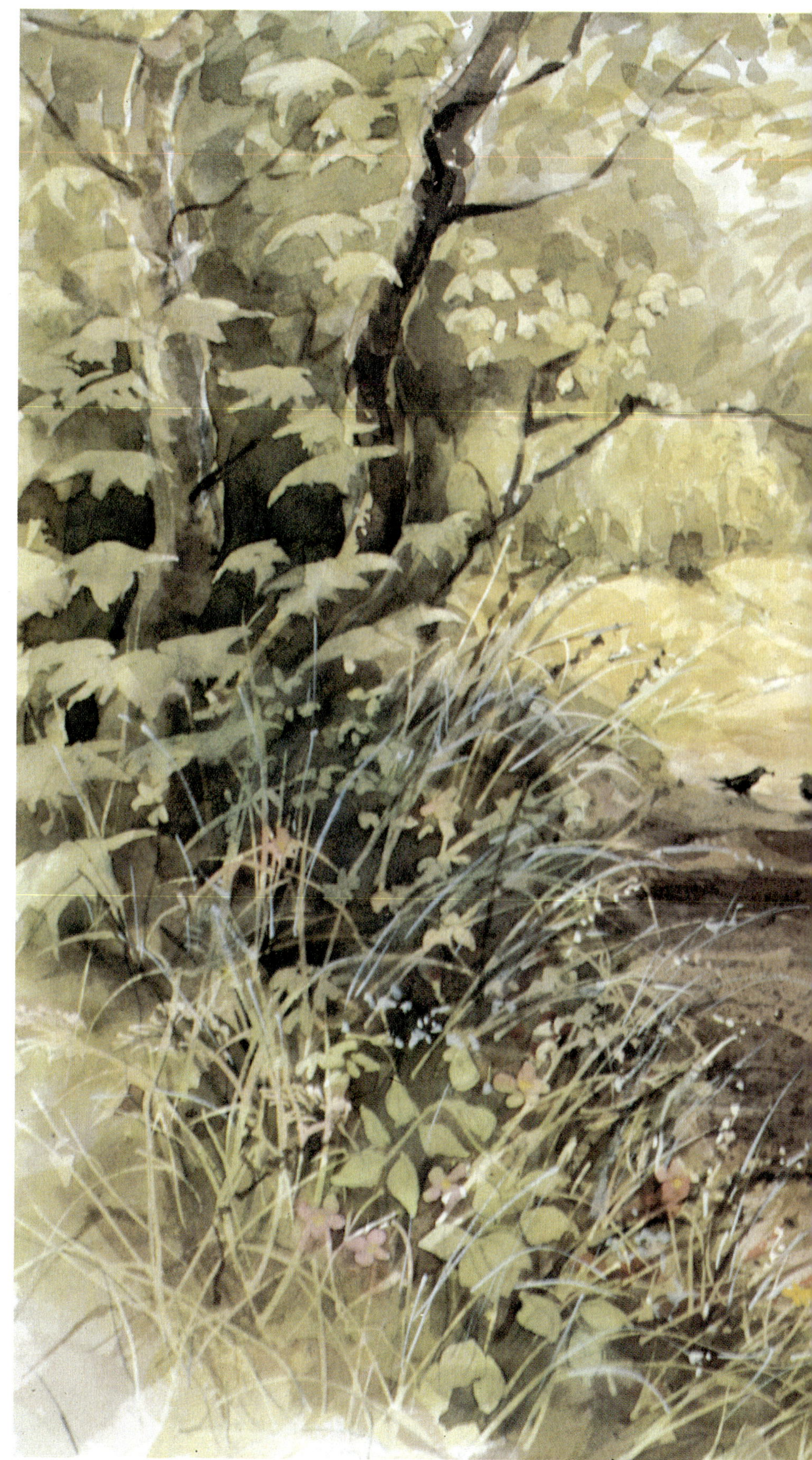

Leafy lane. *This is a scene typical of the sheltered valleys in the Gwane Valley near Fishguard. I love this sort of 'sun-and-shadow' subject, and here I had the added bonus of puddles from a recent shower, as well as a cheeky pair of crows. Farmers in Pembrokeshire frequently paint their gates a cheerful red.*

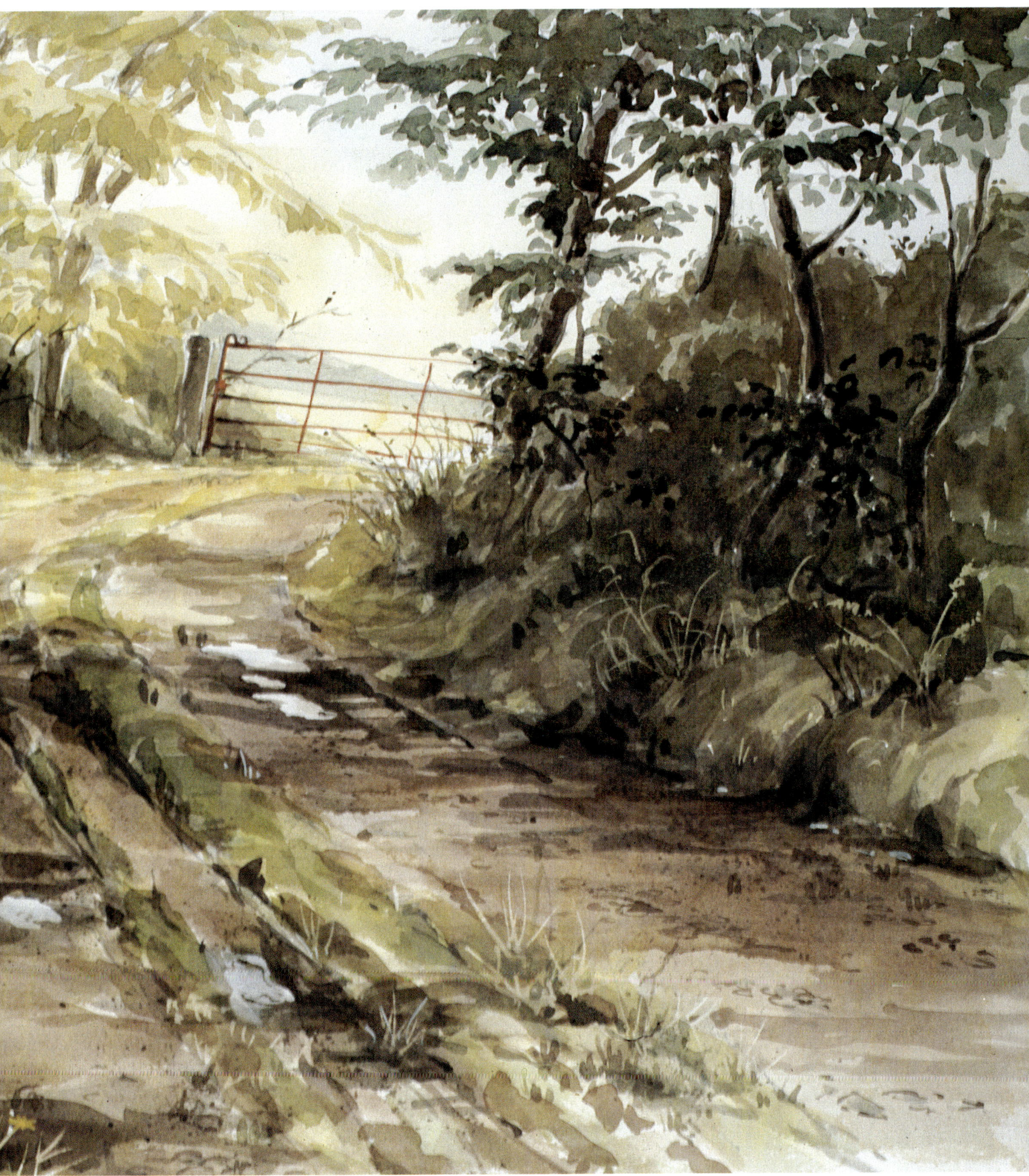

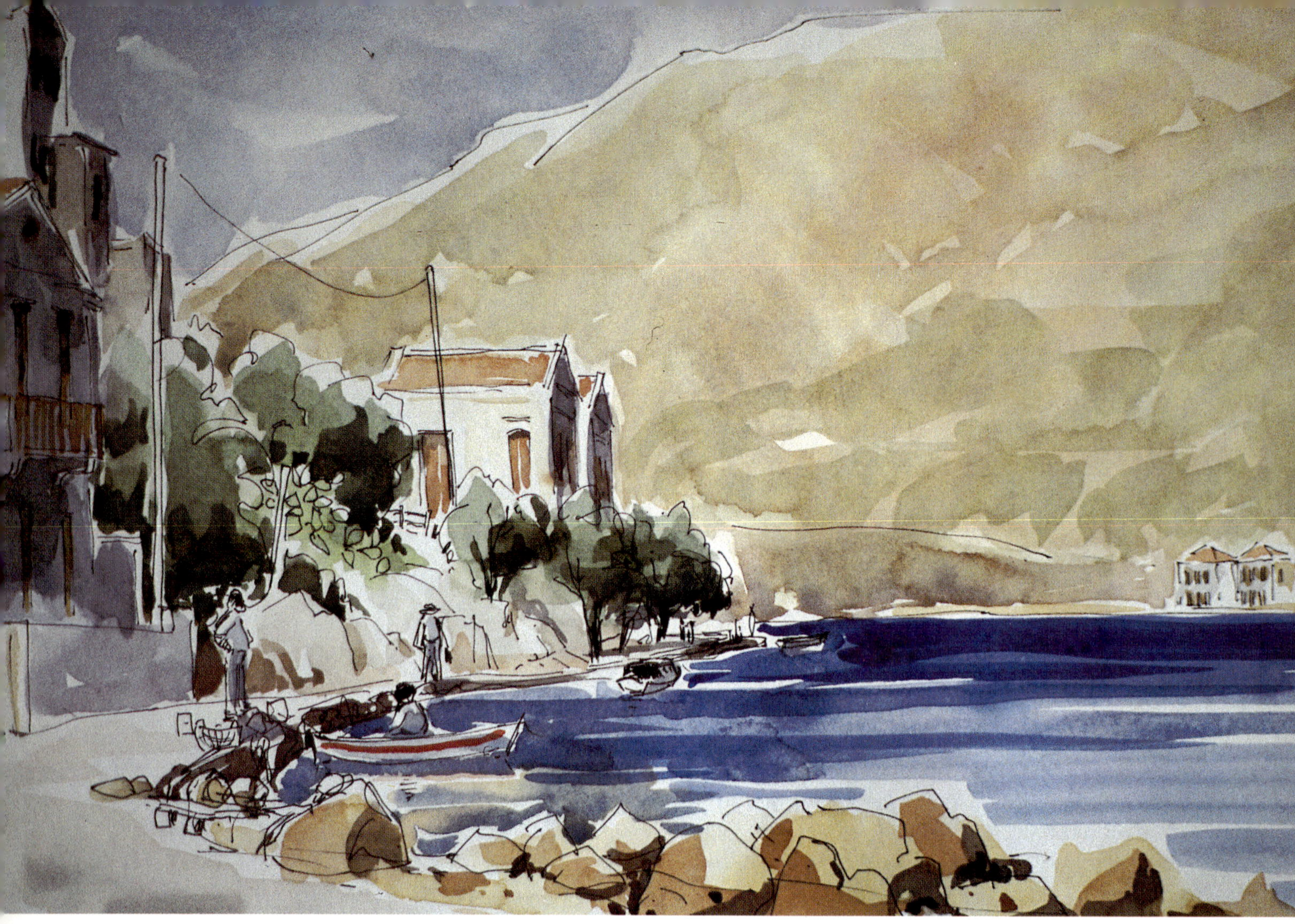

particularly suit your work. A tube of opaque designer's white (not watercolour white, as that is transparent) has saved many a painter's life, and may also be mixed with your normal watercolour paints to re-define 'lost' areas gently.

I am often asked which is the best form in which to buy paints: the tubes-versus-pans controversy. As far as I am concerned there is no contest – tubes win every time, although not for the reason you might expect.

Small tubes are, for me as for many artists, complete anathema. Miniscule pinheads of colour dotted around a small plate do not encourage gay abandon in the initial stage of a wash. I like to be able to dive into my colours at will and in extravagant amounts, and to have enough liquid to sweep my washes across the paper with the largest brush I have. Scrabbling about at the bottom of a bag in desperate search for 'the' tube of colour while watching paint dry is not a lot of fun, and rarely gives the best results.

My solution is a simple plastic ice-cube tray fitted into a wooden box with a tight-fitting lid. I buy large, economical tubes of good artist's pigment in my own choice of colours, and fill each individual compartment with these. The compartments are generous enough to take a 24 brush. Good-quality paints do not dry up quickly, and, should they begin to harden, a soaking in glycerine and water will soon solve the problem.

Symi waterfront. *Look at the wonderful deep blue of the sea, and at how warm and glowing the near boulders and distant headland look in comparison. This is a very simple subject made exciting by the Mediterranean contrasts.*

PAPER

Choosing a suitable surface on which to paint can be a bewildering process. There are so many different makes, types and weights available that most people give up and stick with the easiest option. This is a pity. So much can be gained by trying a new surface that it is well worth making a small effort to try out a few unfamiliar ones.

The type of paper you use must be your individual choice, but, as with your pigments, good quality is important, and an inferior grade will only lead to disappointment.

You can, of course, paint on almost anything, but it is better to use a paper which has been specially prepared for the watercolour artist. The texture of the paper (or 'tooth', as it is termed) is what responds to the brush and creates the unique watercolour effect.

Hand- and machine-made papers

Watercolour papers can be divided into two main types: hand-made and machine-made. A hand-made paper is easily recognizable by its deckle edge and the randomness of its texture. It may also have slight variation in thickness. Machine-made papers have cut edges, and the texture and thickness are uniform.

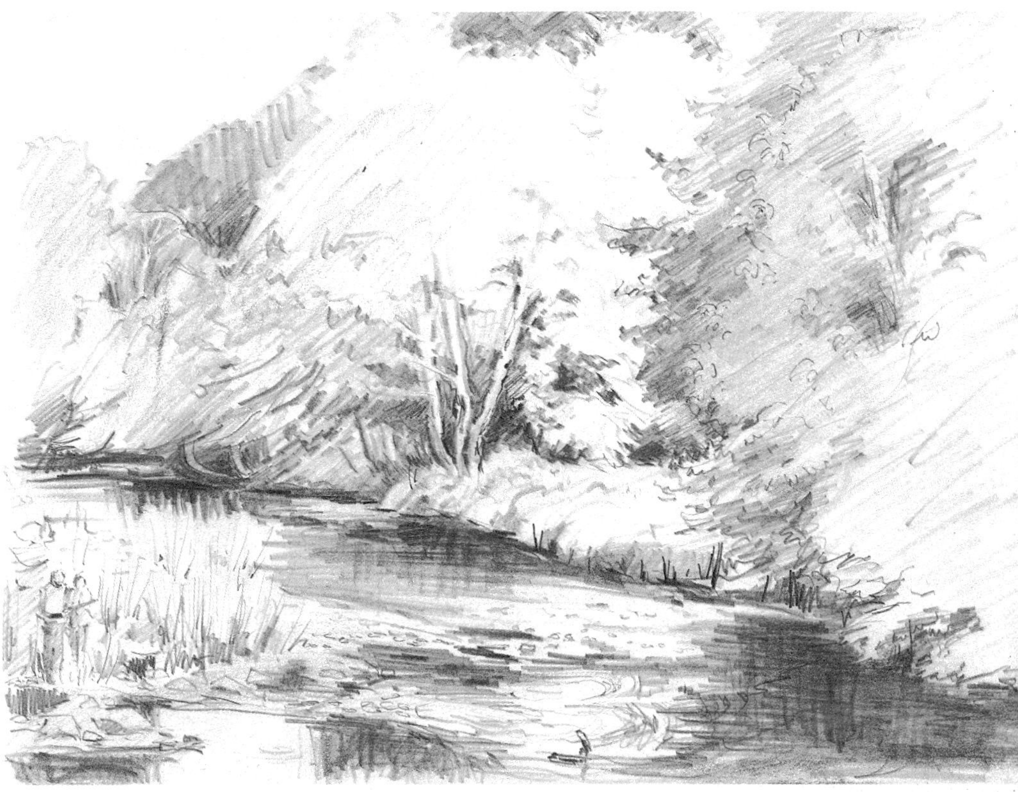

Drawing lesson by the river. *The figures on the left give a sense of scale to the composition.*

One is not necessarily better than the other – just different – though the hand-made product can be more expensive. The best papers have a large rag content, and have also been well-sized.

Some papers are more absorbent than others, giving rather diffuse outlines, while others allow the paint to flow across the surface almost at will. Good papers retain moisture long enough for most of the initial work to be done without re-wetting.

(Overleaf) **Dale.** *These simple 18th-century cottages are attractive because of their position at the edge of the sea, huddled under the bank of dark protecting trees. I kept the colour range quite narrow except for the startling blue house, a well-known feature in the village.*

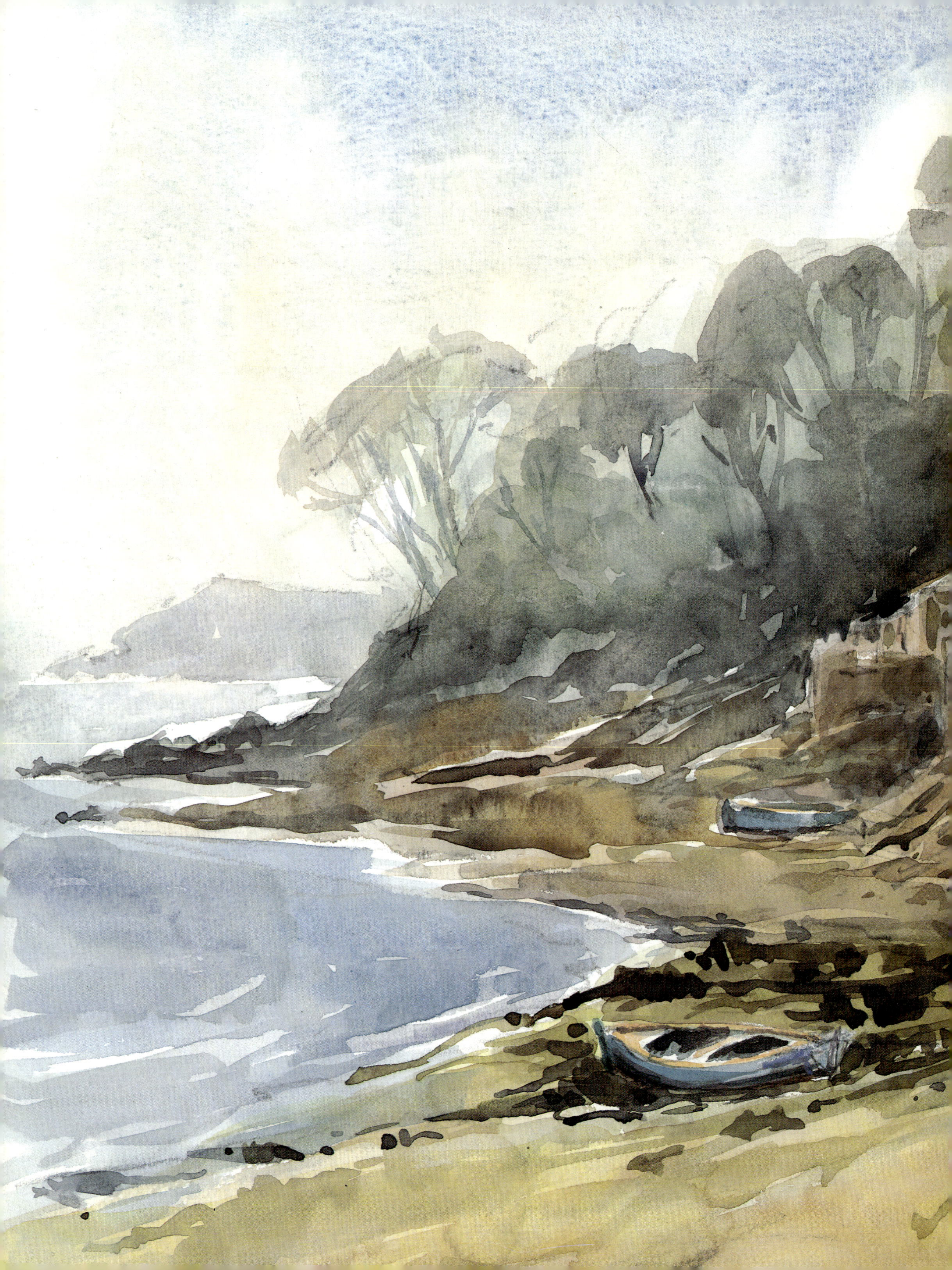

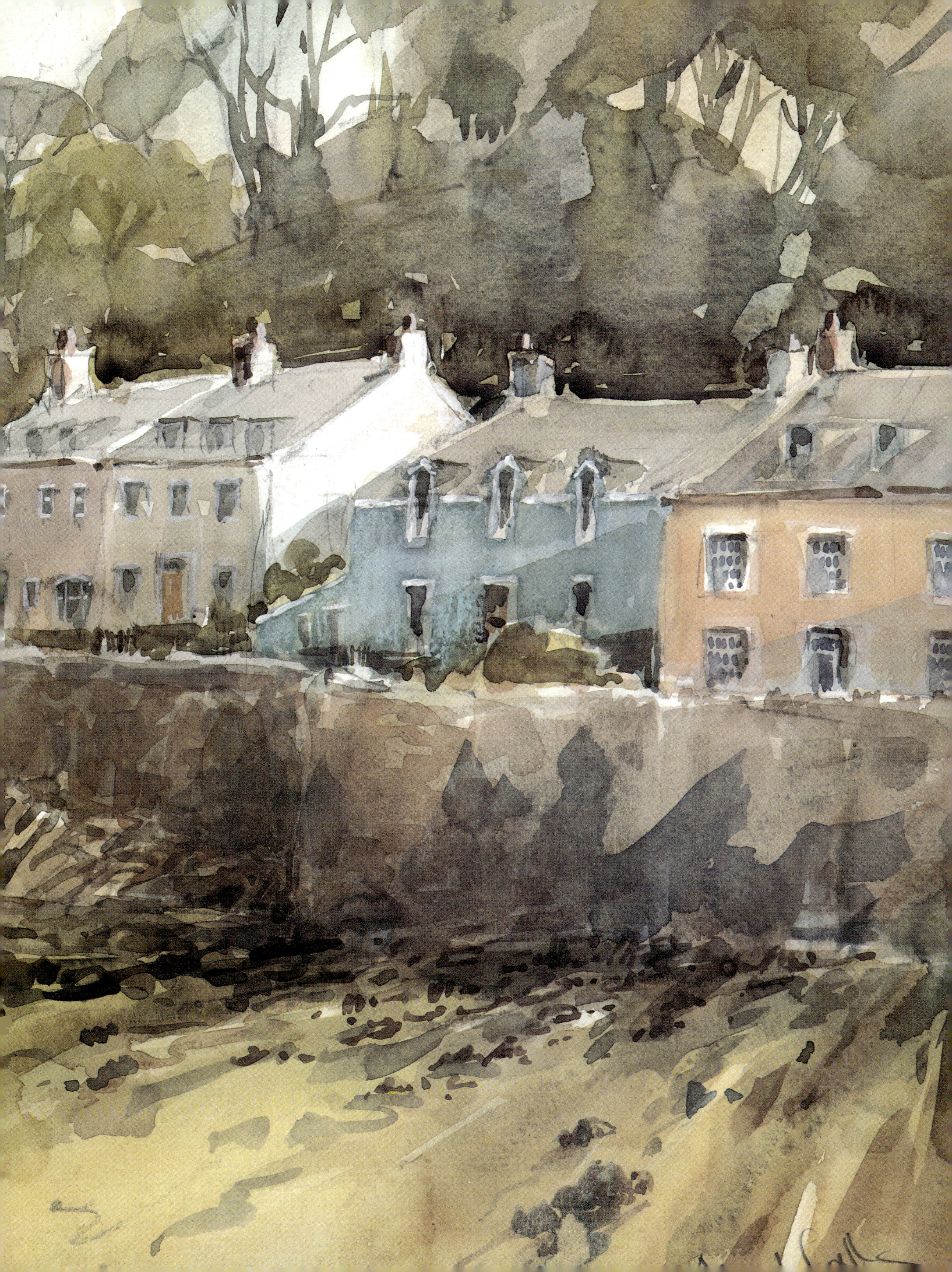

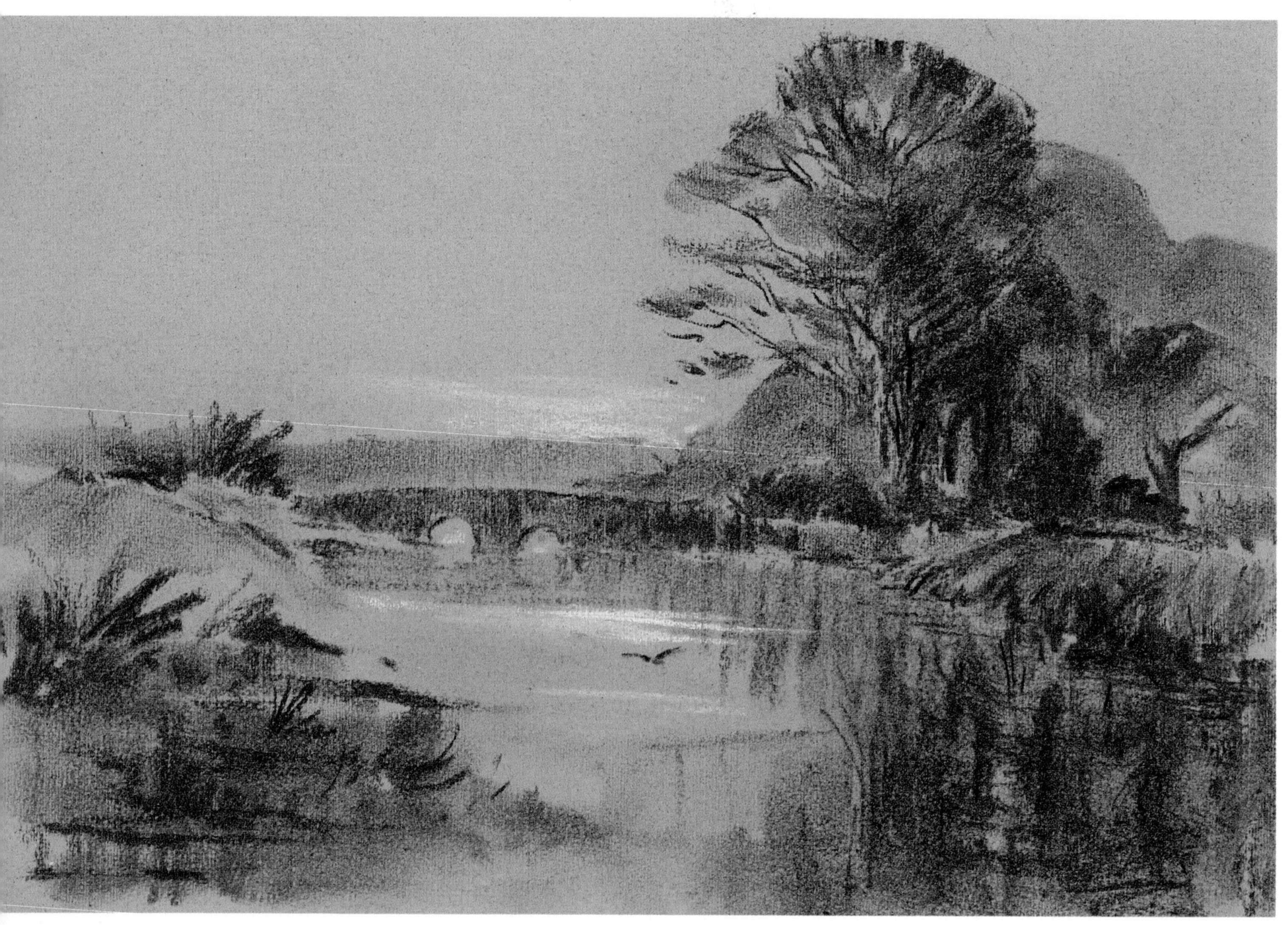

Texture

A sub-division of papers is dictated by their texture, and they are sold under the headings of Rough, hot- or cold-pressed, or Not. Rough paper is just what the name implies: paper with a strongly textured, 'lumpy' surface (just how lumpy depends on the make). It is best-suited to large work, where fine detail is less important than a broad, bold statement. The texture of the paper plays an important part in determining the finished look of the painting.

Hot-pressed papers (in America these are termed cold-pressed) have a very smooth, almost polished surface. They are a delight to work on and often produce the most surprising results when used freely with plenty of water. They lend themselves particularly well to fine, detailed work, but it is a pity to confine them to this alone.

Not papers have a less marked texture: just enough to give a 'bite' and to encourage granulation. These are the most commonly used as they allow for both wet-into-wet work and sharp definition, and are suitable for virtually any subject.

Colour

Watercolour paper is not always white, but can come in many shades from blue-white to ivory, cream, grey or even tan. While it is frequently the luminous effect of white paper shining through transparent paint that you will be after, there are occasions when a more subtle effect would be more desirable. (I am thinking of painting in bright sunlight, when pure white can be hard on the eyes.)

Still waters and bridge. *Tinted paper is of enormous value. It sets the mid-tone from the start, leaving you free to concentrate on the lightest lights and darkest darks. Here I used white pastel for the light on the water, and charcoal for the trees.*

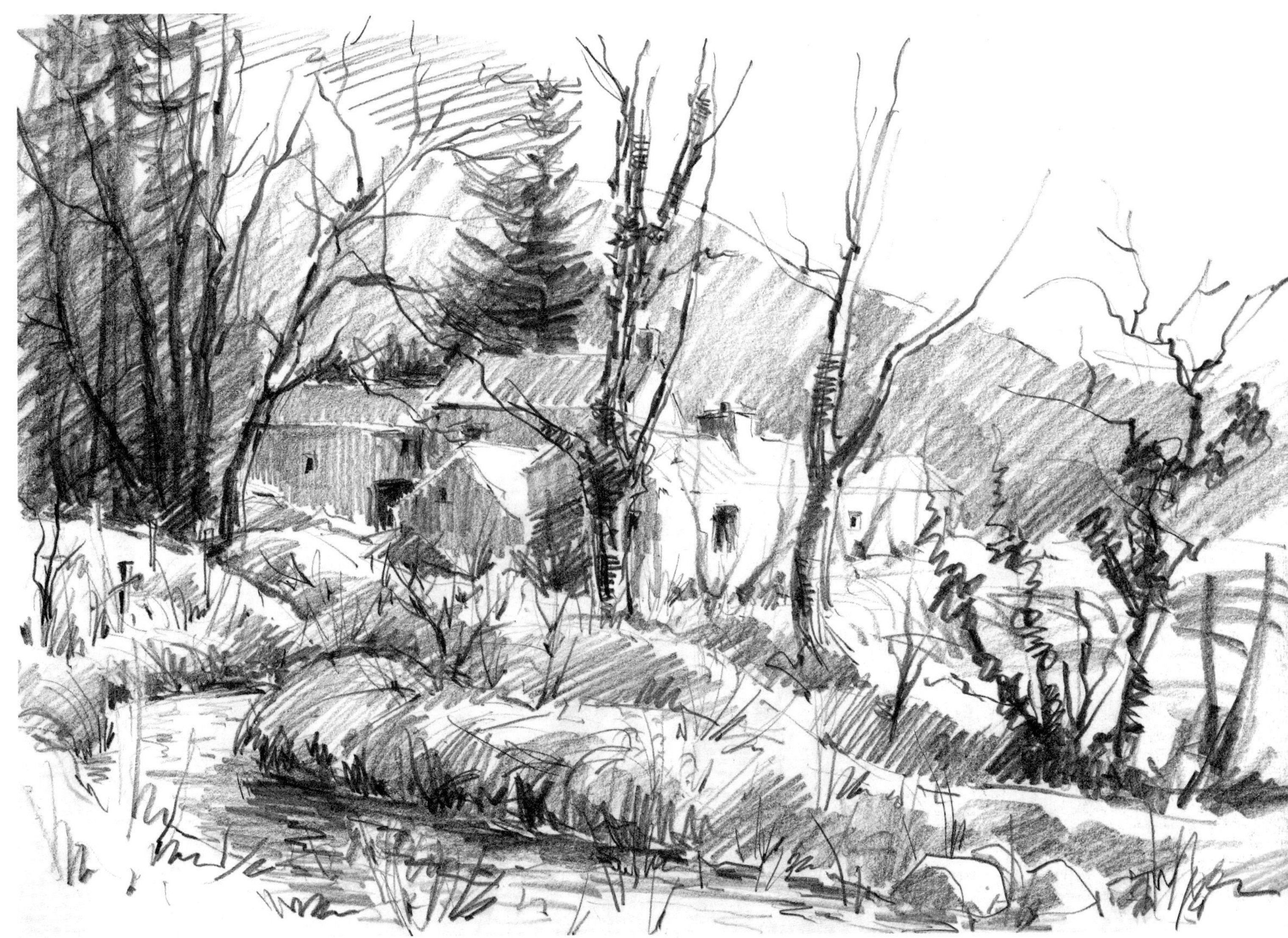

Weight

There is one more sub-division worth considering: that of the thickness or weight of your paper. In general this varies from 70 lb (150 gsm) to 300 lb (640 gsm) or even 400 lb (850 gsm).

The heavier the paper, the more abuse it will take, and the more generous it will be to your painting. Thin paper requires the tedious process of stretching, and even then may cockle and tear. Sponging or scratching can be hazardous and may well leave you contemplating a hole, or even the complete disintegration of a painting.

For a few pennies more, a 140 lb (300 gsm) or, better still, a 200 lb (425 gsm) paper will be far kinder. There is also something very satisfying about setting to work on a paper of good thickness and quality.

It is always good policy to vary the size of your painting according to the subject matter and to what you want to say. You must avoid uniformity and repetition in *all* aspects of your work, and having at hand a choice of blocks, pads, and single sheets will encourage this and tempt you into greater experimentation.

Mill by a stream.

BRUSHES

The brush acts as an extension of your hand and brain, and is the tool that you use to express yourself and reveal your skill to the onlooker.

A single stroke can express a ship, a field or a cloud, and the more economical the artist, the better the result. A painter needs constant practice to perfect control over hand and brain, just as a dancer must exercise daily at the bar or a pianist at his instrument.

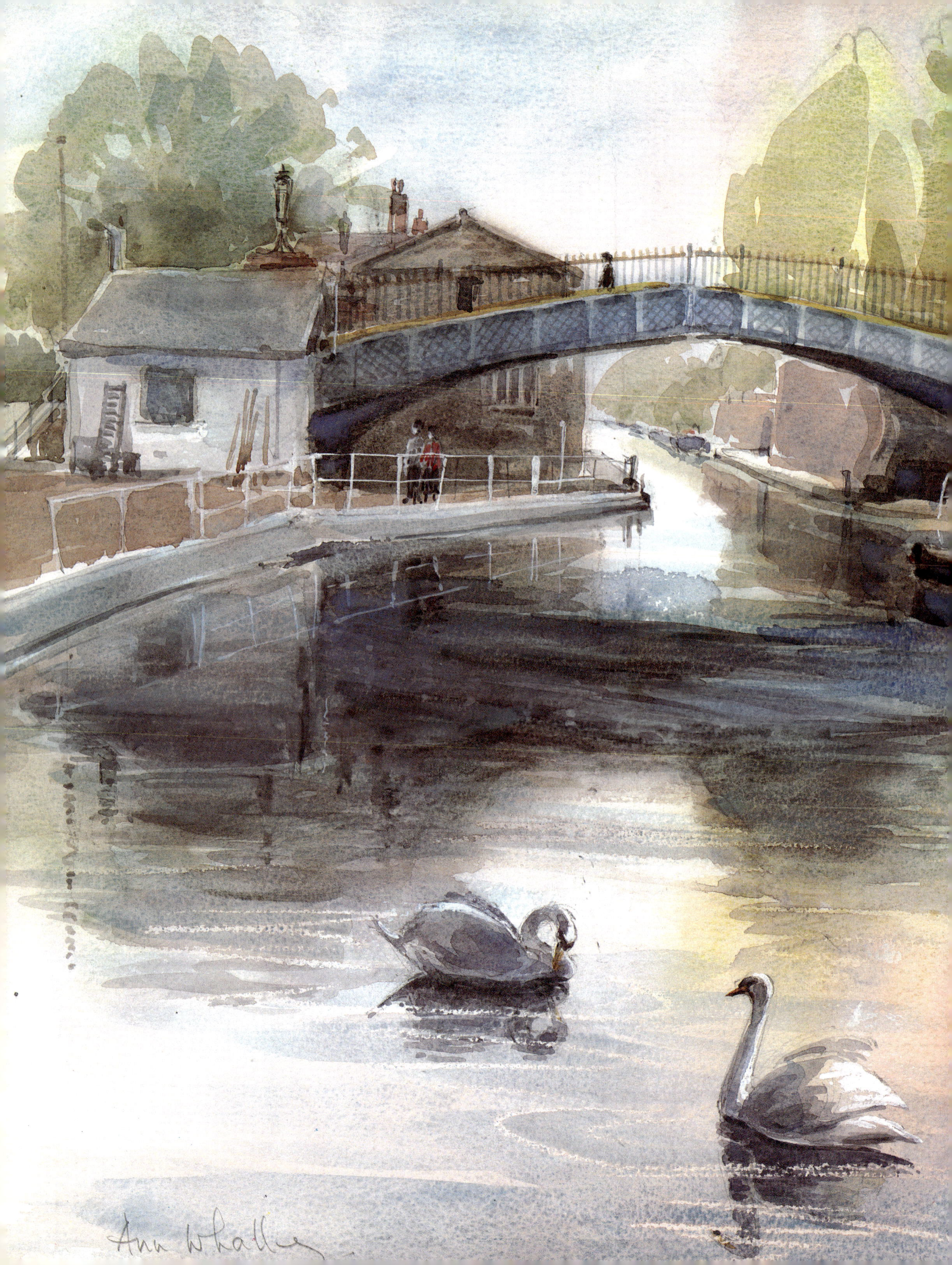

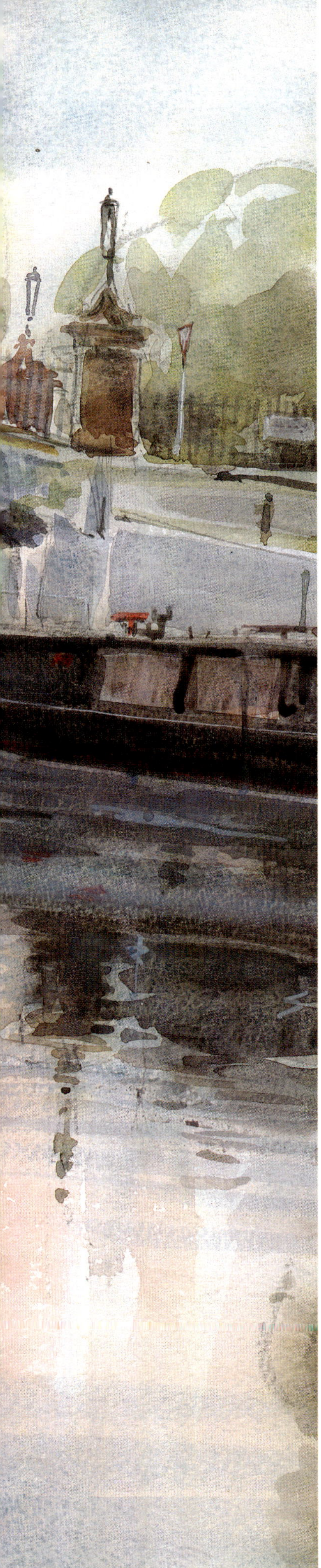

Brush shape

There are basically two types of brush: round and flat. I use a round brush for all general-purpose work such as washes and building up a painting, and various sizes of flat brushes for single-stroke stone walls, textures and so on. Brushes can also be pressed flat and used on edge for masts, rigging and other details.

Brush types

Sable and squirrel are ideal for millionaires, but for the rest of us a good nylon brush does very well indeed. More important is the size of the brush, and therefore its water-holding capacity.

If your brush has a decent point (always keep the plastic cover on when not in use, and suck your brush to a good point after work) you will be able to paint from start to finish perfectly well with a size 20 brush. The problem with attempting fine lines or small areas with a brush with three hairs is that the water runs out long before the line, and one ends up nibbling away at it in a series of small jerks, so that what should have been a smooth sweep becomes a fragmented mess.

Practise painting from a standing position, using your whole arm and shoulder freely rather than the restricted poking movements of your fingers alone. Of course, there will be times when a smaller brush will be more convenient, but anything smaller than a 6 or 7 is unwise. The abstract concept of liquid paint working over a surface to give quality to your work, whatever the subject, is essential for good watercolour.

Little Venice, London.

MISCELLANEOUS

The more painting aids that you can collect about you in the studio, the more likely you are to attack each painting with an open and inventive attitude.

A range of pencils in various grades is essential: HB and B for drawing up a painting, and then anything from 2B to 6B for sketch work and tonal planning. Other drawing implements such as charcoal, conté, pastels, pens, stick-and-ink and felt-tips will give you free rein. Anything that makes a mark is a legitimate drawing implement.

Watercolour painters need not exclude other media from their repertoire. Coloured inks, for instance, are wonderfully rich in colour and highly transparent. They mix most interestingly with watercolour, creating texture, and are very effective as glazes (see pages 27–9).

Pastels also have an important role. For all its tremendous range and flexibility, even watercolour cannot achieve everything. A brilliant clump of flowers may be just what the painting needs, and a delicate touch of pastel the only way to achieve it. White or pale pastel can put back lost sparkle and add interesting and sympathetic textures, and I have rescued many paintings this way.

A range of different-sized sketchbooks will be invaluable (especially when filled!) and a small one in your pocket at all times helps to generate the habit of sketching. Sketchbooks are a painter's diary – an important record of things seen and done – a personal account not intended for public view.

Other necessary items include a fine-grain natural sponge for wetting paper and removing pigment which has become too heavy; a large water pot; a putty eraser which won't destroy the surface of the paper; some large mixing surfaces such as tin plates; razor blades (for scratching out); boards of various sizes; and containers to put things in such as a brush-holder, pencil case and carrying bag of some sort.

I don't regard an easel as essential for the watercolour artist, and knees usually come at the right height to angle your board out-of-doors. In the studio, prop up your board at an angle of about 45° so that washes run down satisfactorily.

Some cartridge-paper mounts cut to a range of opening sizes are useful for assessing a painting, and a small viewfinder aids composition (I use an empty slide frame).

The better you know your paints, papers and brushes, the more enjoyment you will get from your painting, and the better the results you will achieve.

Just one word of warning. Having experimented in every direction and at last found and mastered a good approach, don't assume that it is *always* going to be the best approach, and settle into a set way of working using the same old paper and colours. Always believe that there is a better way, and new methods to be explored, and never be tempted to paint the same picture over and over again. There are no spontaneous discoveries to be made the second time around – only the tired re-working of an old idea.

If you can approach each new painting as if it were something no-one had ever seen before – a new world just waiting to be discovered and needing your best analytical and technical skills to describe – then your work will always be spontaneous, lively and honest.

CHAPTER TWO

ATMOSPHERICS

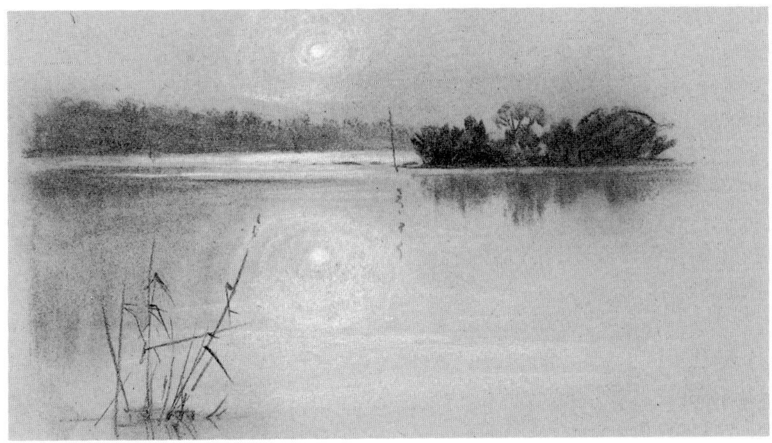

Atmosphere is generally thought to refer to the elusive qualities which pervade scenes of mists and mystery. I use the word in a slightly different context. Everything in the world has the potential for enchantment, however ordinary and mundane it may seem, and any scene can be touched by magic and transformed into something special, if only the artist has eyes to see.

It isn't always the exciting things in nature which offer the greatest potential. Hurricane, tempest and flood may be splendid experiences, but they are rarely very paintable. As I see it, atmosphere is more likely to be found under less dramatic circumstances and nearer home. To the receptive mind, there is atmosphere to be found in every prospect, however unpromising – all you need is imagination and the desire to enhance rather than copy what you see. My dictionary defines atmosphere as 'the feeling conveyed to one by one's environment' – no reference there to nature's histrionics.

When we talk of atmosphere in painting we really mean the creation of mood, and the means of achieving it when contending with problems of light (or lack of it). While it is true that spectacular light may result in scenes of high drama, I prefer to find my dramas in scenes which to others may appear quite unremarkable. Wet pavements on a damp day or clouds reflected in still water can be wonderfully evocative of remembered pleasure – it all depends what you make of them.

In my mind, there is nothing that lends itself better to atmospheric interpretation than water. From a painterly point of view, its essential asset is its ability to reflect. Everything about water – be it in the form of wide oceans or the merest puddle – is dependent on external forces. Water moves because the wind blows or because objects cross it, and its colour comes from whatever is reflected into it. If you accept this, it follows that any study of water must also involve every facet of landscape and seascape painting.

GLAZING

Colour mixing is most commonly thought of as the blending of pigments on a palette prior to brushing on to the paper. Another technique which lends itself well to the creation of atmosphere is that of glazing. Glazing is a way of introducing great depth and luminosity into both light and dark tones, and consists of washing in one transparent layer of colour over another. It is a technique much used by oil painters, although then it becomes a rather long-winded process, as each layer of paint must dry completely before the next can be applied.

The same is true of watercolour, but to a lesser degree as watercolour dries so much more quickly. I use the technique of glazing in most of my paintings to create colours which I can obtain in no other way, and to retain a glowing luminosity in even the darkest of my dark tones. Like all new techniques, glazing requires a certain amount of experiment and practice to achieve the effects you really want, but it is time very well-spent. If you think of it as being rather like using sheets of different-coloured tissue paper one on top of the other, you will soon grasp the concept.

If you have trouble controlling wet-into-wet washes, glazing offers a way of retaining spontaneity without the paint running away with you. It also rids you of the daunting prospect of starting on a pristine sheet of white paper. By its very nature, glazing simplifies a painting by drawing together and harmonizing whole passages and by softening edges through gentle overlaps.

All of you must at some time have gazed despairingly at a delicate evening sky, vainly attempting to define colours so elusive that you are unable to give them a name. Is it lemon? No, there is blue somewhere, and perhaps some pink, or is it purple? It is certainly quite impossible to mix on a palette anything that would come near. This is when glazing becomes the only answer. If you can master the technique, a whole new range of possibilities will be opened up.

Aureolin yellow glaze

Rose madder glaze over yellow

Cobalt blue glaze over yellow and rose

Three stages of glazing.

Firstly, make sure your paper is heavy enough not to go into hills and valleys when soaked (anything over 120 lb [255 gsm] should be suitable) or stretch the paper firmly. Have your board tilted to about 20° so that the washes can move, and find your widest, most water-holding brush – you must be able to sweep abundant quantities of liquid paint across the paper without running out half way. Use only the purest, unmixed pigments to make your washes and prepare them in generous quantities (if you make twice as much as you think you will need, that may just be enough). Most importantly, be sure to plan the painting well before starting work, thinking particularly of any white areas you will want to save. White areas among the colours help your painting to sing.

Let us start with a translucent evening sky. I always begin with yellow as this is the lightest and most delicate colour, and will only become opaque and crude if used more than once; it fails to show when subsequently washed over other colours, so it must be right first time. Aureolin, the most transparent and pure of yellows, would be the one to choose. Once you have mixed up enough paint, take your big absorbent brush and, starting at the top, sweep the paint on in horizontal strokes, avoiding any overlap, but catching the beads running to the bottom of the last stroke. Because the paper is tilted, the colour will blend downwards. Never be tempted to go back over or touch up – get it right the first time or leave it, as the next colour wash will disguise any small lapse.

When you come to any areas you want to keep white, just lift the brush and jump over. Absolutely clean, hard edges are not particularly desirable, and small overlaps of glaze will only be light in tone, helping to add a little colour vibration. Check that the edges of the paper are not collecting too much liquid which could 'bleed' back into the drying paint, and lift any blobs collecting above white areas with a damp brush. Avoid dabbing away with a tissue, or you will find you have lost all the watercolour quality.

Now stop and assess what you have done so far, and wait for the paper to dry completely. Failure to do this will be disastrous. Decide if the colour is right: if too pale, wash in another layer; if too deep, then hold under the shower and let some of the pigment float off. Remember that this too must now dry completely. Estimating how much pigment to use requires practice, so don't worry if you don't get it right the first time.

You are now ready to apply the next colour. Permanent rose or rose madder are the cleanest and most transparent reds. Repeat the whole process, and again sit back and assess the result. It is important that your brushwork is economical and direct to avoid disturbing the yellow layer beneath. Once the red is quite dry, it is time for the final colour, and I find cobalt the most transparent of blues and therefore the best suited to glazing.

It may be necessary to add further layers of red or blue, depending on the effect required. Avoid making all your washes of equal strength, or the result will be rather muddy. For a warm glow, make the yellow or red the dominant wash; for a soft blue-grey, emphasize the blue stage; and for lavenders and purples play down the yellow. Always use a mix of all three primaries even when one of the colours seems undetectable – a sky of only yellow and blue will turn green!

Even the darkest areas of your painting can be built up using glazing, and will avoid those opaque, dead shadows which kill a watercolour stone-dead. To prove this, mix up red, yellow and blue on your palette and apply the result alongside an area built up from the same colours in glazes, and just look at the difference!

As you come to have more control with the technique you will be able to vary the intensity of the individual glazes across the page. Try turning the board upside-down when applying the blue, so that the red and yellow layers are hardly affected at the horizon. The possibilities are unending for obtaining lovely atmospheric effects and creating the illusion of space and distance.

You will come to find more and more uses for glazing. One that I find particularly useful in creating luminous shadows is to paint all the objects in local colour to begin with, and, once this has dried, to glaze in the shadows with pure cobalt. For an even more exciting effect, try using the complementary colours – a light wash of purple over a vibrant yellow, for instance. Any highlights of the sunny side can then be lifted with a damp brush.

WORKING ON THE SPOT

I have already emphasized the importance of getting out into the environment to sketch and learn from first-hand observation. The ability to draw is not a God-given miracle vouchsafed to the chosen few – quite the reverse. It is the result of constant hard slog which needs to be carried out every day. If you fail to pick up a pencil for a week, the next drawing will be that much harder. Fluency only comes with constant, day-to-day practice. The better you draw, the better you will paint – after all, what is painting but drawing with a brush?

There really is no substitute for getting out with your sketchbook and pencil at the ready and seeing for yourself. Apart from the unique information you will gain, the mere fact of braving the elements brings home, as nothing else can, the power and presence of nature. You need the ambience, the sun on your back, the birds singing and the light transforming the familiar into something special. The fact that the wind may tear your paper and the rain complete the disintegration will only serve to intensify the recollection!

Even good photographs which you have taken yourself fall far short of the value of even the roughest sketch made on the spot, although they *can* be used for reference (see pages 99–103). The camera can tell terrible lies, rendering three dimensions as a flat pattern of light and shade, flattening or exaggerating tonal contrasts, and sometimes creating a distorted impression of perspective and depth. Nor can the camera select or, even worse, leave out. I am frequently amazed to find an obtrusive post or tree in my photograph which I completely ignored in my sketch. And how dreadfully insignificant all those soaring mountains have come out!

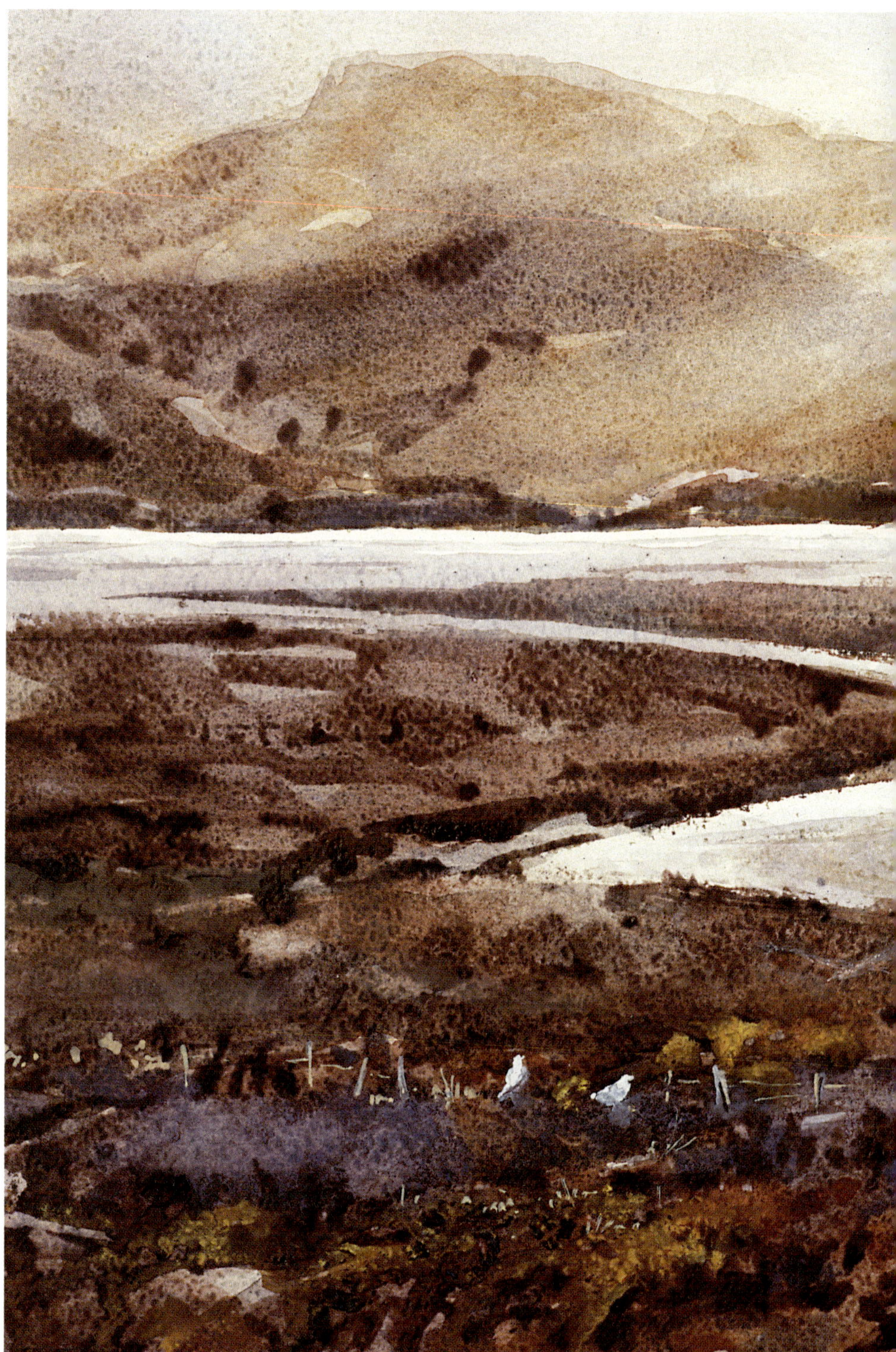

Snaking Barmouth River. *The area between Cadre Idris and the Snowdon range of mountains in north Wales offers some splendid atmospherics – Turner found this too! Notice how little you can see of the actual river here, which is really quite wide, as it winds down to the sea. At high tide all the sand banks are covered and the mountains seem to float.*

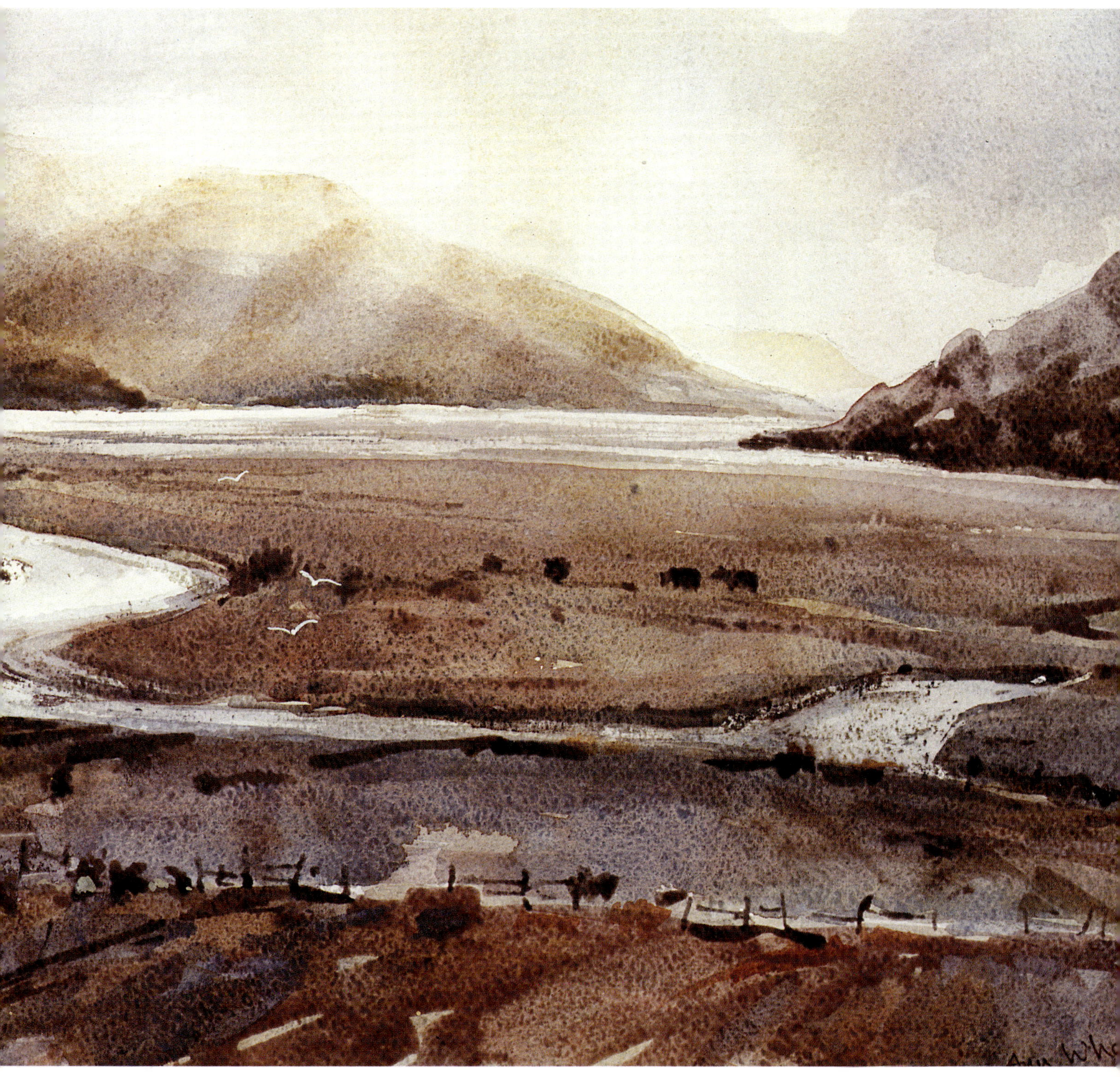

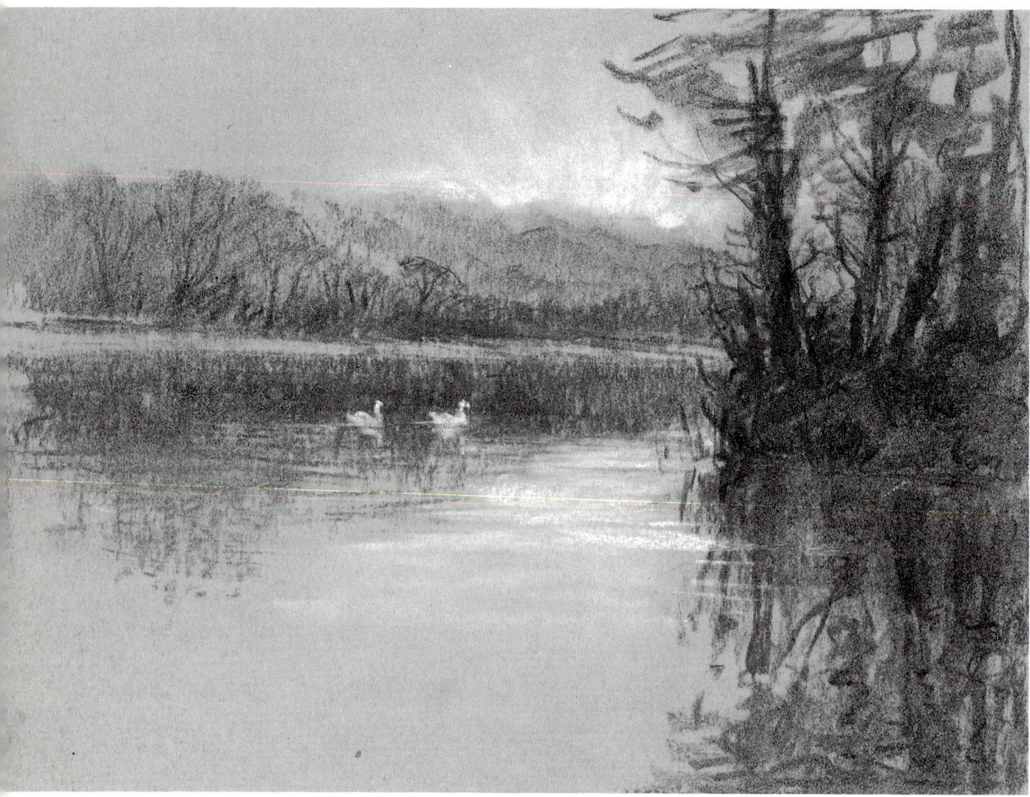

Swans on the lake.

Horses on the beach. *I love the vast emptiness of our coast, but maintaining interest while trying to suggest space in a seascape can be a problem. Here I used an advancing weather front to give drama*

If we accept that a good painting results from the painter's ability to react subjectively to the scene before him and then to exercise his powers of selection to build up atmosphere, work on the spot assumes paramount importance. Have you never been moved to tears or resorted to hopping about with joy because it is all just too wonderful? I can't put into words the sense of well-being that I feel at such moments. All artists must feel something similar at times, or why else would we go on?

Of course, it is one thing to see and be moved by all these wonders, and quite another to get them down on paper for others to share. Nature in the raw is a daunting prospect for any artist. For one thing, nothing ever stays the same for long – clouds pass and the distant sparkle on the water moves with them; mists disappear; and tides ebb and flow. How on earth is one to cope with it all?

It is essential to develop the ability to work fast and to get down at least a broad statement of what is there before it all changes or walks away. A good way to achieve this is to give yourself a strict time limit – say fifteen minutes. This clarifies the mind wonderfully, and soon you will find that you are instinctively putting down only what is essential and ignoring the usual clutter of useless detail. At first you will arrive home only to find that you have left out a lot of vital elements and filled the paper with some fairly useless reference. If you persevere, however, you will soon sort out the wheat from the chaff and end up with some quick, direct, pared-down sketches containing all the information you need and nothing else.

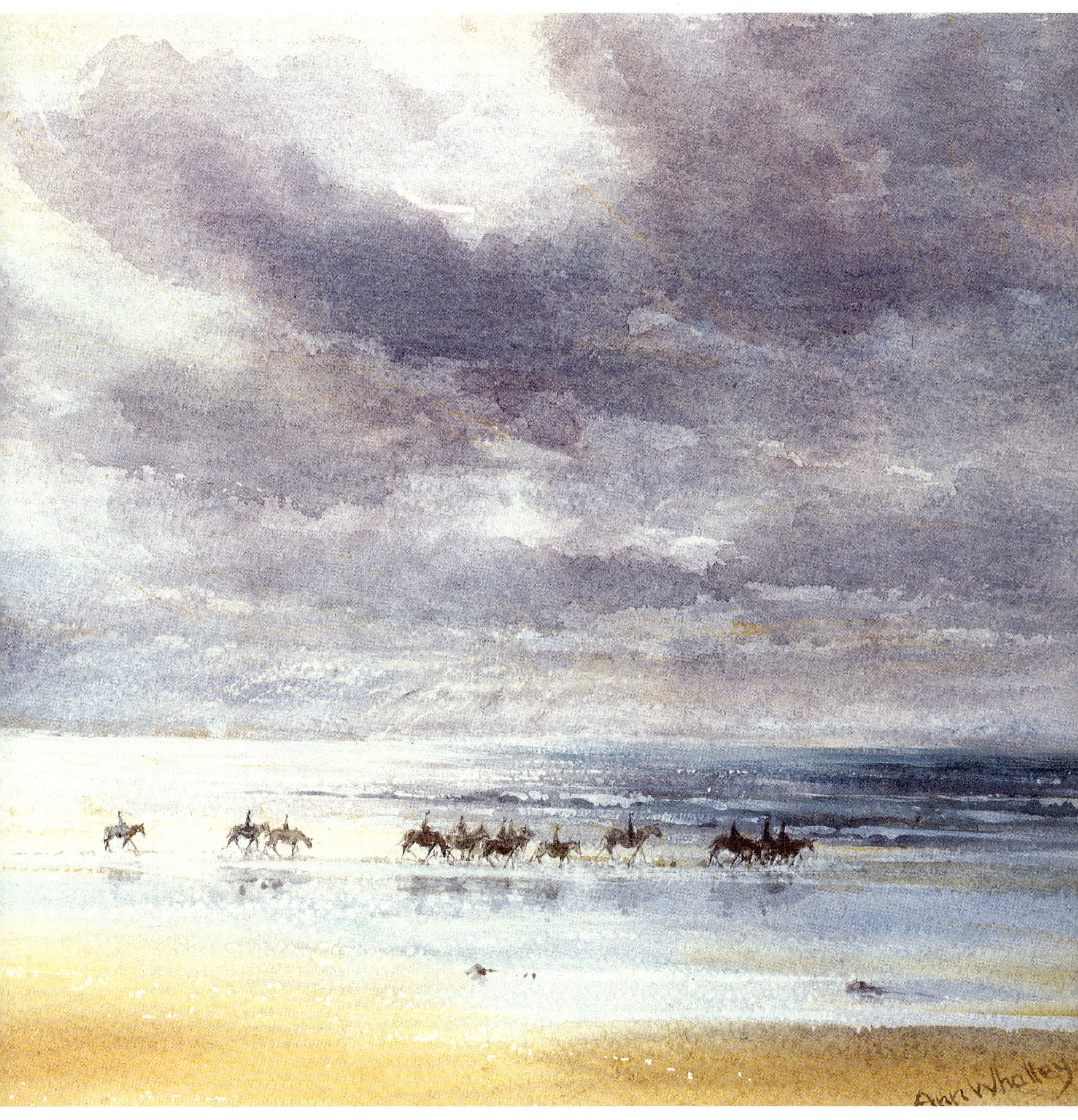

and movement to the sky, which takes up two-thirds of the picture. I toned the sea from indigo under the clouds to sparkling white where the light struck the water, added warmth to the foreground, and finally added the horses and riders to give scale and a focus of interest. Very simple elements are combined to produce an evocative scene.

(Overleaf) **Morning mist, Little Venice, London.** *I caught this lovely effect early one morning before anything stirred the stillness.*

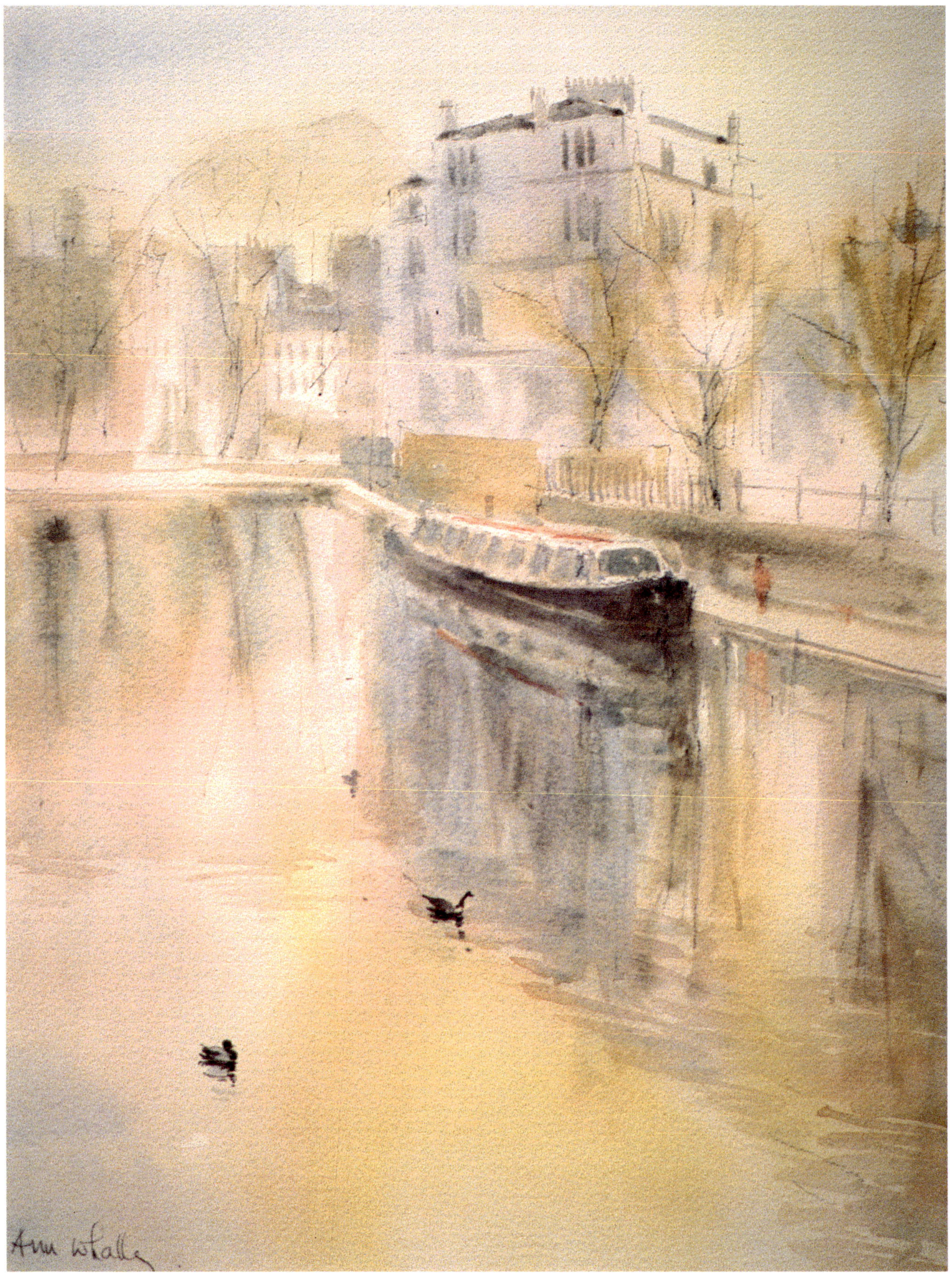

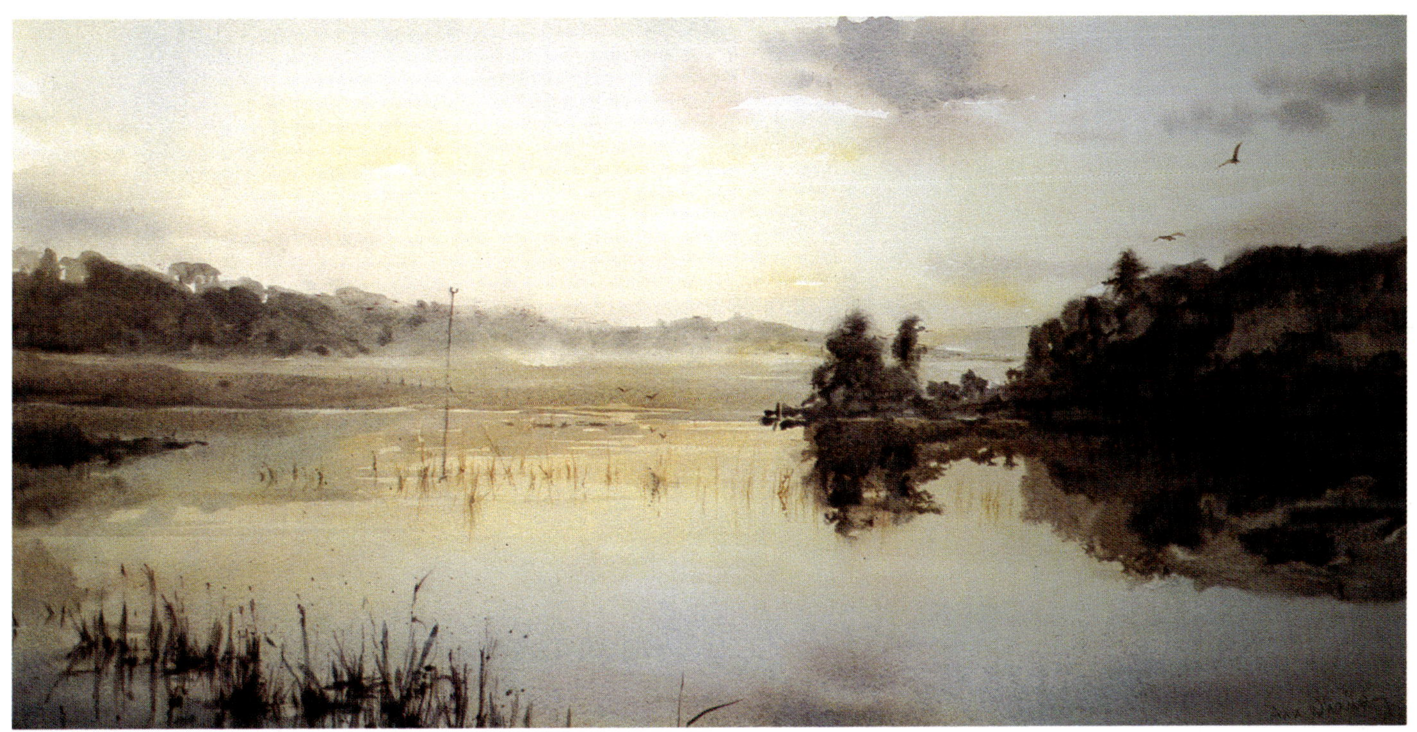

MISTS, FRETS AND FOGS

This kind of atmospheric painting always attracts an appreciative audience. They are also great fun to do. I love to work in pencil most of the time, and find that it does almost all I could ask, but there are times when a softer medium may give a better result. Lovely vague, misty effects are possible using charcoal with white pastel on tinted paper, for example.

I feel that what appears on paper does so as a direct result of what the artist is thinking about as he performs. Pretty obvious, you may say, but useful to bear in mind when wondering why a drawing has failed. Just what were you thinking about when you muddled the whole thing up? You must do the real thinking before you start, and remember that you are not making a copy of the scene, but using it to make a painting.

The more decisions you make early on, the more confident and simple the drawing will be. This saves a great deal of wasted effort and a lot of paper! For instance, ask yourself why you have chosen a particular view as opposed to a dozen others. I still find it all too easy to forget why I chose a scene in the first place, in the excitement of getting it all down, but muddled thinking (or no thinking at all) does not make for good work.

Look closely at the way mist and fog change the appearance of different objects: it is not just that they become less sharp, but the colours change too. Whether there is sun or cloud behind the mists is also important.

Our house stands on a wide reach of the River Cleddau in Pembrokeshire, where the tidal waters may rise as much as twenty feet at certain times of the year, flooding a great basin. A veiled sun rising through the mist above the wide expanse of still water is extremely beautiful. This scene, with its wheeling gulls, statuesque herons and leaping fish, has been the subject of many paintings.

When tackling this kind of subject, I invariably start off painting very wet-into-wet, swirling on pure colour and encouraging it to run almost at will. While the paper is still quite wet, I make a slightly thicker mix and just suggest the far bank and trees, again keeping my colours as clean as possible. There is no place here for muddy, tertiary greys or apologetic half-measures. The reason I am painting this scene is because of its glory, and this is what I want to get on to paper.

Cleddau sunrise. *This is the view which greets me through my bedroom window. As the light grows, the distant river seems to 'smoke', while the still water mirrors perfectly the delicate colours of the sky. I have painted this scene many times, and there is always something fresh to say.*

Sea frets are an all-too-common phenomenon along our west Wales coasts. They can suddenly appear from nowhere, and blot out a warm, sunny day in a moment. When this happens halfway through a painting, the temptation is to pack up and go home, but it would be more constructive to sit tight and begin a new painting. Isolated among the ghostly forms of rocks and cliffs, experiment with this new world, expressing its unfamiliarity and strange silence. Even if your painting doesn't turn out a masterpiece, think what you have learned by being there, and how much is stored away in your memory for future use.

Mists and fogs are very rarely dull grey in colour, but suffused with subtle shades of gold and pink, blue and lavender. Look hard for these shades and flood them in as washes of pure, unmixed colour, letting them mix on the paper instead. Let the first washes dry completely, and then repeat the process where necessary (again with pure colour), gradually adjusting tone and colour as you build up glazes to create a luminous, atmospheric impression.

As you near the end of the painting, drop in the tiniest amount of sharp definition in the foreground (just enough to place a few close objects clearly). This will help to create an impression of distance and space. Remember that, in watercolour, it is always possible to tone down or modify, but that once the sparkle is lost it is gone for ever.

Sunrise. *I used pastels to illustrate this scene quickly. It was a January morning with the sun rising late through a thick mist. I kept detail to a minimum and concentrated on the relationship between tones and colours, and on the atmospheric effect.*

Mist frequently lies more densely at ground level, so that the tops of trees and hills seem to float free above an invisible landscape. This can be quite fascinating, as can succeeding ranks of soft-edged hills gradually paling and changing colour as they recede into a blue distance. It is not only the bright, sunny days that tempt artists out to paint, and there is just as much interest in gentler conditions.

(Opposite) **Rovinj in a cloudburst.**

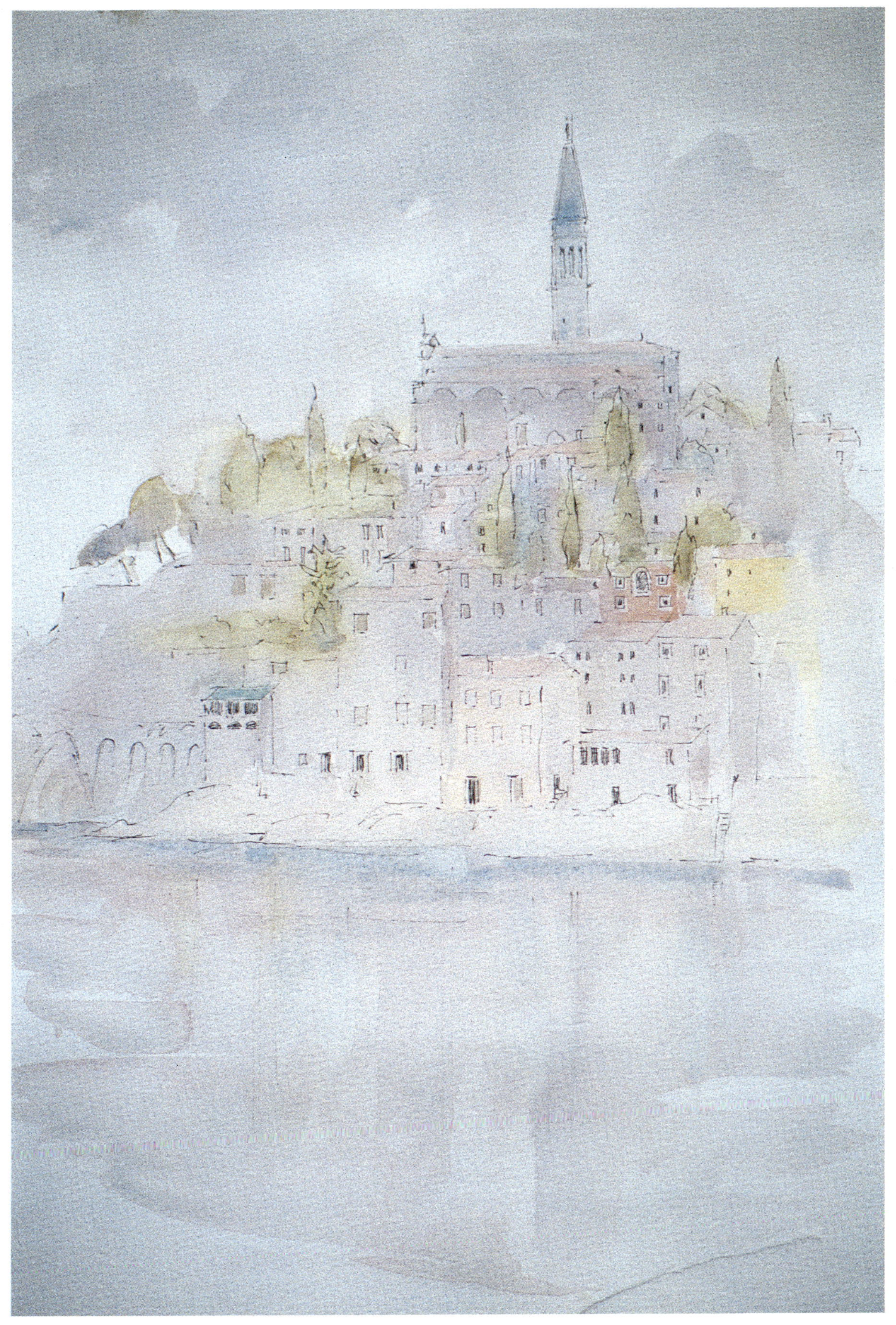

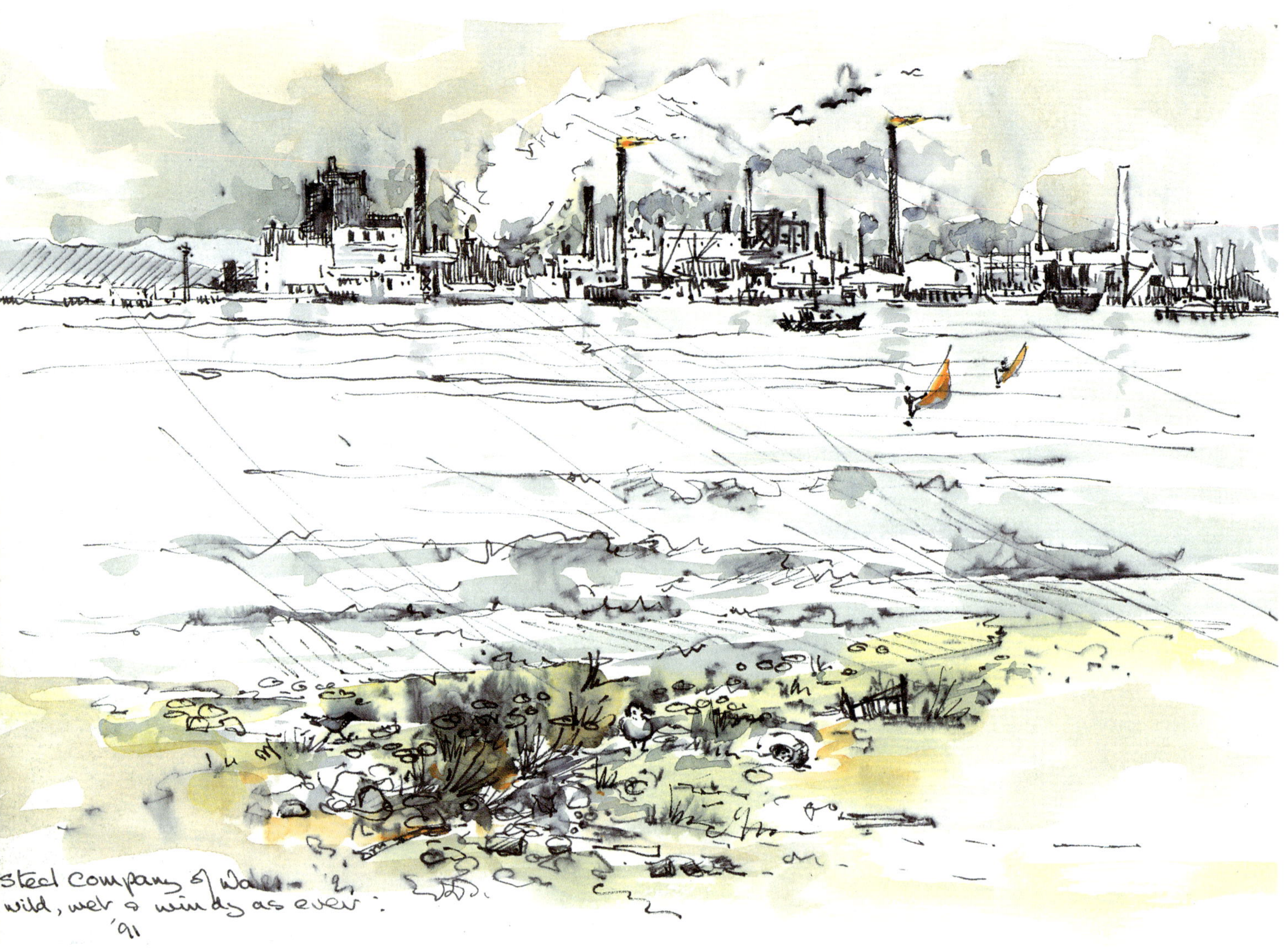

Port Talbot in the rain.

RAIN

Mists and fogs usually form at ground level and dissolve up into clear air above, but rain falls from a dark ceiling of cloud. This causes a far greater diminution of light, reducing all the tonal values. Instead of tones graduating from black to white, we now see pale grey moving towards dark grey on the monochrome scale. Colours become muted too, and the whole scene loses its hard edges and sharp definitions. As a result, it requires a special effort to look for colours among the greys, and to distinguish between warm and cool areas. There is so much subtle richness in low-key subjects that they need never appear drab or colourless.

To expand on this colour/light concept, it may be that you will need to add a new combination of pigments. It is always constructive to re-think your customary palette from time to time, and it is amazing how enlivening this simple act can be.

Try introducing cerulean as your blue, for instance: mixed with light red it gives a lovely warm/cool tint, and is equally interesting with the siennas and umbers. Try permanent rose instead of alizarin, lemon in place of gamboge, and then see what happens when you introduce raw umber. Try a few experiments and soon a whole new set of subtle greys will become available. As all these combinations (with the exception of cerulean) are very transparent, they lend themselves well to the technique of glazing (see pages 27–9), which is an excellent way of softening outlines as you overlay delicate shades in a slow build-up.

Try to express falling rain in an impressionistic way – by implication, as it were.

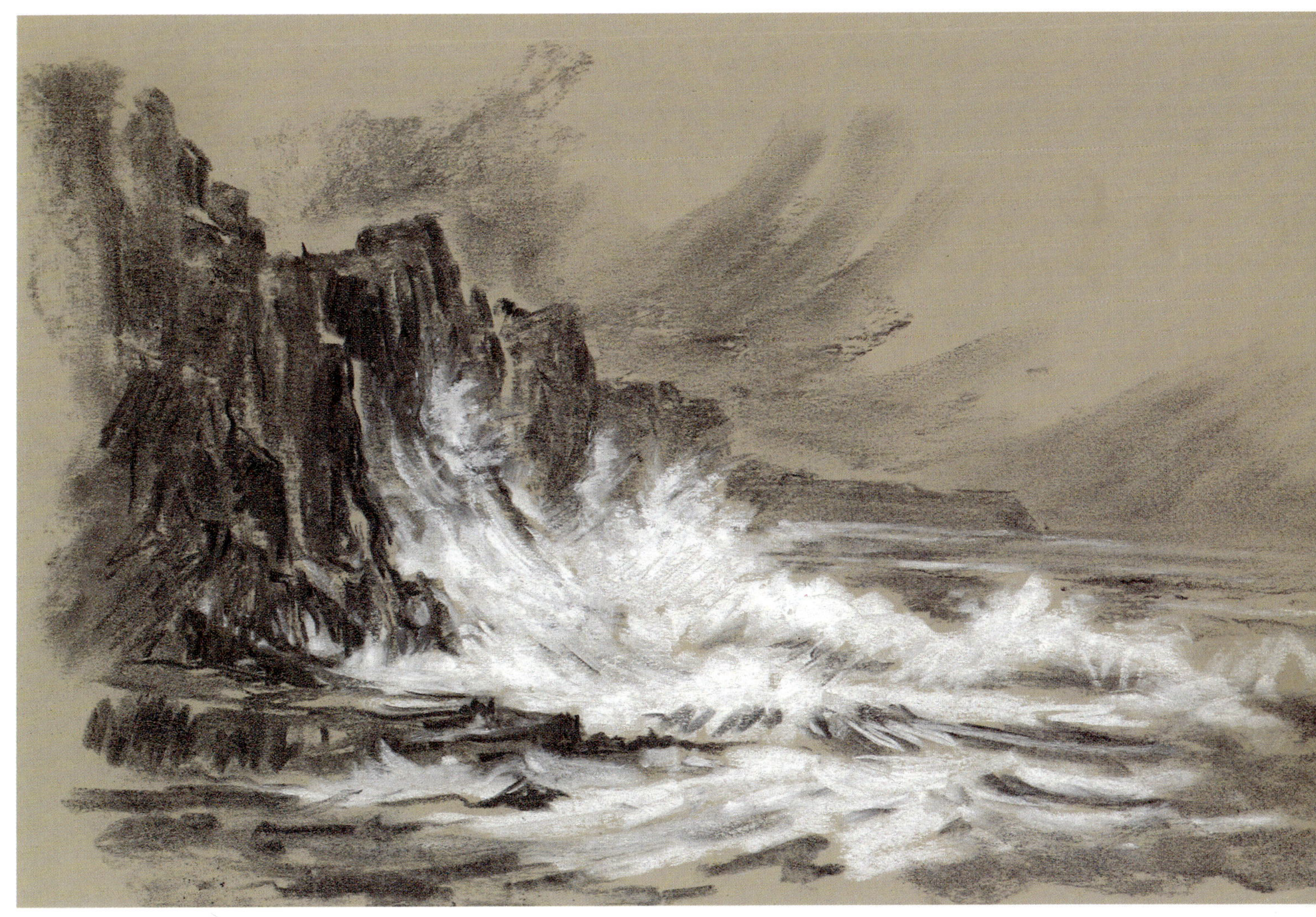

Concentrate on wet surfaces and reflections; heavy skies and scurrying figures under umbrellas. Leave out as much unimportant detail as possible. You probably won't be able to see it very well, anyway, and, as a general rule, if you can't see something, don't put it in.

WIND AND STORMS

Oh dear, I hear you protest, I can't paint wind – I can't even see it! Very true, but the evidence of its force is only too clear: trees swaying and bowed over; leaves fluttering down and birds battling to stay in the sky; breakers pounding the cliffs; and sudden dark squalls across a lake. Small streams turn into rushing torrents, and even the artist may be hard-pressed to stay upright!

The depiction of extreme conditions demands extreme measures. Be forceful and energetic with your brushstrokes, and in the way you apply the colour. Look for strong contrasts of tone, and search for well-defined forms to hold the whole structure together amid all the violent movement. Use solid features such as immovable boulders to act as a foil to rushing water, and note how the water builds and divides around them.

Wild sea and cliffs. *Expressing a scene of wild water such as this in monochrome calls for exact tonal variations and careful use of white pastel to depict the foam and spray. Everything should enhance the movement and vigour. Use a soft pencil or charcoal, and work as freely and quickly as possible once all the decisions have been made. You are conveying an impression of excitement, from which fine detail of strata and so on would only detract.*

Keep your statements simple and your intention clear. Be selective in what you choose to paint, avoiding proliferation and confusion. If *you* are confused, how do you think the viewer will feel?

SNOW

A fall of snow transforms everything. All the familiar values are reversed at a stroke when a snow-heavy sky lowers darkly over a strangely luminous white land. Streams wind between frosted banks like ominous black snakes, with the occasional grey feeler of ice creeping out over a still backwater.

Contrary to what might at first appear, snow scenes are anything but monochrome. Skies and shadows verge towards deep purple or blue, while dead grasses and leaves seem in contrast to glow with colour. Look carefully at the colour of the snow itself. How often could you say it was really white? In shadow, it can range from the palest pure cobalt to deep amethyst or lavender; and where it is caught in the slanting rays of a winter sun it may be anything from deep gold to a delicate rose. Look for the contrast of cool and warm, light and dark, and use every excuse to experiment with counterchange. This is the practice of using tonal contrast in such a way that light objects are highlighted against a dark background, or dark shapes silhouetted against light. Dramatic interest could be created in a snow scene, for instance, by depicting white roofs against a deep sky, or bare trees against a starkly white hillside.

The sudden contrast of dark and light tones draws the eye and becomes an immediate centre of interest. Clearly this must be planned from the start, and is often the reason a particular subject was chosen. Always look for these little moments of drama and try to record them – so often they rely on the play of sunlight and are fleeting. Do not be afraid to use really dark tones in your watercolour when you are introducing some delicious light, bright detail, as the dark areas act as a necessary foil and add strength and depth to the work. Paintings based only on light and mid-tones *can* be effective, but a few rich darks bring it all to life.

While tonal contrasts are the most common method of achieving counterchange, it can be done through colour very effectively. Use your knowledge of the colour wheel and consciously place bright primaries against their complementary colours. Rich yellow against deep purple, for instance, will certainly draw the eye and liven things up. In a perfect world you will of course have planned all this in the initial stages, but it can be done later. Do you remember my suggestions about glazing on pages 27–9? As inks are so much more brilliant than watercolour, a glaze of ink and water may enliven parts which have lost their impact.

Alternatively, a more subtle type of counterchange may take the form of textural contrast, by placing a finely detailed balcony or aged stone wall beside a quieter, more neutral area. Look for these moments and your work will come alive.

The study of landscape under snow is tremendous fun. It is even possible to transform a rather unpromising summer sketch by removing all the leaves and reversing everything until it becomes a thoroughly wintry scene. To look convincing, snow demands a light, sensitive touch and no over-working. Keep the

Cleddau locked in winter.

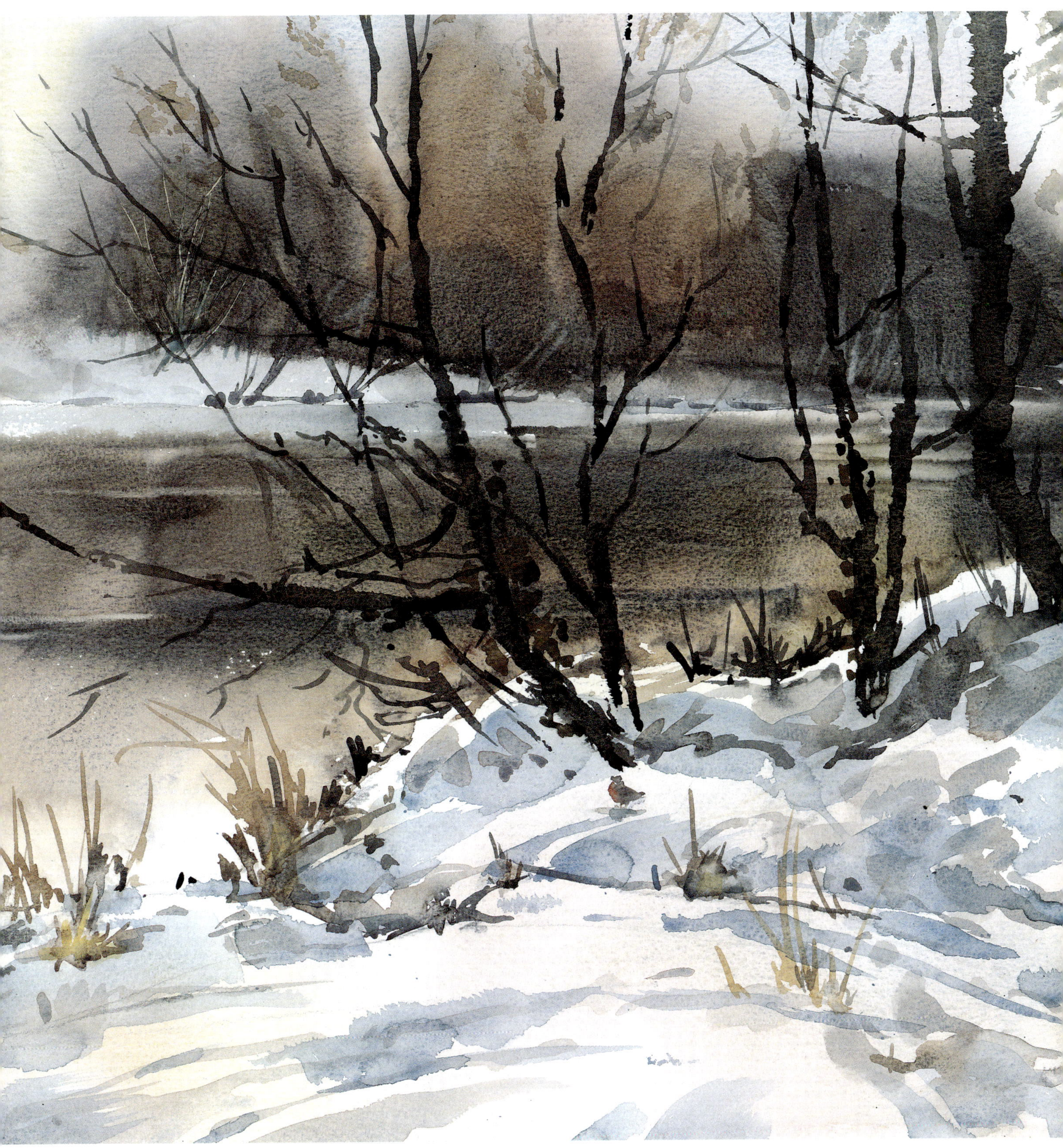

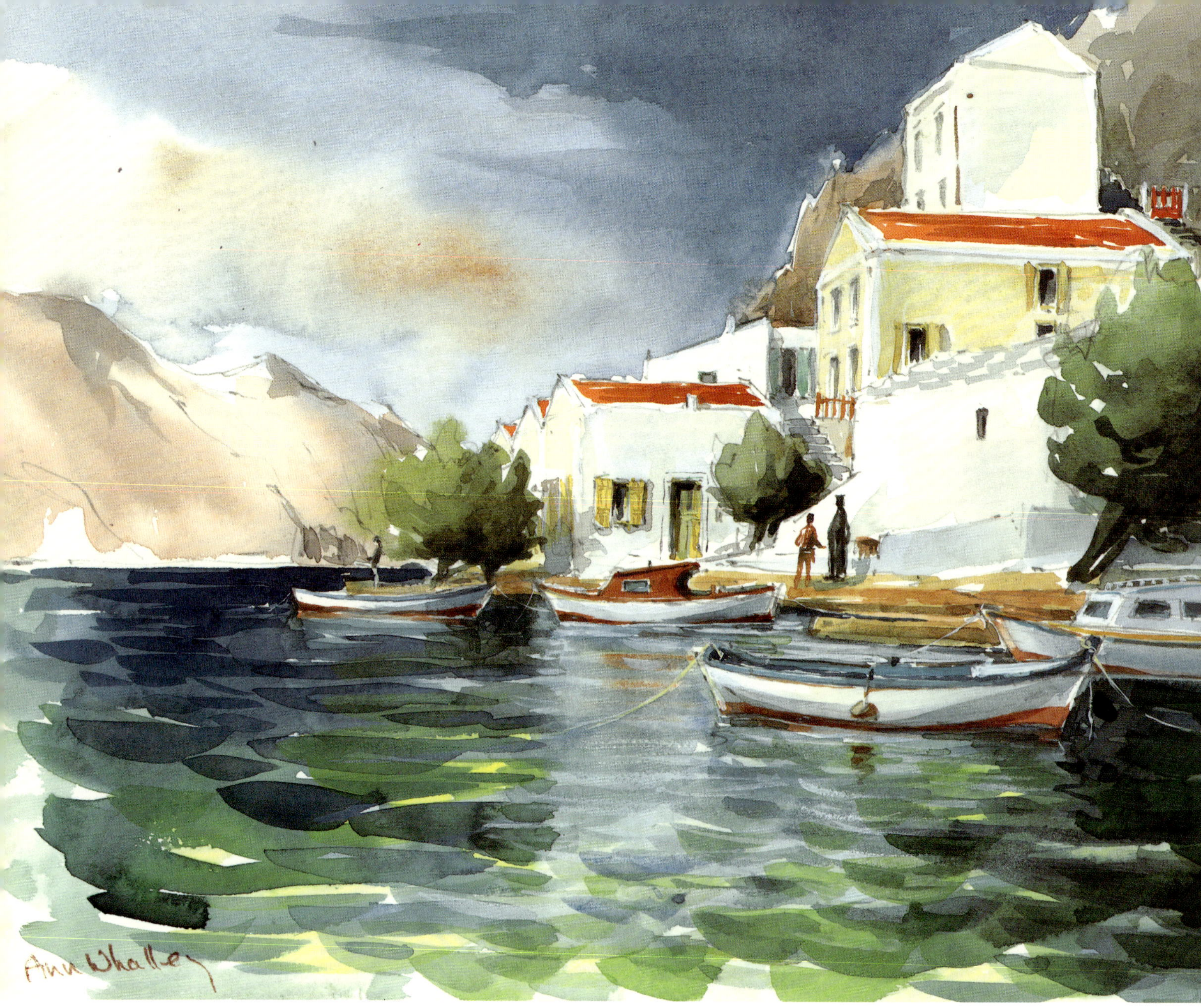

colours clean, and put in a few definite contrasts. If you don't believe me, try taking a sketch that you think has failed and changing it into a winter wonderland – you may end up with a masterpiece!

SUN, WARMTH AND LIGHT

While we do have some lovely warm, sunny days here in Pembrokeshire, I really associate this joyous ambience with more southern parts, and in particular the countries surrounding the Mediterranean. I am always delighted to leave for a while the greys and browns, the cold winds and rain-sodden paper and head south to warm seas, bright colours and exotic surroundings.

So many things are different that it is hard to know where to begin. The contrast in tonal values is always a shock. Lights really *are* light and bright, and darks deep with glowing colour and reflected light. People, buildings and boats shine in the sun, fascinating in

Pedi cottages. *What a difference a little Mediterranean sun makes! Just look at the 'wine-dark' sea and brilliant white buildings with their rich red roofs. This was a quick sketch made on the spot to catch the wonderful feeling of Greece, and to show that 'atmosphere' does not only mean storm, rain and mist!*

their detail, and the sea is every shade of blue and green you could imagine. The dominant impression is of flooding light and bleached-out colour, of golden roofs lighter than the sea, and white buildings against a backdrop of purple-brown hills.

Some preparation for the impact of all this is essential. Arm yourself with an array of blues, yellows and earth colours, as you will be sure to need them all. Add a cool and a hot red, and some lamp black to mix with yellow for the hot, dark green of Mediterranean trees. Take a big, absorbent brush and a plate or large palette (your paint will dry quickly in the sun), and throw in a few pastels to catch the brilliance of massed geraniums and oleanders.

Tonal contrasts will be at the heart of most of your paintings in the sun. Many people confuse tone with colour, as it is often difficult to assess values. Squinting through half-closed eyes can help to make things clear. I find that tilting my head sideways to view the scene works well, as everything becomes an arrangement of abstract shapes and tones. A simple tool is a graded tone strip, easily made with pencil on a piece of card, or, more sophisticated, a rectangle of smoked glass with some card stuck across the back. Hold this up like a mirror at an angle where you can view the scene you are painting, and, because of the resulting deeper tones overall, contrasts become apparent.

I would advise you to spend at least a day making tonal sketches instead of rushing in straight away with colour. As well as coming to terms with light, shades of white on white and the problems of light bouncing from one surface to another, you will also absorb many of the special characteristics of the place. Never feel that you are wasting your time in this. An illustrated diary, full of pencil and colour sketches of incidents, places and people, with notes and comments interspersed, may be the best memory you could take home to savour over the years.

A graded tone strip is easily made with a pencil.

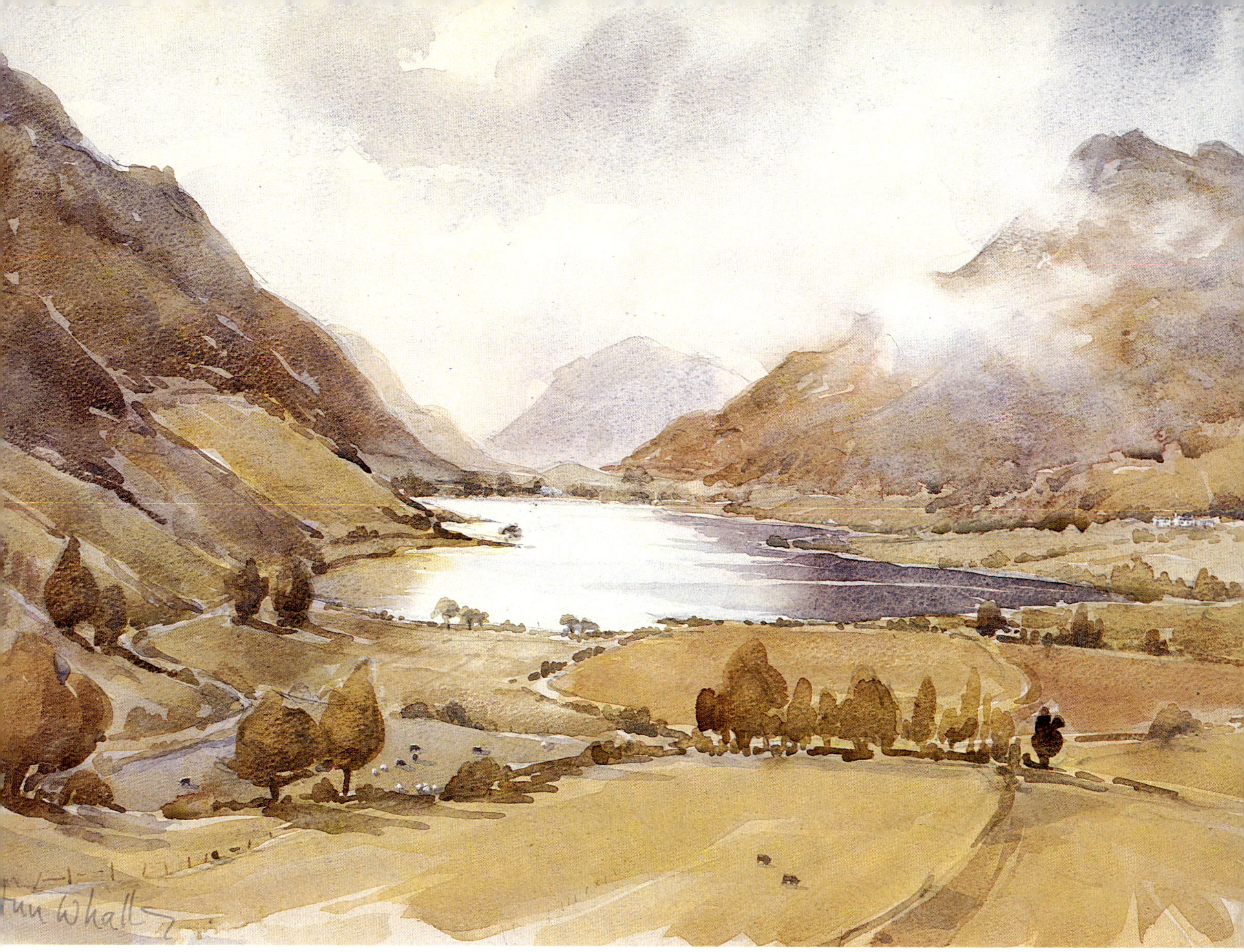

DULL DAYS

Not every picture needs to excite; in fact too much of a good thing can be boring, and a whole exhibition devoted to drama can leave your audience punch-drunk. Overcast or hazy days, which cast a diffuse light over everything, have a gentle depth of feeling that is wonderfully beguiling. There is a delight in soft tones and colours used to describe a subdued scene of quiet melancholy. The depiction of merging shapes defined in halftones demands close attention and a great deal of concentration, and will help to extend your range.

Serious study of atmospheric effects can be uncomfortable on occasions. I have endured wind and rain, heat, flies and ants, curious bullocks and inquisitive tourists, wet feet and frozen fingers. Long ago, however, I decided that this was the price I would have to pay for my fun. I was in France in the spring looking for some non-existent sun. After two wet days of painting my bedroom, the view from my bedroom window, the kitchen table and my husband, I ended up under a dripping umbrella in the middle of a saturated field, battling against the elements in order to paint a brave group of red poppies nodding in the raindrops. The painting actually turned out rather well, and was the first to be sold at an exhibition of my work in France. So it is worth suffering a little for one's art!

Tal-y-Llyn lake, north Wales.

(Opposite) Figure 1.

CHAPTER THREE

REFLECTIONS

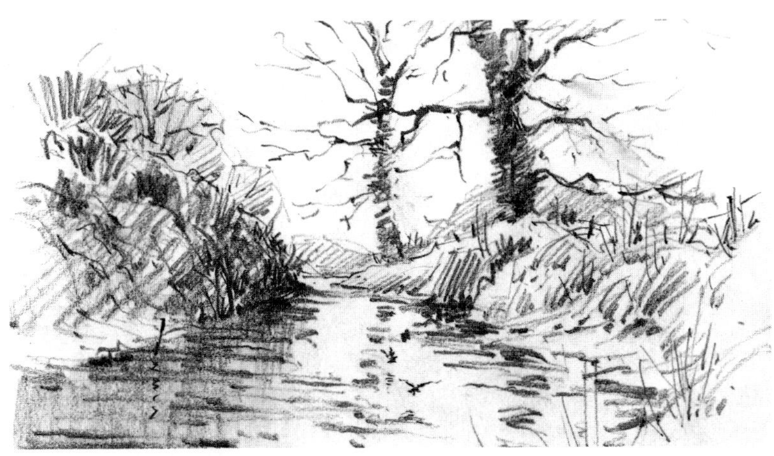

We come now to the problem of reflections. So often I see otherwise undaunted painters raise their hands in despair over this subject, asserting that they just can't get to grips with it. Once again, calm observation must come to the rescue, and soon the apparent chaos of colour and movement will become ordered and reasonable. There is a rational explanation to it all, provided that you grasp one or two simple principles. The main point to remember is that water, in whatever form, almost invariably repeats itself endlessly.

REPETITIONS

If, at first sight, a watery scene seems impossibly complex, stop and *look* at what is in front of you. The same wave will come along again soon and will break at the same spot, and the same ribbons of colour cast by a moored boat will snake towards you in the same way again and again.

The reason for this is simple: water moves because of external forces acting upon it. If you pinpoint these, therefore, understanding will begin. Ask yourself *why* the sea builds and breaks at a certain distance; or *why* the river ripples and eddies, or flows smoothly, and you are more than halfway to the solution. If you find water a challenge and long to paint it with conviction, awareness of the rules governing its behaviour and appearance may help to clarify matters.

CALM WATER

Water acts as a mirror for its environment. Waves and other movements are visible solely because they reflect the tones and colours of everything around them. The angle of incidence is always equal to the angle of reflection.

From Figure 1 it becomes clear that the wave face turned towards

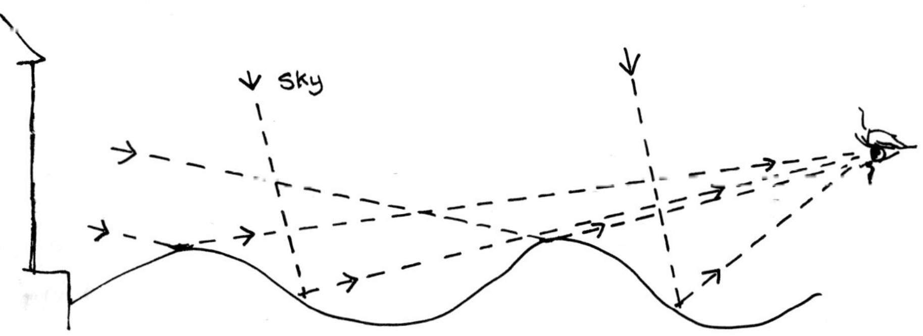

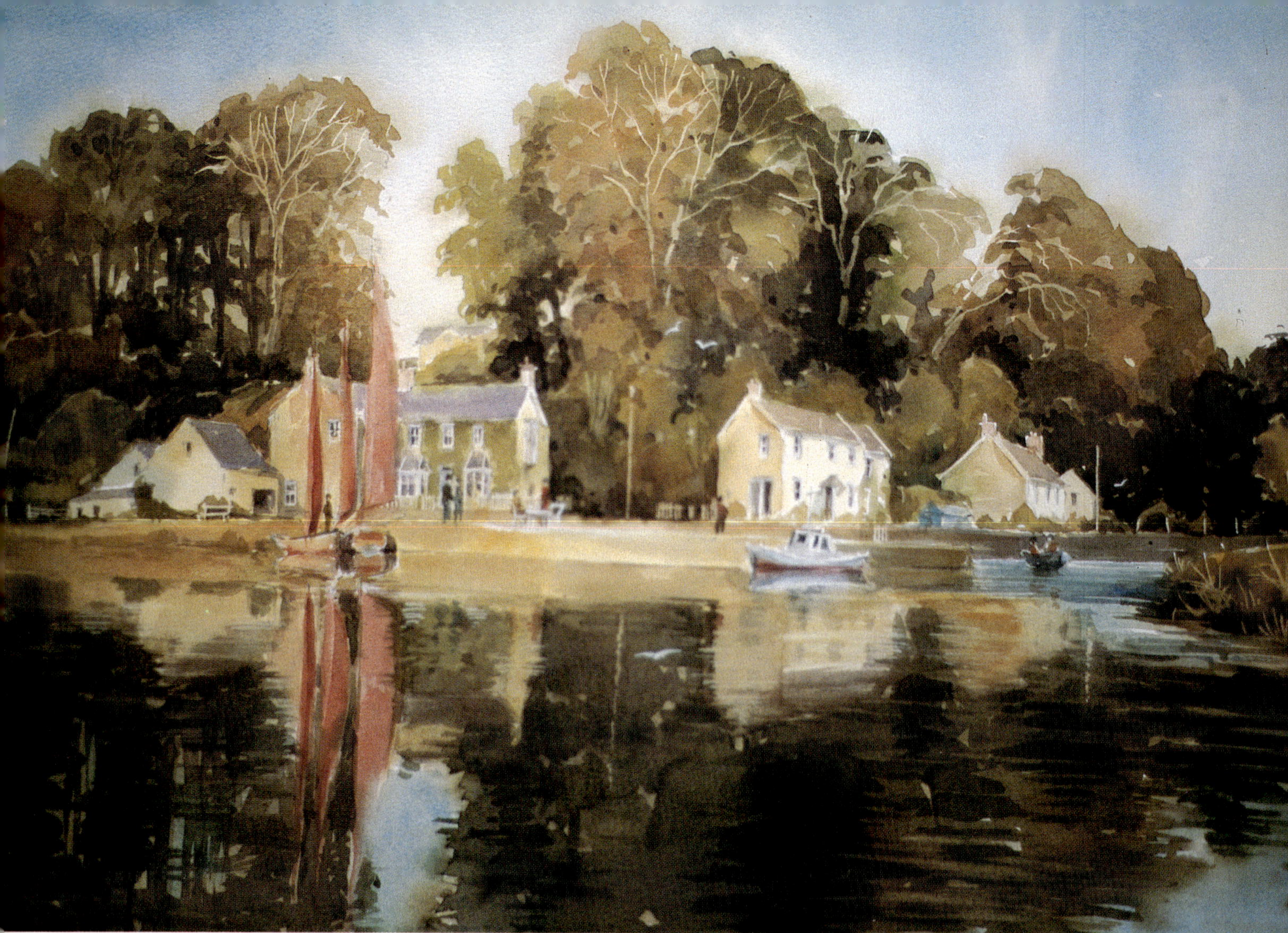

you reflects what is above (the sky), while the face turned away from you reflects objects nearer to the horizon. Knowing this makes immediate sense of the strange, horizontal-striped effect of many reflections, where the blue of the sky intermingles with the deeper colours of trees, boats and other objects.

It also accounts for the odd effect of the Mediterranean sea, which appears darker at the horizon than it does in the foreground. This is because the lighter back slopes of the waves – reflecting a paler horizon – are hidden, while the

Creswell Quay. *This is one of the many small riverside villages near our home, all of them equally attractive. I chose this one because I liked the way the pale houses stood out against the towering trees, casting their reflections right to my feet. An added bonus was the two red-sailed dinghies at the quayside and the blue-hulled rowing boat. Without these, the painting would have been much less interesting.*

(Opposite) **Venetian backwater.**

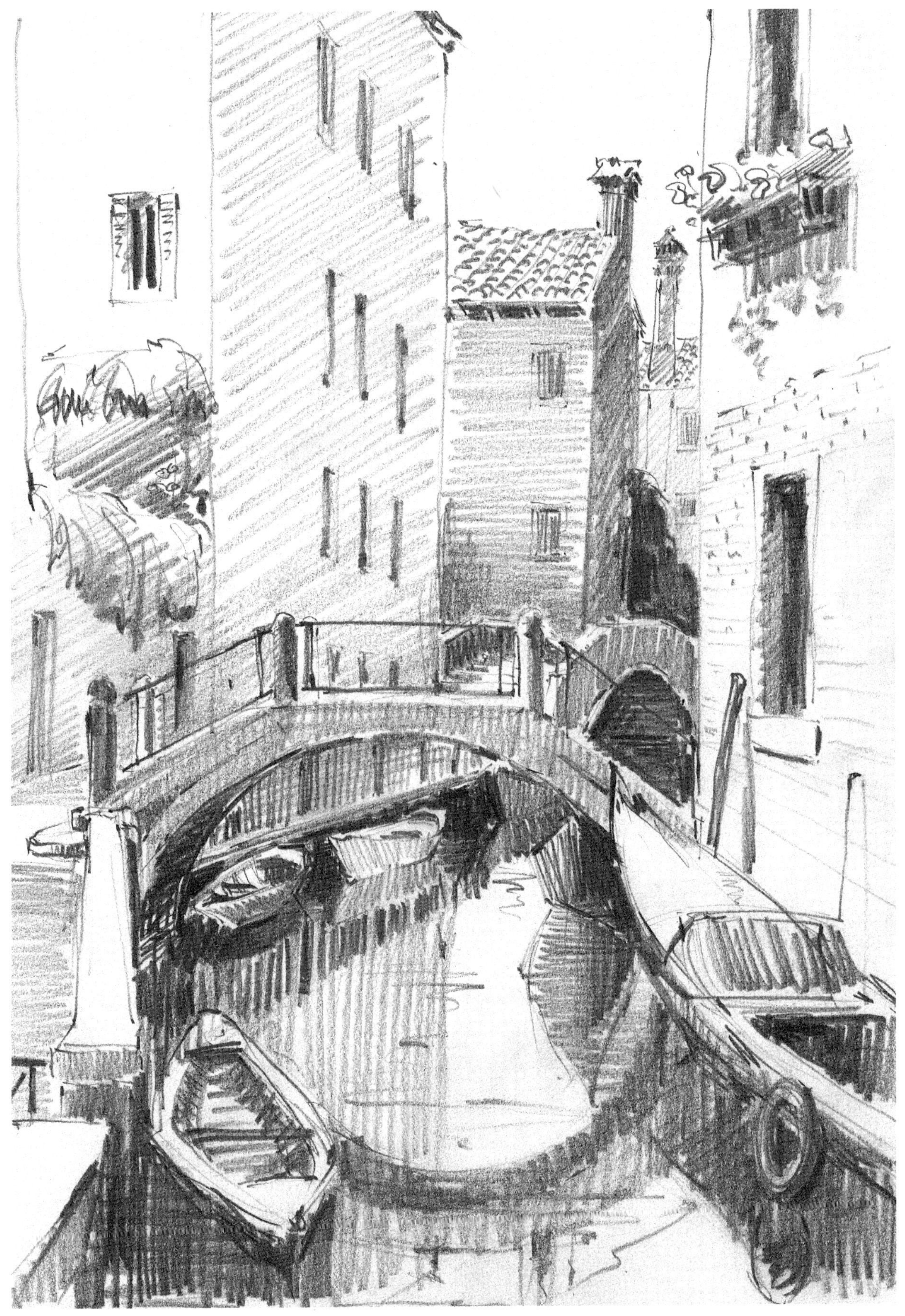

darker front slopes mass together in perspective and reflect the deep blue overhead (thus Homer's 'wine-dark' sea!)

It is not true to say that a reflection, even into mirror-still water, is an exact reversal of what you see before you. Rather, it is the upside-down repeat of what you would see if you were *floating with your eyes at water level* (Figure 2). Look closely, and you will see that this is the case. It is as if you were looking up from *beneath* the objects instead of across or down, and this is why one sees in reflection the underside of features such as boats, arches, trees and so on – aspects which may be hidden from direct view.

Arising from this, it follows that only objects at the water's edge are reflected in their entirety. Objects placed further back will have their bases obscured by the bank, and only the very tops of trees even further away may appear reflected in the water. As a general rule, therefore, remember that you see only what would be visible from the water level.

Figure 2. Turn this diagram upside-down to see what I mean about eye level.

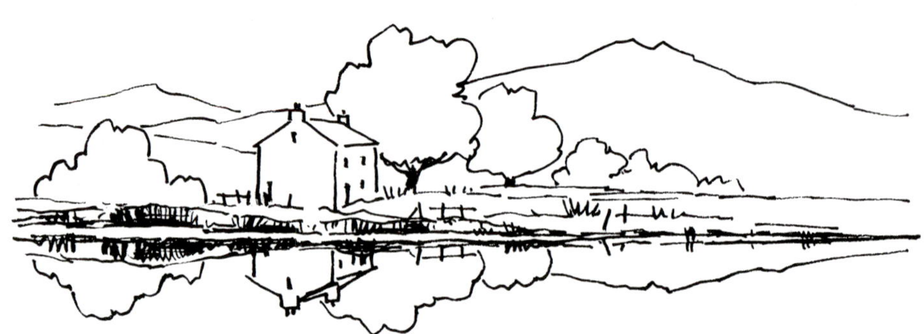

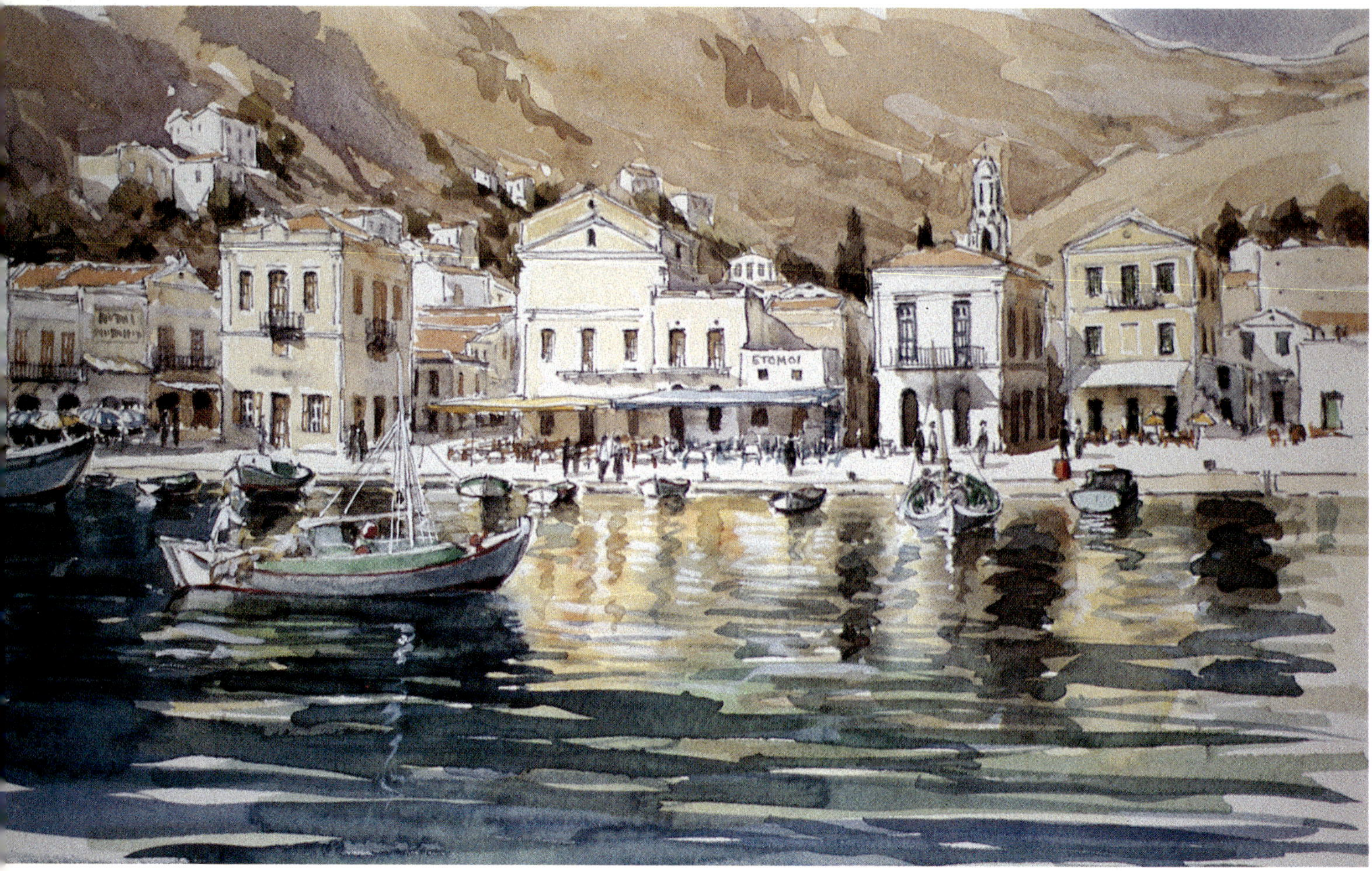

Symi waterfront. *Symi at midday just sparkles with colour, which is repeated in the water below. As the harbour is always busy with small boats, reflections are fragmented into horizontal bands of colour. It was important to get the tones dark enough in the shadows to highlight the sunlit façades.*

RIPPLING WATER

What I have said so far refers only to what would be seen in still water, which is not a condition frequently encountered. Once the ripples start, so does the panic! We have seen from Figure 1 on page 45 that the effect of ripples across an expanse of water is to split the reflection, so that not only buildings, trees, cliffs and so on are reproduced, but the overhead sky as well, the whole seeming to become so mixed up as to induce total confusion in the eye of the beholder.

At the same time, there is also the illusion that the actual reflection has somehow become stretched and elongated to seem far longer than the object being reflected. This is not so: it is still the same size, but the intervention of sky faces to the ripples makes it appear so. If one were able to add up all the object reflections, they would still equal the object's size.

You will have noticed by now that reflections in moving water have a tendency to appear as vertical bands of tone and colour, irrespective of the shape of the actual object. This means that we now have to contend with both horizontal and vertical stripes. The trick here is to reconcile one with the other (these rather simplified blocks can be very useful compositionally, lending strength in a valuable abstract way).

First establish the extent of the reflection with a series of brisk horizontal strokes, narrow in the distance and getting wider apart as they advance towards you. Use a large brush with a good point and plenty of water, and remember to echo the colours of the objects above, but a tone or two darker. Try not to make the lines too

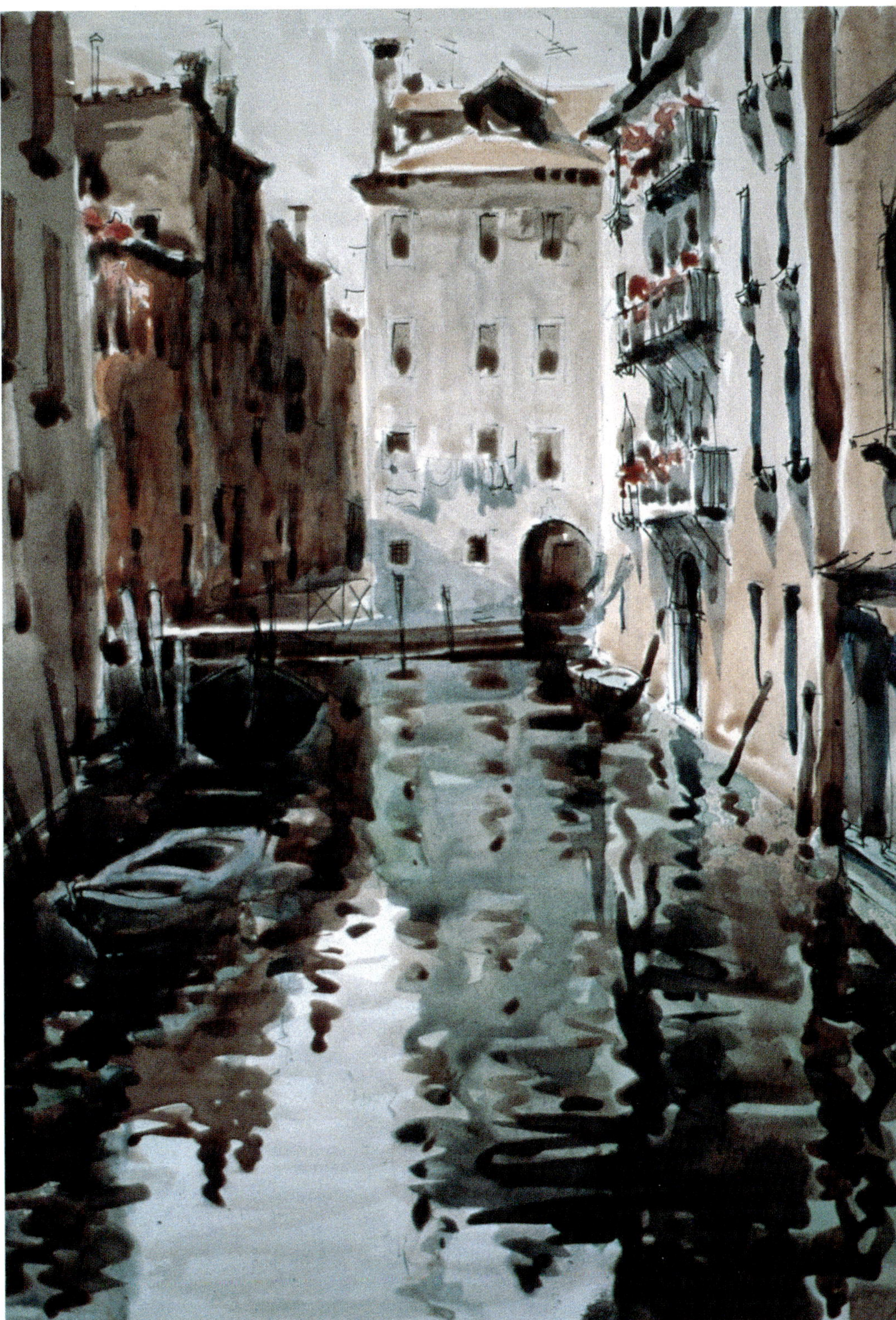

Venice backwater. *An absolute gift to the student of reflection: colour-washed walls and intricate architectural features are all doubled in value.*

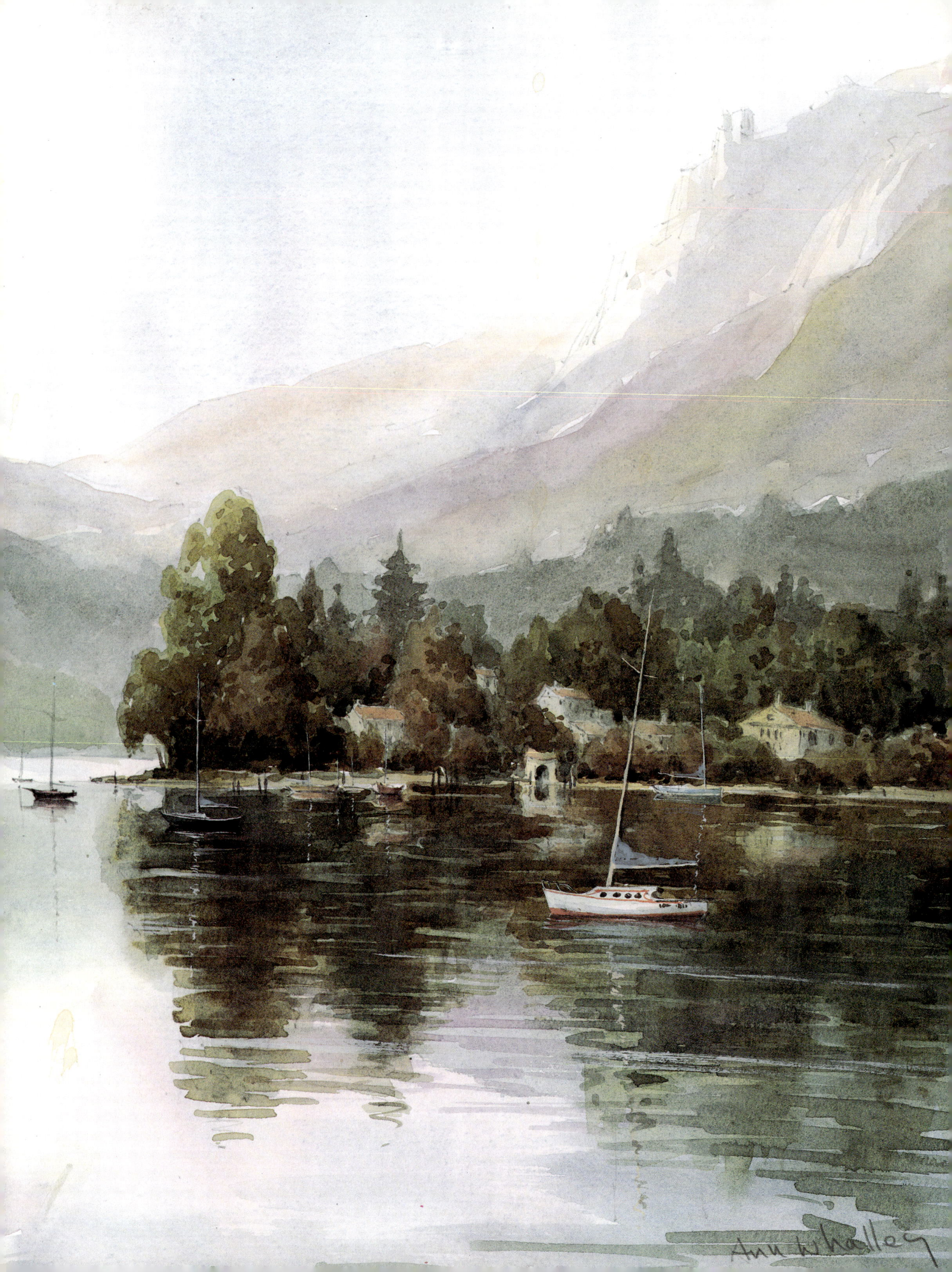
Ann Whalley

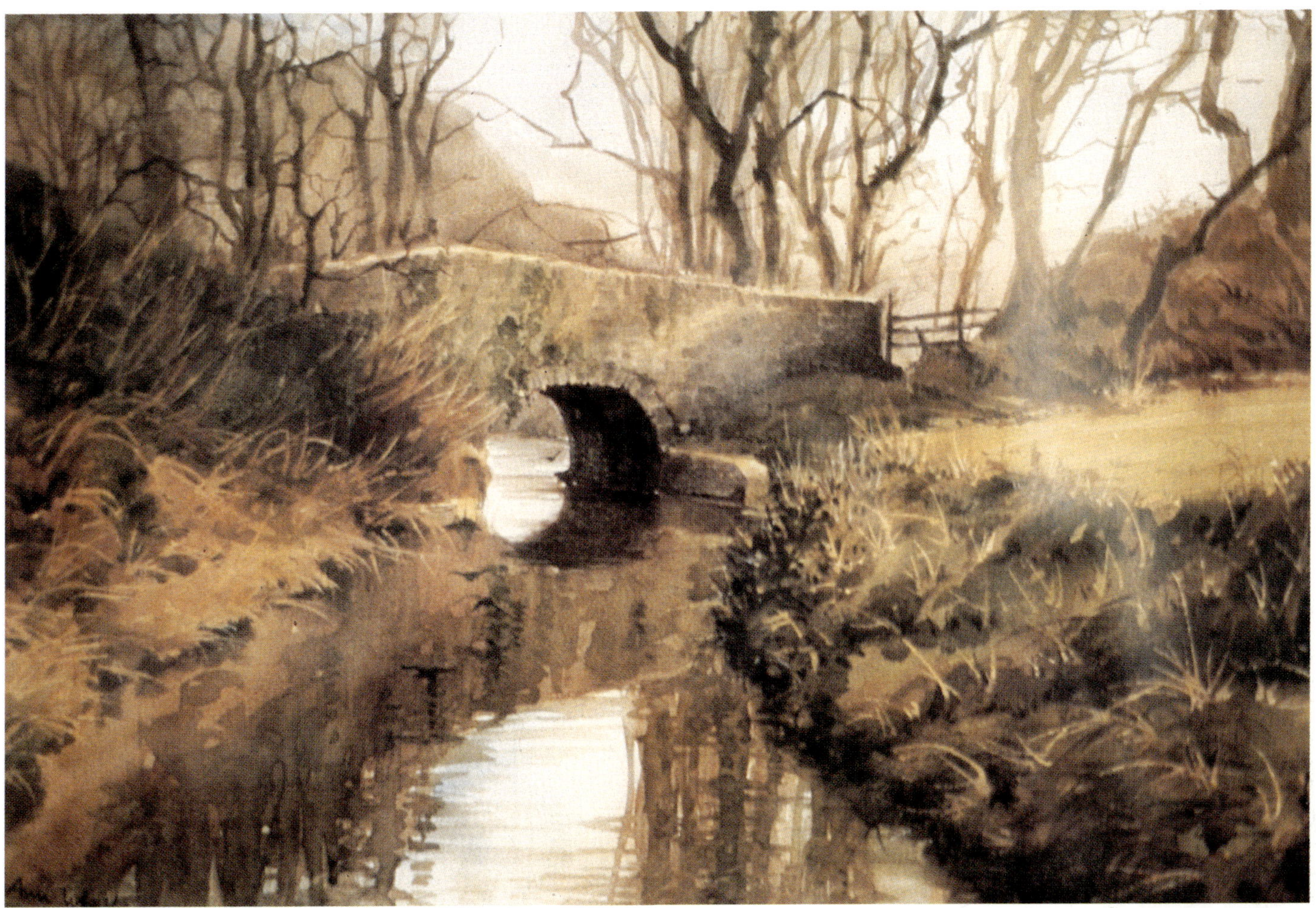

regimented, but break them so that they overlap slightly, while all the time their widest extremity is contained within a rectangular block. Allow one or two ripples to escape sideways, and let the paint dry. If it looks a little too stark or hard-edged, fill your brush with clean water and gently wash over the ripples to soften them – use restraint here or the whole thing will dissolve! A big brush, plenty of water and just one or two light passes with the brush are the answer.

Lake Orta, reflections. *In order to use reflections as a part of the composition, look at everything from the start as an arrangement of tonal masses, considering land and water as one. The reflection area is vital in this picture – cover it with your hand and see the design fall apart.*

TONES AND COLOURS

Water is an absorbent surface which swallows up a percentage of light and colour. A reflection will always be a tone darker and less brilliant in colour than the object. It may also change to a startling degree, and it is important to observe this closely, and to assume nothing.

Pictorially, this characteristic has value, eliminating sharp details, lessening contrasts and creating simplified masses to counterbalance more complex areas of the painting. The great temptation is to try to define every wavelet and every nuance of colour, but you should resist this.

Pelcomb bridge. *I love these old stone pack bridges, which seem part of the landscape with their crowding trees reflected in the stream. This is another winter picture, and is certainly not short of colour, created with the earth colours and cobalt.*

Far more satisfactory results come from a firm resolve to simplify and eliminate, rather than to put in too much.

Often it is the intimate details of reflections which particularly interest and excite me, such as the narrow backwaters of Venice, so full of atmosphere and with such strange shapes; or the brightly painted boats of Greece with the dark, snake-like gyrations beneath them, endlessly re-enacting a strange, silent ballet.

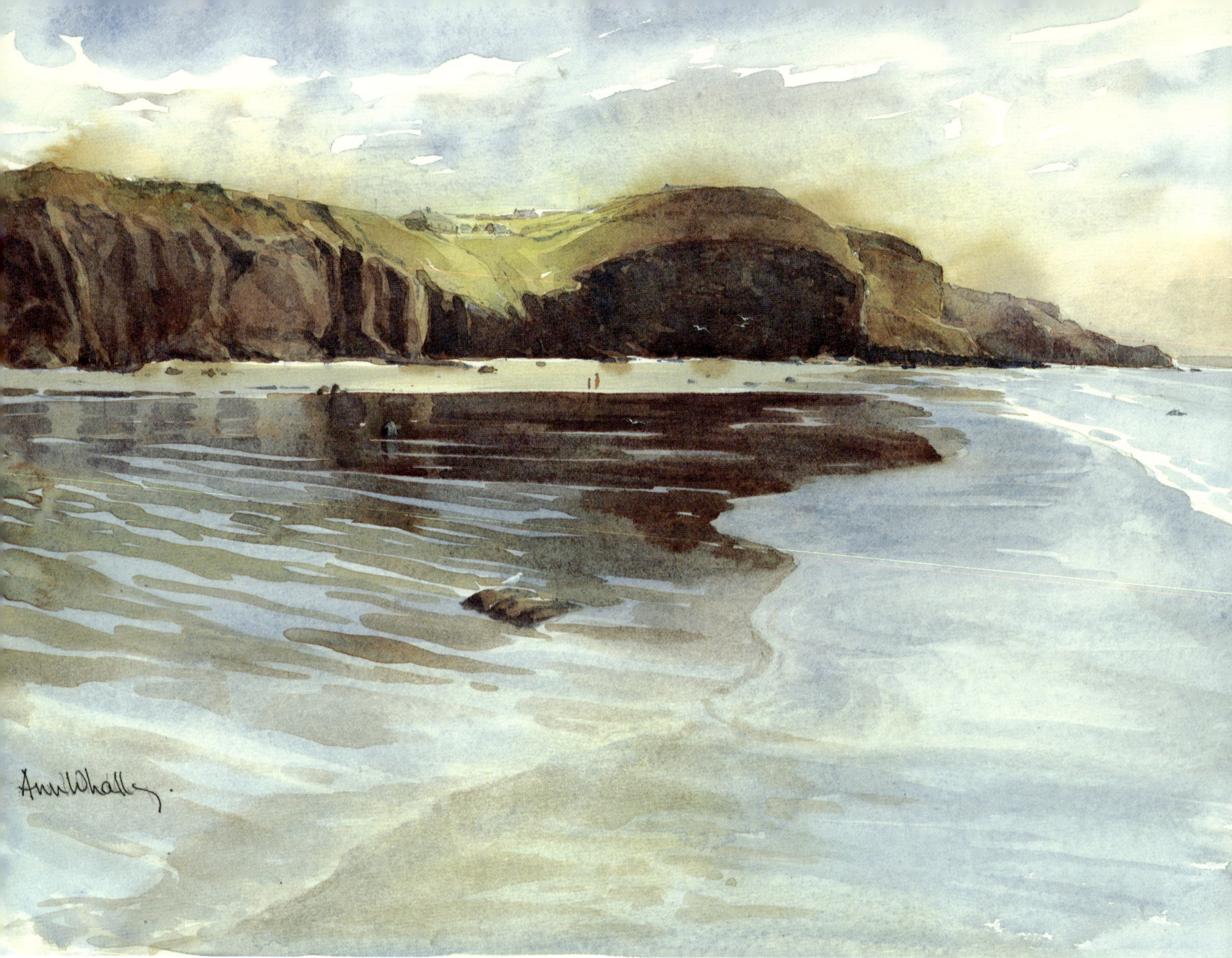

Druidston cliffs. *This painting shows how a large area of shore in the foreground can be made interesting. Very often a receding tide will leave the sand wet, so that the background cliffs are reflected darkly. I began this painting as a series of wet washes, and allowed these to dry before defining the cliffs and dark part of the sand, softening edges where necessary with clean water.*

PRE-PLANNING AND PRACTICE

Good paintings of reflections always look spontaneous, as if they were gaily dashed off in a moment. Unfortunately, it is never that easy. The painting itself may indeed have been carried out quickly by an experienced artist, but hours of study, sketching, photographing, analysing and agonizing will have preceded it.

All the decisions should be made in advance: all the experiments with technique and the order of doing things, the pattern-making and the colours to be used, have to be considered well before you approach the paper with the brush. Painting is only the climax, the final outpouring, when mind and hand work together with the confidence of all the decisions made.

Remember that the rules of perspective apply even to the drawing of ripples. They will appear to become closer together as they recede, and special note needs to be made of the tones.

In fact, tonal sketches are valuable in resolving almost all indecisions (you will remember my earlier insistence on getting the tones right before everything else). Fine detail is not required for this: concentrate instead on capturing the big masses of dark and light, and relating them accurately to the reflections that they cast.

Experiment also with the act of getting paint on to paper. In what order will you tackle the subject? Does it demand a wet-into-wet

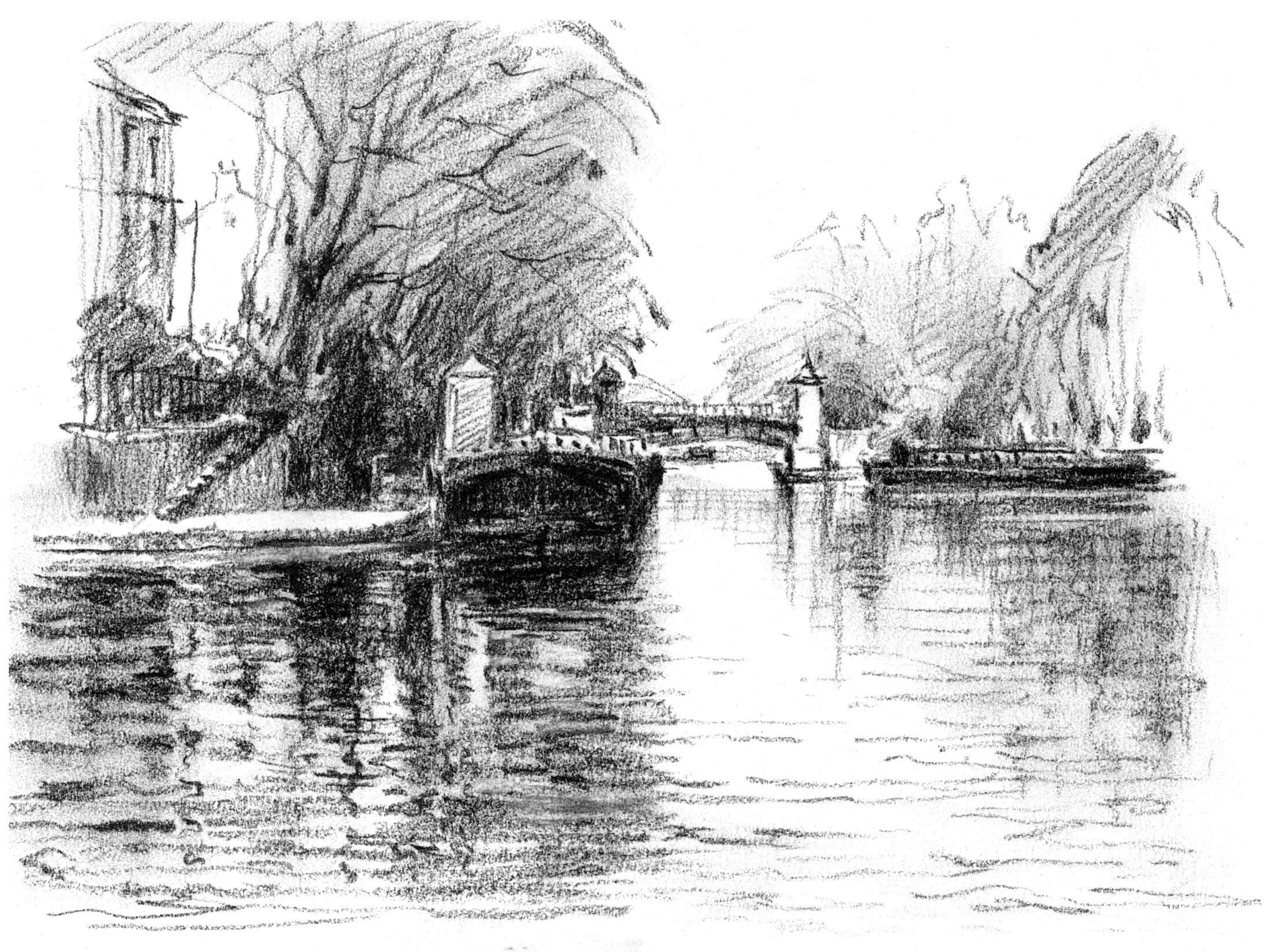

approach, or would a more controlled mix of wet and dry be more appropriate? Does the subject demand that the landscape and its reflection be washed in as one, or would the movement be better explained by the use of short horizontal strokes? These are just a few of the many decisions which have to be made.

There have been times when I have unashamedly looked to the masters for help. Think of the way in which Monet tackled similar problems, and study his methods. Bonnington, too, made water a lyrical element in his work; and Cotman's wonderfully evocative hidden pools and streams deserve your attention. Never miss the chance to make use of the genius of the past – and indeed the present – and don't be too proud to make copies to discover their technique. At the same time, consider the aspects which they found important and worth recording; where they placed the emphasis and what they disregarded.

It may seem that there are an awful lot of rules to observe and digest on the subject of reflections. I do feel, however, that the phenomena I have described are essential knowledge for all landscape artists. With experience, they cease to be so dominant in your thinking and can be pushed back into the subconscious, rather in the way that a learner driver has to think how to change gear but later performs the operation quite automatically.

In time, you too will automatically register all these points and retain them for use when needed, leaving you free to turn your thoughts to more abstract values and the subjective expression of what you *feel*, not just what you see.

Small canal in Venice.

CHAPTER FOUR

WIDE WATERS

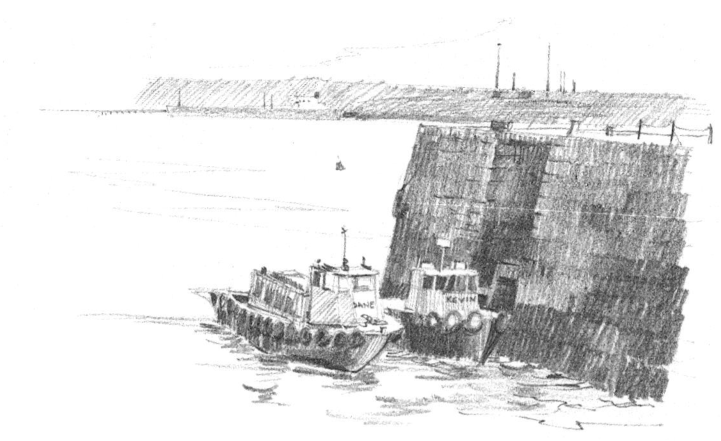

In the last two chapters I have been at pains to stress the need to study and understand fully the ways of water and its environment, and the dangers of taking anything for granted without question. 'Why' is the most important word in an artist's vocabulary. Only when we have begun to understand our surroundings can we progress into the realms of interpretation. The painter does not seek to copy nature: a camera does that. The purpose of painting is to express a vision of the world that is deeply personal and subjective, and this may have little to do with an exact rendering of a view.

Ours is a world of illusion, and our job as artists is to translate what we see with added perception so that others may also discover a world beyond mere actuality. In order to achieve this, however, we must first become masters of the real world, and of the unchanging logic within which it works. You cannot manipulate what you do not understand. The world as it exists is a joy to paint, and subjective values grow slowly as a result of the natural development of an artist.

To many people, sea-painting is the most difficult of subjects, and it can certainly present the artist with some knotty problems. For one thing, the sea is never still, but has a constantly changing shape and colour. The light can alter from minute to minute, as can the wind, while reflections writhe and gyrate in apparent chaos. There is, however, a peculiar sense of exhilaration in coming to grips with the worst the sea can throw at you – often quite literally!

BEING THERE

I remember vividly a wild day last winter, when my youngest son and I had literally to cling to each other for support as we vainly struggled to record great Atlantic breakers pounding the cliffs below us. We could actually feel the ground shake beneath our feet, while great columns of foam shot into the air far above our heads. Eventually, soaking wet and exhausted, we gave up and went home to work in the studio – but had we not been there suffering, very little emotional involvement would have resulted, nor would the experience have been locked indelibly into our memories.

Having said this, assessing exactly what is happening in the maelstrom sufficiently clearly to be able to paint it is another matter altogether. Being given to moments of stark panic myself,

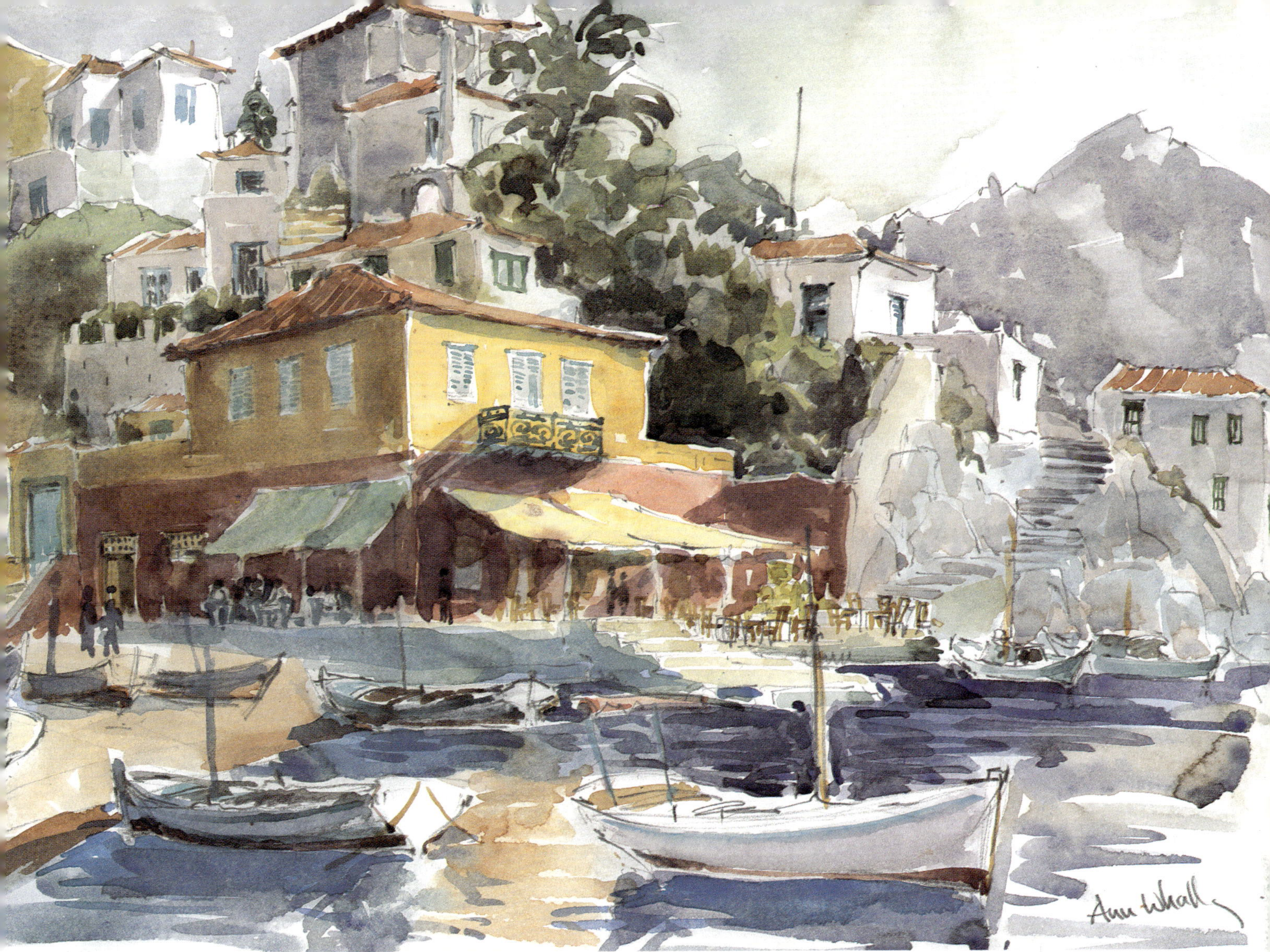

I have found a disciplined and rather formal attitude of mind to be of some assistance. It helps to have all necessary materials, colours and equipment out of your bag and to hand before you start. This seems to lend a certain confidence, however misplaced. I follow this with a protracted period of contemplation of the scene.

Observation is greatly helped by an awareness of certain fairly basic 'rules' applying to the sea. For, despite its seemingly random movement, the sea is in fact a structured surface of orderly, repetitive forms, and, as such, is capable of being demystified by the painter.

Hydra waterfront. *All around the Mediterranean similar clusters of dwellings hug the shore, bringing village life right to the water's edge. With no tides, sea walls are unnecessary and water, boats and tavernas all mingle in happy and colourful proximity.*

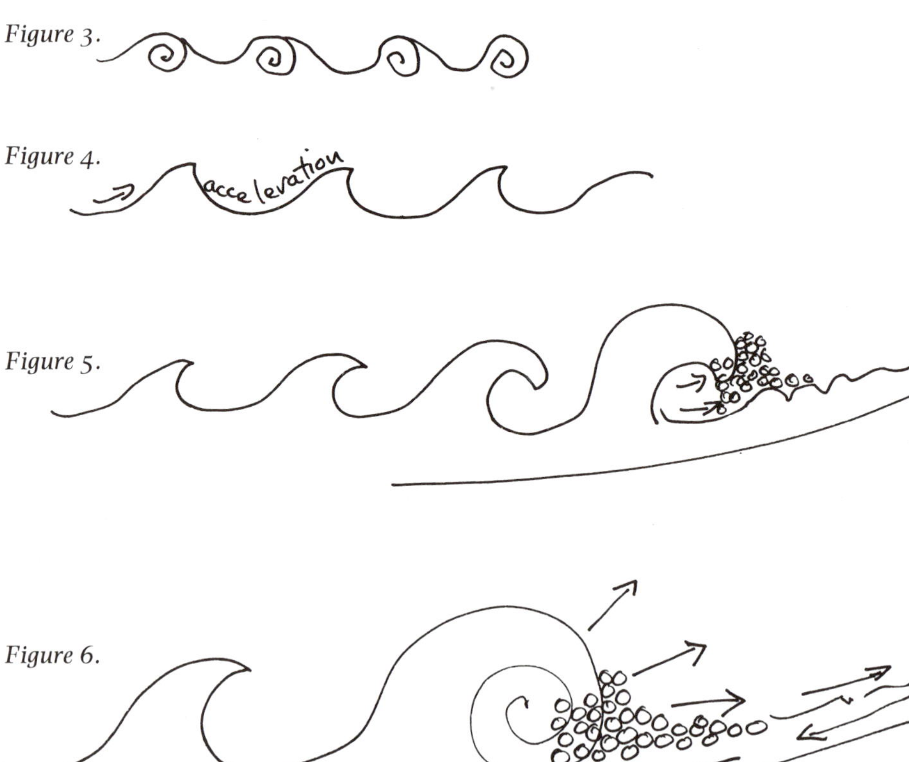

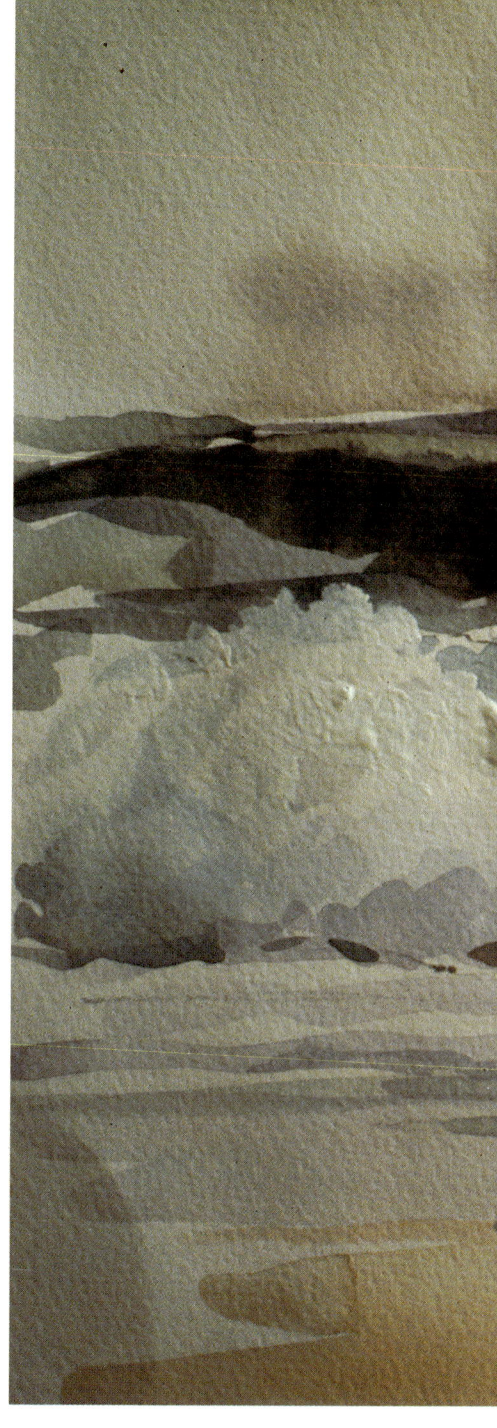

WAVES

A wave is a movement of energy, circular in motion, and not a flow of water in any one direction (Figure 3). Its apparent movement towards the shore is deceptive. The wind causes waves to form and seem to move, but it is only the ridges which move, while the mass of water merely goes up and down. Out at sea, these ridges are driven in the direction of the wind in an uninterrupted progression. If the wind strengthens, the ridges become higher and further apart. They also begin to change shape (Figure 4).

As the waves approach the shore, the sea-bed rises and the water becomes increasingly shallow. This causes the waves to slow down and start to pile up one upon another, more and more steeply until they can no longer support themselves and begin to tumble (Figure 5).

This movement is aggravated by water receding from the previous wave, causing an undertow (Figure 6). As the circling water rises to an optimum height above the mass, the surface tension breaks and trapped air explodes outwards and forwards as foam, spewing out ahead of the main mass of water.

Charged with bubbles of compressed air, the leading edge of the breaker tumbles down the forward slope of the wave, bouncing over the undertow as foam. It is forced up the slope of the beach, high above the general level of the water, until forced by gravity to halt and run back, leaving behind a lacy pattern of bubbles.

Once explained, all this becomes quite basic and reasonable, but how many times have you sat on the shore and despaired of making any sense of it all? Now you know what is happening, and why, the next time you are faced with this scene you will be able to anticipate the action, wait for it, and know that it will repeat itself endlessly. You will therefore begin to see form and pattern in what once

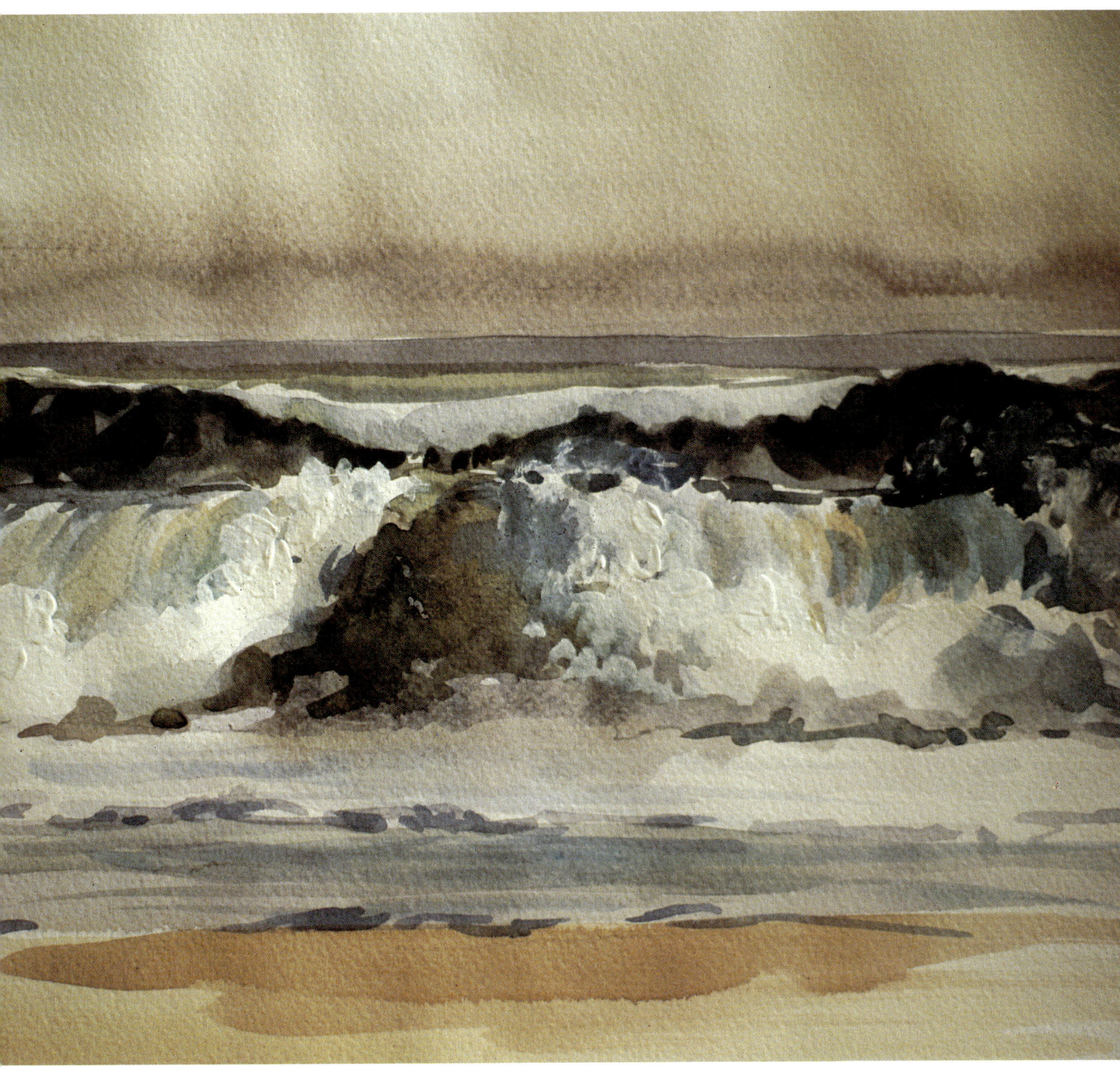

seemed random chaos, and be able to translate it into paint with greater confidence.

The fact that we live on a sphere becomes very apparent when we look out to sea. The higher we are above sea level, the more sea we

Breaking wave. *This could be anywhere beside the Atlantic, but is in fact at Trafalgar, near Cadiz. Look at the way the foreground breaker and the building wave behind it take up all the 'sea' area, with only the thinnest band of ocean above. The darkest part of a wave comes just below the collapsing crest. I sat on the beach to do this, thinking of Nelson and times past.*

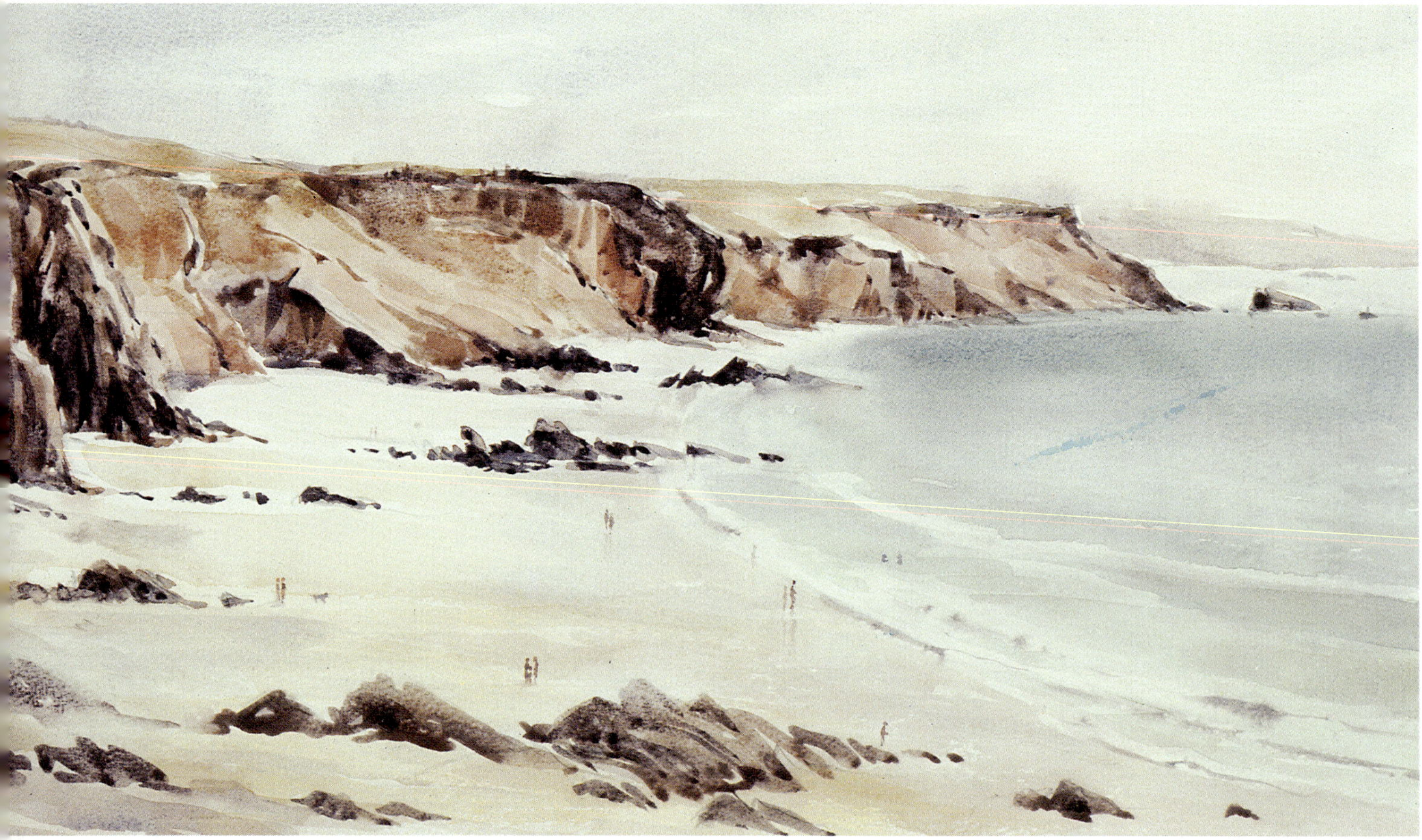

Marloes beach. *I sat on the cliff-top for this painting, and you can see how the horizon has climbed up the painting because of my raised viewpoint. These great, smooth Atlantic beaches sweeping to the horizon are what make such scenes for me.*

Figure 7. A high viewpoint.

Figure 8. A low viewpoint.

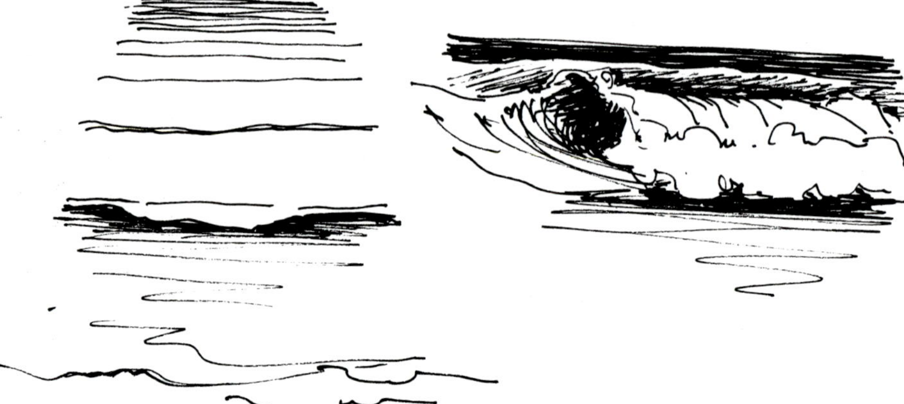

see, and the more marked the curvature of the horizon becomes.

Standing at the water's edge, one is able to see only about three miles at most, depending on the state of the tide (if the tide is coming in, there will actually be a bulge of water). From the top of a high cliff, however, one can see for twenty or thirty miles. One can also see a distinct gap between one wave and the next, the intervals diminishing with distance.

Back at sea level, all one sees is the nearest wave occupying most of the sea area, and then a series of diminishing ridge tops forming a narrow band across the picture.

Always a tricky design question, positioning the horizon becomes critical in a sea painting. Reluctant though I am to make rules, it would seem logical that the higher you climb, the higher up the paper goes the horizon (Figure 7). You can measure this for yourself: compare the relative space occupied by the sea and shore as opposed to the sky, as you climb up from the beach. I am always struck by the narrowness of the horizontal band of sea when seen from the shore (Figure 8), and it is a common fault to give it too much depth, creating an uneasy, tipped-up appearance.

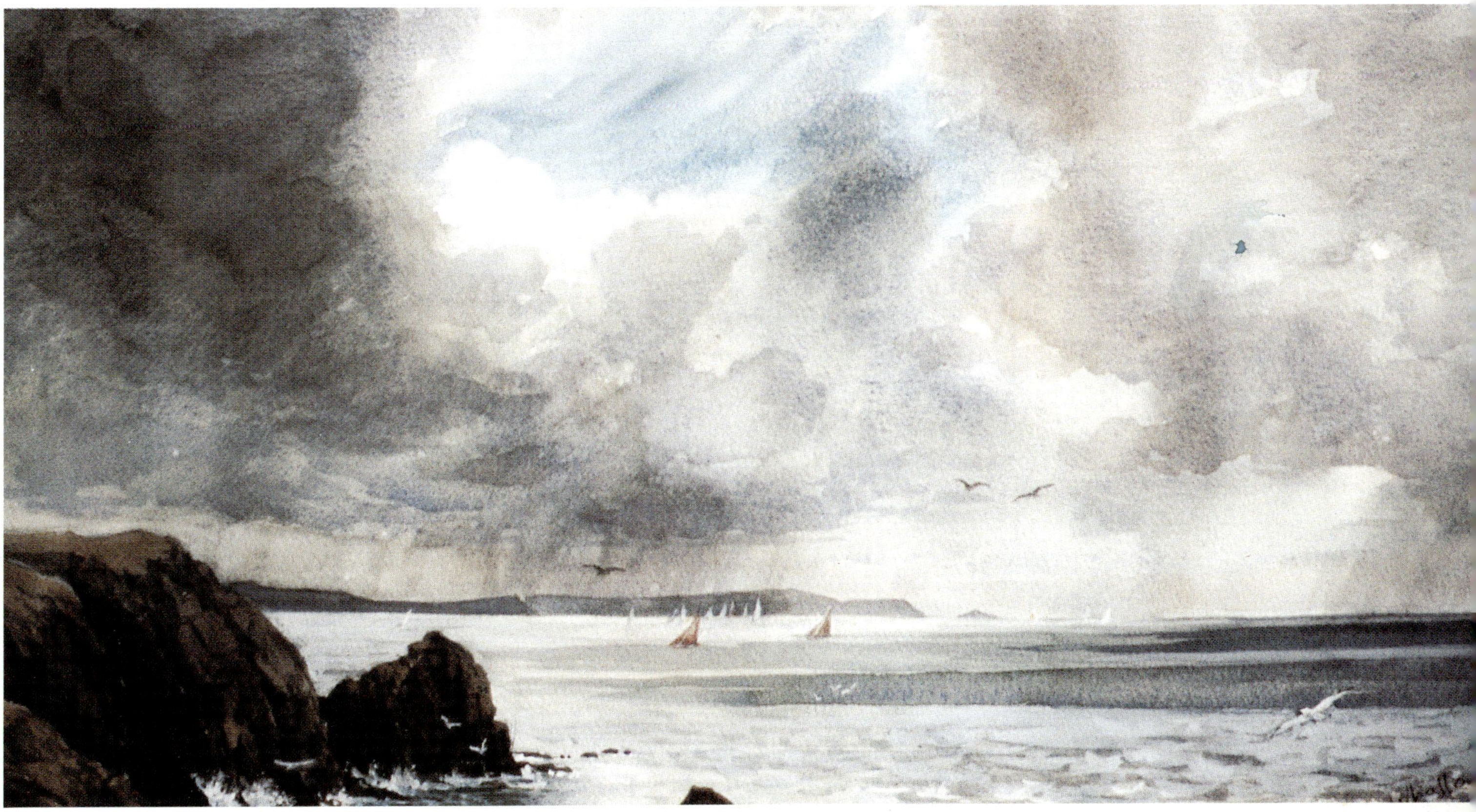

Storm, St Brides. *Big skies go hand-in-hand with sea painting, and are very exciting to do. Take particular note of the dramatic light across the water. The swirling clouds and keeling sailing boats add to the impression of strong winds.*

SKIES AND CLOUDS

One cannot be unaware of the sky when working near the sea – a great concave bowl curving away and down until it disappears behind the horizon. The role played by the sky in all marine painting cannot be over-emphasized. Often it takes up two-thirds of the painting surface, and the whole atmosphere and colour of the painting will depend upon it.

If you remember that water is like a multi-faceted mirror, reflecting everything around it, the opportunity to build up atmosphere becomes limitless. Notice the marked difference in

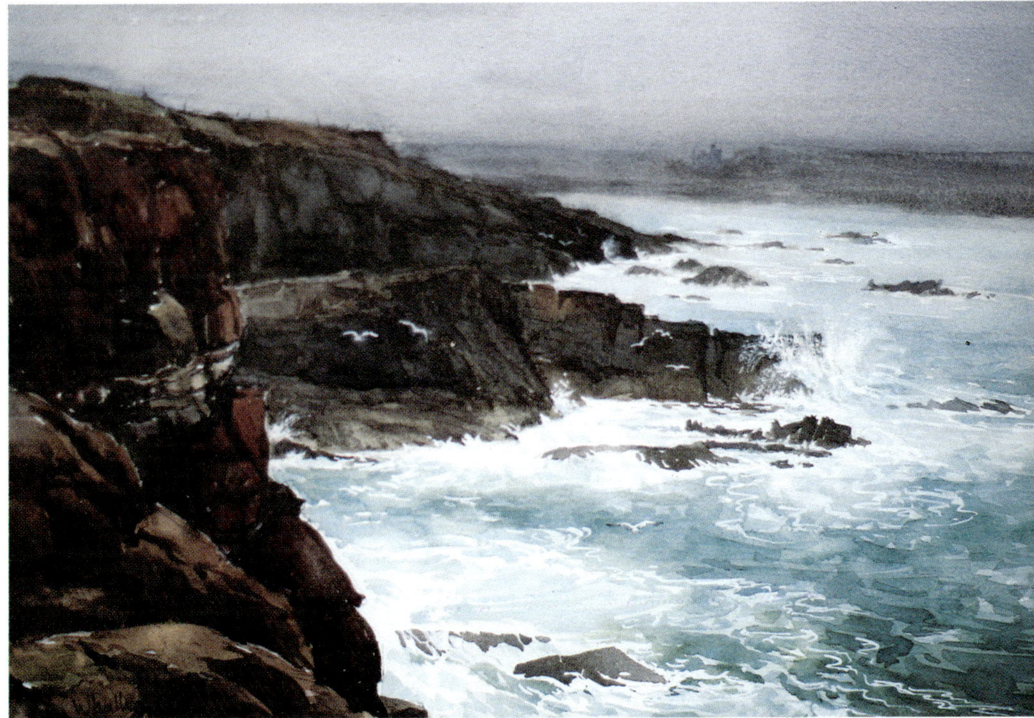

St Brides coast, winter. *This is a very low-key work, and relies on some rich, deep colour in the cliffs and water. The placing of the birds and spume carries the eye from the foreground to the distant foggy headland.*

tone and colour from zenith to horizon, and the effect that this has on the water. Passing clouds show as bands of colour, and can be used to add interest to a concrete sea. If the sky should happen to be a rather dull blue, then invent a better one.

Any clouds that are present will obey the laws of recession, becoming smaller and closer together as they go away, with the further ones frequently half-hidden by the nearest. As you are looking up into the underside of a huge sphere, you see only the nearest clouds entirely. The undersides of the more distant clouds are all you will see as they drop away into the haze.

Take note of the position of the sun, and of how its light defines the form of the clouds. Different weather produces different types of clouds, from high cirrus to massive cumulus and heavy rain clouds hanging low over the horizon. Practice and observation will enable you to give your clouds a three-dimensional quality, but do be sure that the sun shines from the same direction for the rest of the picture!

DIFFERENT VIEWPOINTS

From both an interest and a compositional standpoint, it is often more satisfactory to adopt a viewpoint which looks along the coast, rather than straight out to sea. By doing this, you can introduce many more elements into your composition, such as cliffs, buildings and great curves of beach. When sketching, do take special note of the sweeping curve of beach and breakers as they converge to a point on the horizon.

Figure 9.

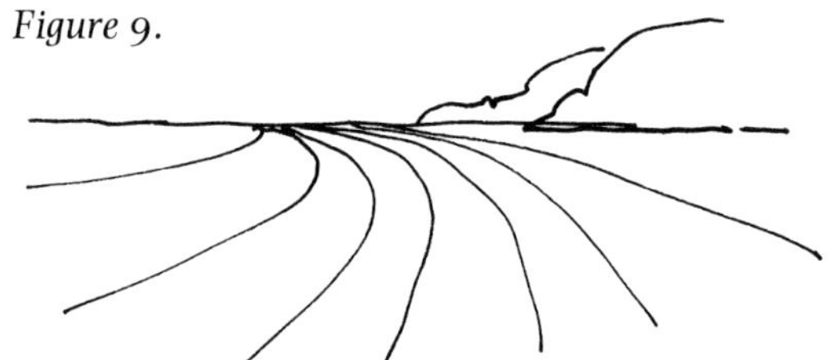

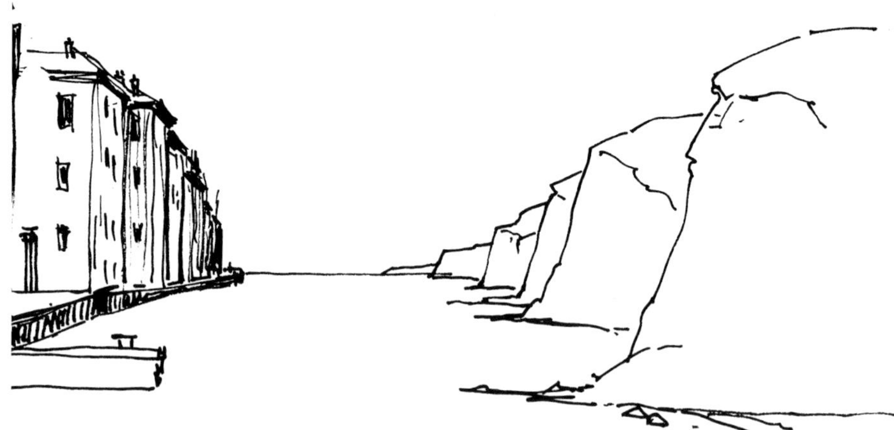

The convergence shown in Figure 9 is just another optical illusion of perspective, and applies equally to phenomena such as cliffs, moored boats, buildings and so on. It is exaggerated considerably by the horizontal plane of the sea and the low eye level.

Depending on your eye level, the tops of objects become lower and the bases higher as they recede into the distance. You may think this an obvious point, but I have seen some paintings with strangely tilted seas and boats floating in mid-air! The use of perspective when drawing figures is discussed on pages 65–6.

If absorbing all this seems a little alarming at first, try starting on a small area and concentrating on that – the eddies in a rock pool, for instance. Whatever you decide on, always seek to simplify movement by accentuating the most pronounced motion, and exclude as many irrelevant or distracting details as you can.

DRAWING AND SKETCHING

Drawing the sea in any number of different media is just as much fun as painting it, and it is perhaps wise to leave colour until you are confident in expressing structure and movement. As one needs to work quickly, I often choose a tinted paper for sketching, using charcoal or soft pencil with white pastel.

I put in the immovables first – rocks, sea walls and so on – and then begin to define the main movements of water, noting the white patterns or foam, and the way the movements are dependent upon and break around fixed objects. I continue to build up the contrasts, reserving my lightest lights and darkest darks for the area of greatest interest (focal point). Look for variation of tonal values in your pencil work, and remember that shadows are not all a uniform mid-grey, but can and

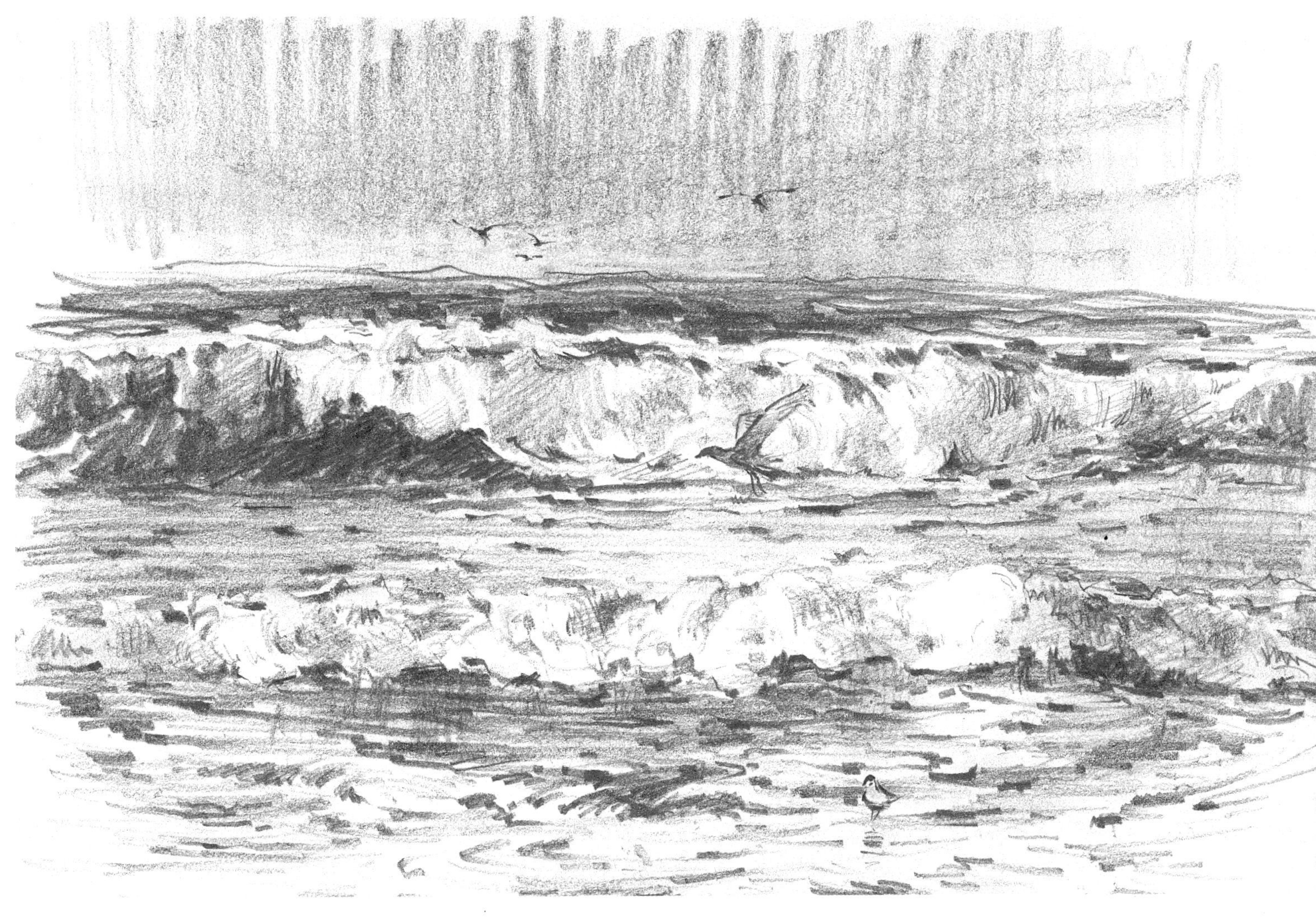

should vary from palest grey to black.

When I sally forth on a sketching expedition, I am one of those people who take the kitchen sink along too! It may be that I end up using only a pencil, but there have been many times when it has been valuable to have a choice. Different media suit different situations, and also bring sparkle to a jaded and repetitious way of working. There was an occasion in Rovinj in Yugoslavia when, in a misguided flush of generosity, I lent most of my materials to a forgetful student, only to find myself left with just an assortment of coloured inks and a large brush. As I had walked some distance and found a particularly delectable view, I was not going to admit defeat. So, with no water or mixing palette, and in a foul temper, I sloshed ink around in gay abandon and – much to my own surprise – produced a lively piece of work quite different from anything I would have done with more conventional materials.

Take every opportunity to vary your media. Use watercolour on ordinary cartridge paper; gouache on brown wrapping-paper; ink and wash for quick architectural notes; and felt-tipped pens on almost anything. Experiment whenever you can – anything to get away from being 'safe'. When tackling a complex subject, sketch in the main structure freely, ignoring for the moment all those delectable details and concentrating on the main strengths of form and tone. Set the darkest darks and lightest lights as soon as possible, and build out from the centre of interest. Otherwise, with no focal point, your design will fall apart.

Breaking waves.

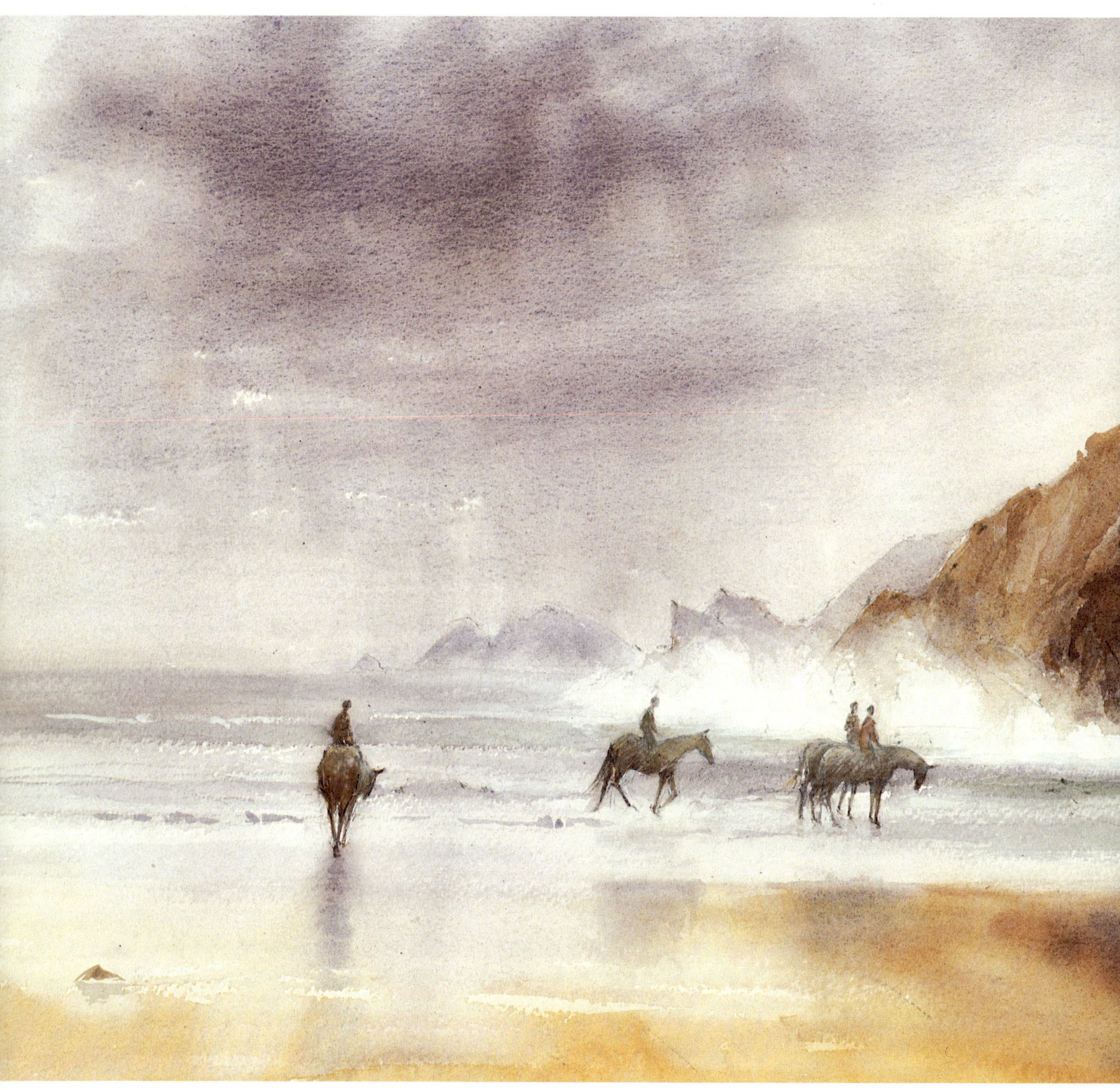

Horses at Pen-y-cwym cliffs. *This is a favourite of mine and shows my sons exercising the horses by the sea. I used the breaking waves to silhouette the figures and kept details to a minimum.*

When you feel confident that you really understand what you are looking at, start to work directly with watercolour. All your preliminary 'searching' work will now come into play. Work as simply and as broadly as possible at first, concentrating on the large values and ignoring detail until later. The painting should 'work' at this point. When you are satisfied, catch it all together with one or two well-placed points of detail, to set the scale and direct

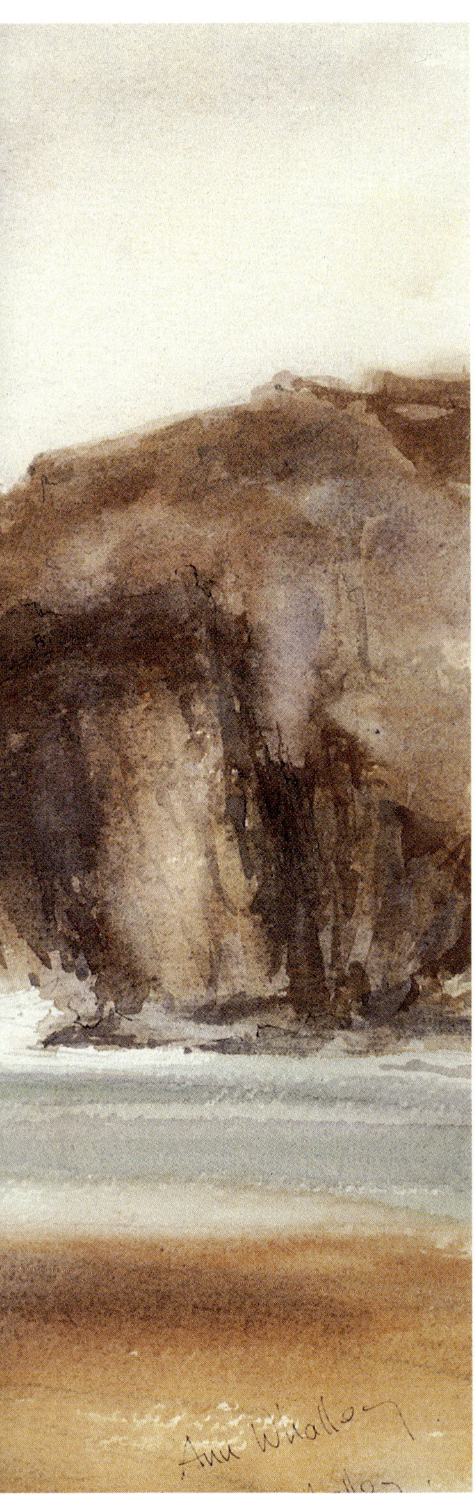

the eye. These should be very well-observed and accurate, while at the same time not being over-emphasized and leaping out of the painting.

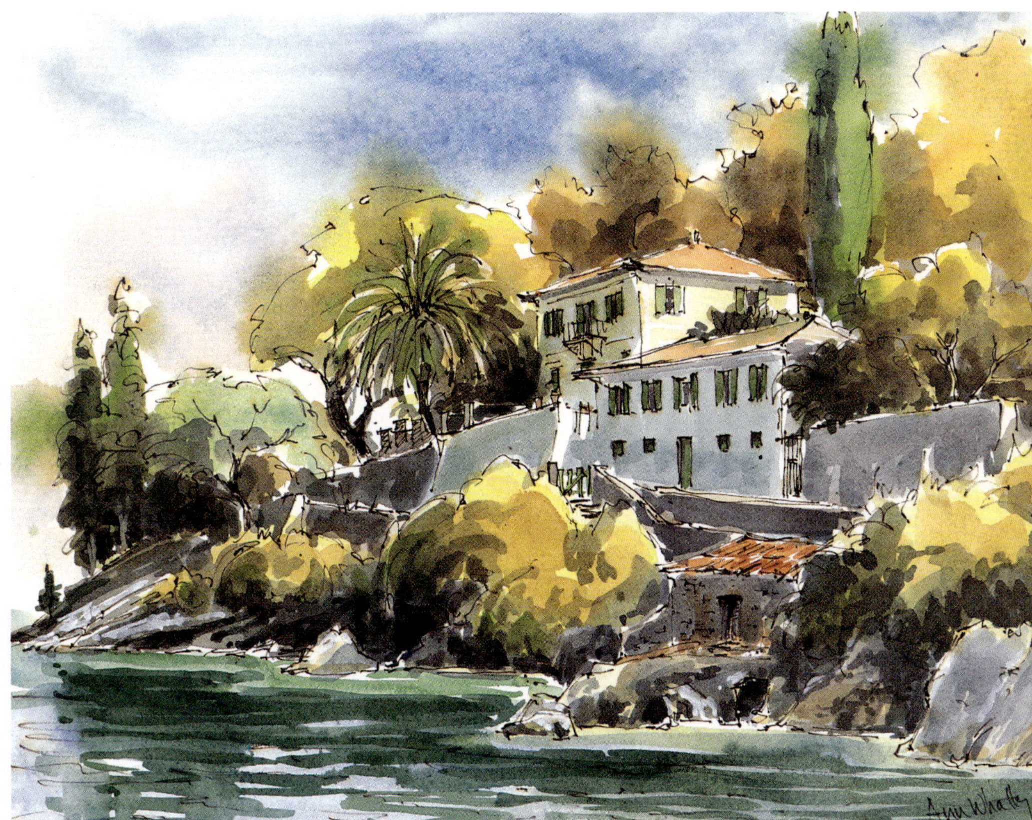

The Manor House, Paxos. *This picture shows the wonderful green trees and Italianate architecture of Ionia.*

THE MEDITERRANEAN

As an insatiable enthusiast for travel, especially around the Mediterranean, I spend my winters dreaming of being abroad, and the rest of the year in a state of happy delight and curiosity about every place I visit. However much I may cherish my beloved Pembrokeshire or defend its often churlish climate (so suited to vaporous water-colour), it takes very little to lure me off, full of glee, to sunnier climes. There is also nothing like a change of scene for sharpening up the perceptions.

I invariably advise my students to travel light – excellent advice which I am quite incapable of following myself. There are some extremely compact 'complete-watercolour' kits on the market now, in which you may like to invest if you plan to do a good deal of travelling. These are miniaturized boxes containing colours, a water bottle and pot, a palette and brushes, all in a box no bigger than two by four inches! I have one of these myself, and it is wonderful for times when a large bag would be a distinct hindrance. For a two-week painting stint abroad, however, this is just not enough, and I can usually be recognized as the archetypal lady-artist toiling along beneath a welter of encumbrances in totally inadequate bags. This is not because I enjoy carrying things – far from it – but because the more I travel, the more I find it necessary to have with me a wide means of expression. Now that I have also discovered pastel, my problems are immense! The sensible course of

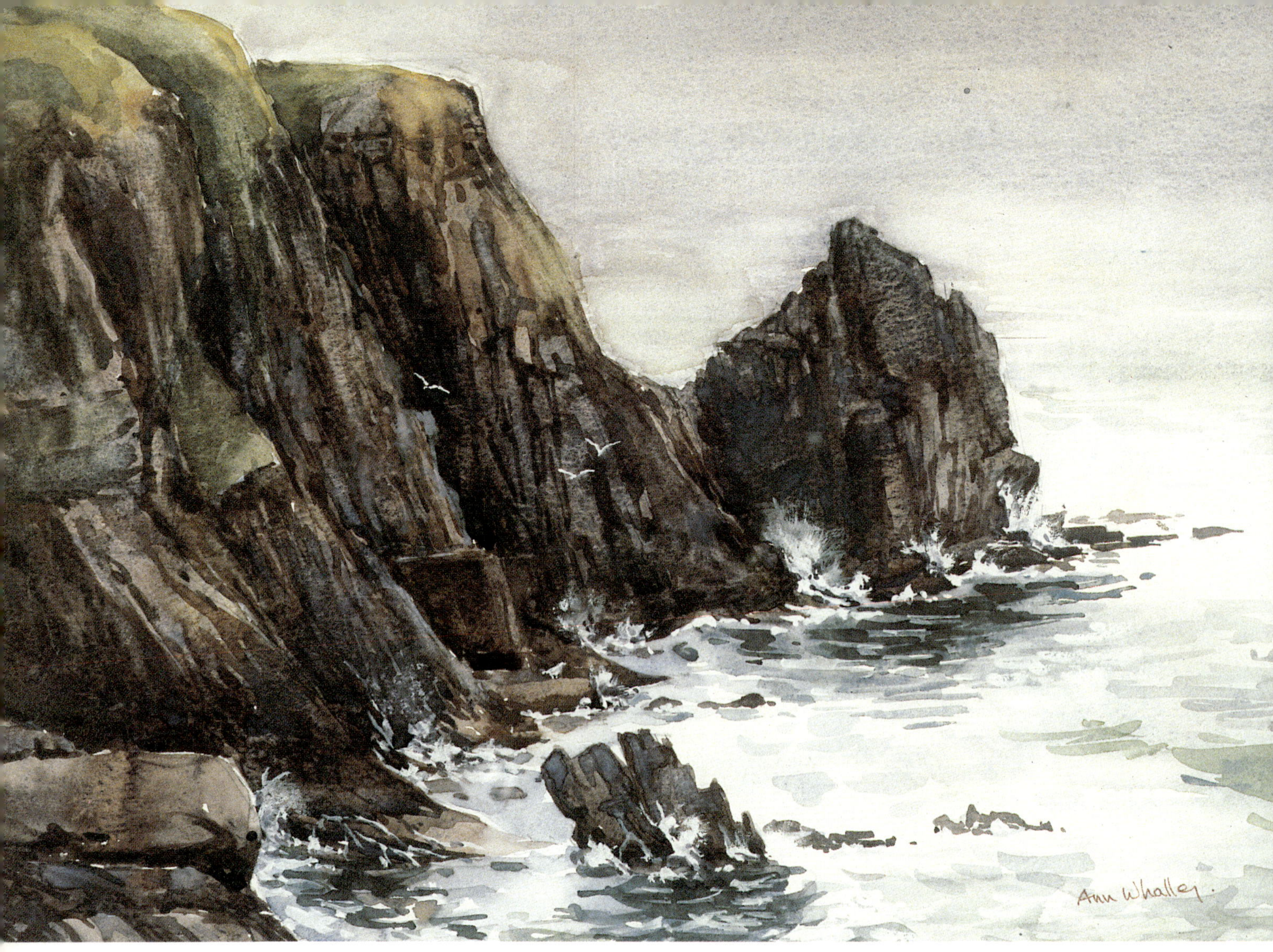

action is of course to find a happy medium, and to try to limit yourself only to the materials you really need, which is something you will learn with time.

Many of the more uncomfortable problems which beset the marine painter are less evident in the Mediterranean – perhaps the warmth and general relaxed ambience have something to do with this. There are no tides to speak of; no finding oneself awash and floating out to sea; or looking up to find acres of sand where a moment ago were breaking waves. Buildings come right to the water's edge, so that the sea comes gently into the town, creating an intimacy not often found beside oceans.

There is fascination in the unfamiliar shape and detailing of buildings, the colourful people and boats, the simpler way of life, and in the amazing range of colour taken up by the sea. If you go to the Mediterranean to work, be sure to take every blue, green and turquoise pigment you can lay hands on – you will need them all. As ever, the raw material of painting lies not so much in the objects depicted, but in the way that light falls over them. The passage of the sun across the sky and the moving shadows that this creates have a great impact. One great advantage of working here is that one can rely on tomorrow being the same as today, with a bright sun shining in a blue sky.

St Anne's Head. *This is Pembrokeshire's 'Land's End', where the jagged cliffs plunge into the ocean and the next stop is America. The rocks here are very old and deeply indented and worn.*

WALES

I have to admit that the same cannot be said of the part of the world in which I live. Many a cloudless day of bright promise has ended shrouded in impenetrable fog, isolating the dismayed artist in a limbo world of damp vapour.

There are two ways of coping with this: to go home in despair, or, better, to start another painting and try to capture something of the mysterious forms of rocks and cliffs before they dissolve completely and the paper follows suit. In such circumstances, quick tonal sketches are all one can hope to achieve before galloping back to the studio to develop the idea before the memory fades.

Of course, not every day descends into gloom. Here at the edge of the Atlantic the air is clean and unpolluted, and we enjoy an enviable clarity of light which even in winter has a soft translucence. Inevitably we get frequent storms and strong winds, but these are all fuel to the marine painter, bringing as they do dramatic skies and great seas. Our wide beaches are swept clean, while small villages huddle in the lea of high cliffs or at the mouth of wide river estuaries.

Go out of your way to find stimulating visual elements to particularize your scenes. Jetties and piers contain linear interest, both in themselves and in the reflections that they cast. Boats of all kinds, buildings at the waterside, odd rock formations – all serve to focus the eye and bring your scenes to life.

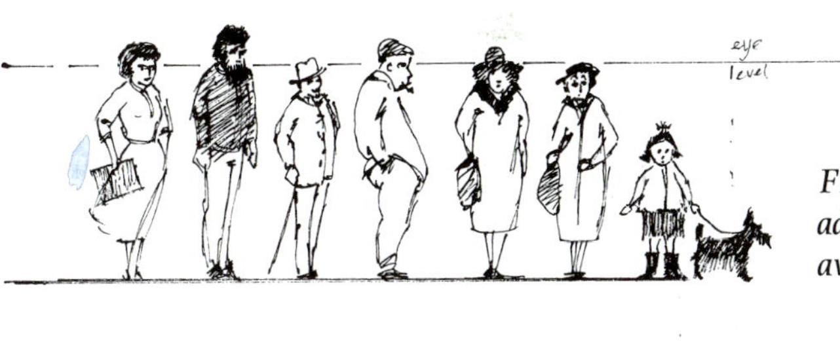

Figure 10. Most adults are of an average height.

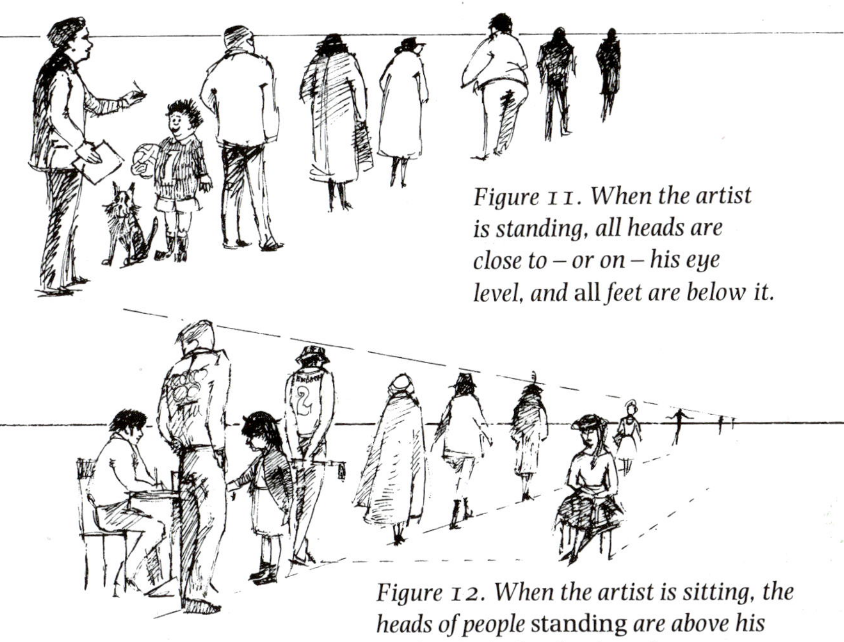

Figure 11. When the artist is standing, all heads are close to – or on – his eye level, and all feet are below it.

Figure 12. When the artist is sitting, the heads of people standing are above his eye level. The heads of people sitting are on his eye level.

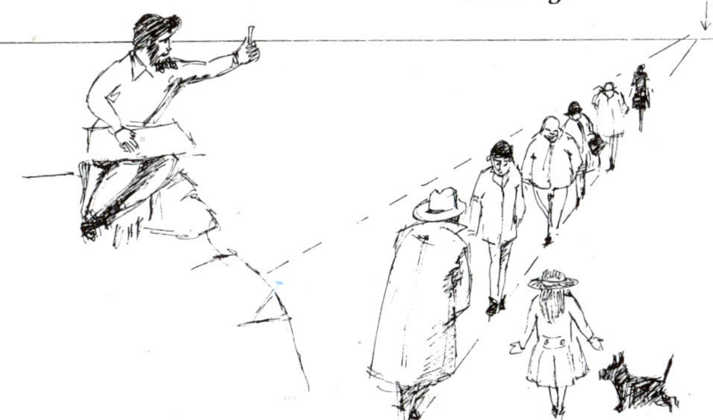

Figure 13. When the artist's position is elevated, all heads and feet are below his eye level. Watch out for children and dogs!

FIGURES

Some water subjects demand the inclusion of people. They need only be the roughest suggestion (a few brushstrokes will often be enough, and no more defined than any other part of the painting), but a waterfront scene with no people leaves me a little uneasy. What do they know that I don't? Use your figures to pinpoint centres of interest in the composition, and make use of counterchange (see page 40).

The introduction of figures can not only help to bring a scene alive, but also brings a sense of scale to the composition. If you get the scale of the figures right, noting where the heads and feet come in relation to the buildings and other features, the rest should fall into place. It helps to relate the figures to the size of doors and windows. A door is usually about six feet three inches high, and this will act as a useful guide.

Recession can be a problem, but all that is needed is observation and some very basic perspective. If, for instance, you are standing on fairly level ground, you can assume that your eye level will be more or less the same as that of your figures – in other words, all the heads will be at a similar height, even if some are further away than others (Figure 10). This means that, as the people diminish in size as they recede, all the heads will remain at a constant height, and it will be the feet (well below your eye level) which go up (Figure 11). If you are sitting down and the people are standing, however, your eye level will be below theirs, bringing the heads lower and the feet higher as they recede (Figure 12). Suppose now that you are looking down from a window and are above the people you can see. This time, both the heads and the feet will rise as they go away (Figure 13). Easy really, isn't it!

Unless you are building your picture around one or two close-up figures, details of clothing and so on are best kept to a minimum. It is better to concentrate on the figure as a whole, defining general proportion, movement and characteristic pose. We find no difficulty in recognizing friends in such ways from the other end of the street or glimpsed for a fraction of a second from behind.

When painting people in groups, try to see the group as a whole, allowing one figure to merge in with another. In a group one can usually only define clearly the heads and legs and not much else. Use fluid paint and don't worry if the colours mingle a little – this will help to make the figures part of the painting as a whole.

Wherever possible, make use of the shadows cast across the ground. These help to 'attach' the figures to the earth and also provide a few valuable horizontals and dark accents. Unless lit by a low sun or lamp, figures are mainly dark in tone, but avoid making them so dark that they jump off the page. With practice, you will be able to treat people with the same nonchalant confidence that you use for the rest of your work.

Painting successful seascapes can be summed up quite simply: it is all a question of observation. Spend more time looking than doing, and never stop drawing. Develop a sense of urgency and learn to work fast, while never confusing speed with carelessness. Simplify wherever possible, and try at all times to recognize the overall structure behind confusing detail. One learns more about what an artist regards as important by what he leaves out, so try studying some old masters (and some not so old) with this in mind, and it may help your own sense of values.

Above all, remember that there is no shortcut to success, and no magic formula. Ultimately it is all up to you and to how hard you are prepared to work.

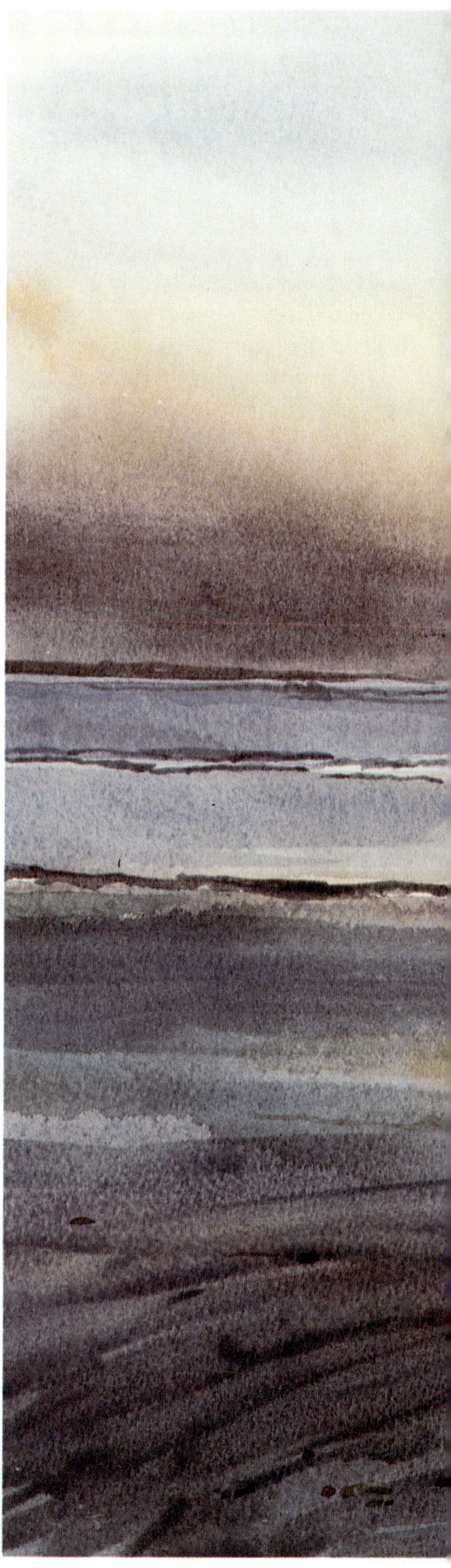

Sunset. *It is possible to get in all the colour of a sunset and still avoid a garish effect, as the reality is very different from the impression. The whole sky is rarely a mass of colour – the colour is restricted to a relatively small area – and the sky's brilliant appearance is largely the result of deep, cool shade at the horizon and at all parts not directly lit by the sun.*

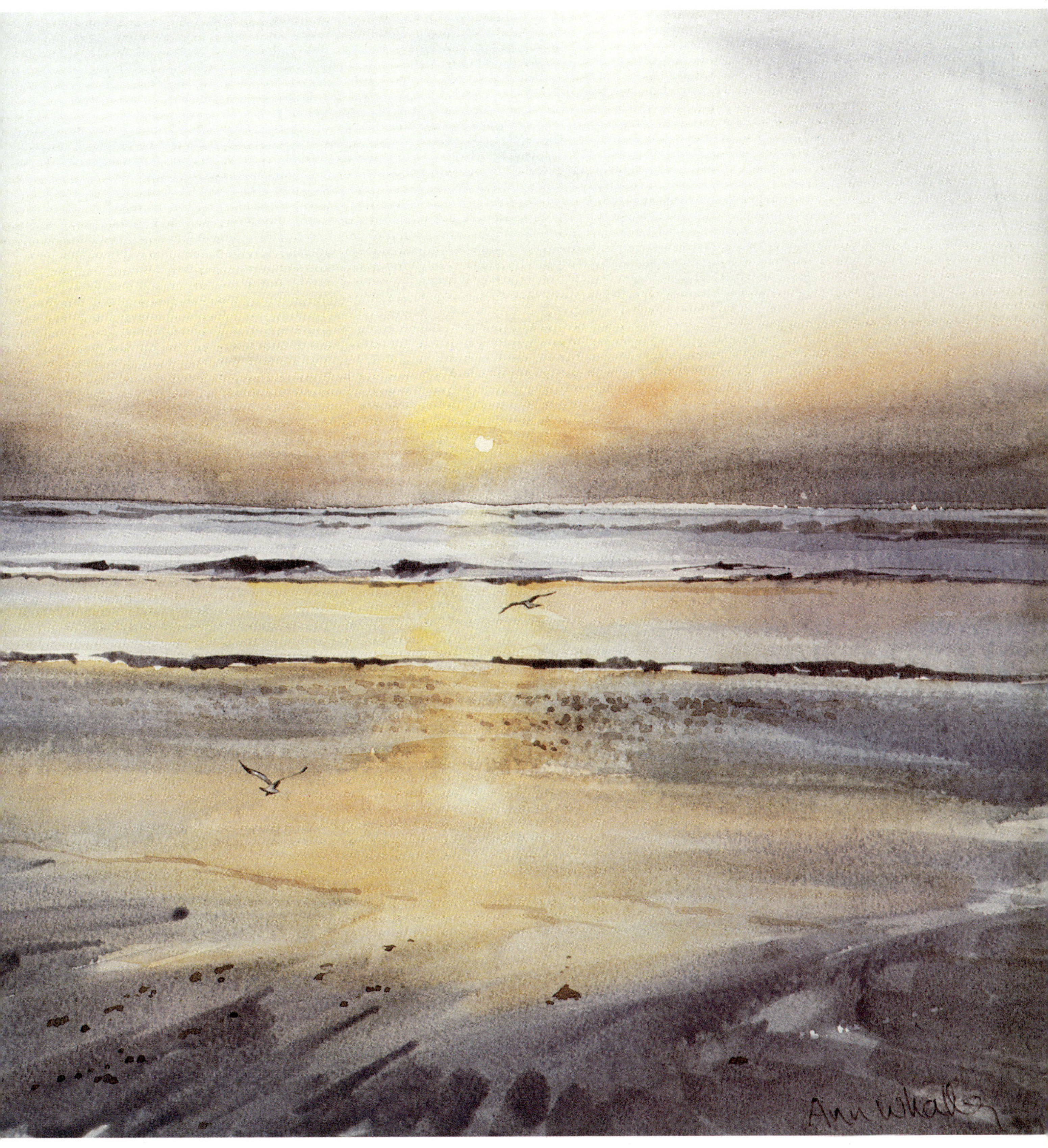
Ann Walker

CHAPTER FIVE

STILL WATERS

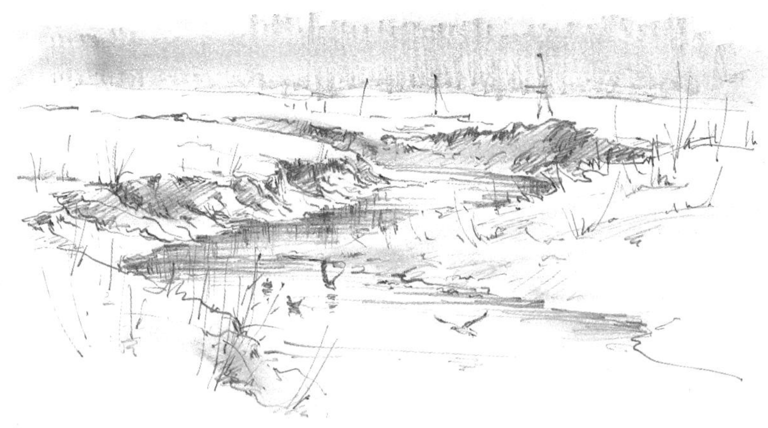

How privileged we painters are, wandering about the countryside with our sketchbooks and paints in a perpetual state of wonder. I remember a time some years ago when I had taken a group to paint on the shores of a lovely little lake in northern Italy. On the first morning I was up early, standing at the lakeside listening to the stillness and watching the pale opalescent mist gradually turn to gold. Above me hung strange shapes of gnarled trees, their fingertips dipping to meet their reflections in the still water. Then the mist cleared, and the scene resolved into its daytime bustle of boats, ripples and busy people, but for a brief moment I had been alone and enclosed in a world of enchantment. Such moments stay in one's memory for ever.

I have no need to go as far as Italy to find such scenes. I have only to look from my bedroom window to see the tide rising over the marsh in plumes of vapour. Such effects are by their very nature elusive, and do not last long except in the memory; and from memory is probably the best way to paint them. It is the *illusion* that you seek to capture here, not the reality, and for this your own subjective recall is the best means.

INFORMATION-GATHERING

I know that there are artists who are able to sit down in front of a scene, evaluate composition, tones and colours in a trice and then proceed to paint a good finished work on the spot. How I envy them! I am invariably so delighted with all I survey that, however good my intentions, I end up attempting to include everything and every colour just as it is.

It is infinitely better to approach the whole thing thoughtfully, allowing time to absorb the scene, analyse the elements which make up the whole, evaluate the colours, and then make a few dummy runs, sketches and so on. If you do not muster the self-discipline needed to do this, you will waste a lot of time and paper.

I have now resigned myself to considering most work done *in situ* as sketching and information-gathering for use later in the studio, or what Wordsworth referred to as 'emotion recollected in tranquillity'. I suspect that there may be many like me, finding a great deal more success when painting from work done on the spot in the quiet and peace of a studio.

Hanging trees over Lake Orta *(see finished painting on page 72).*

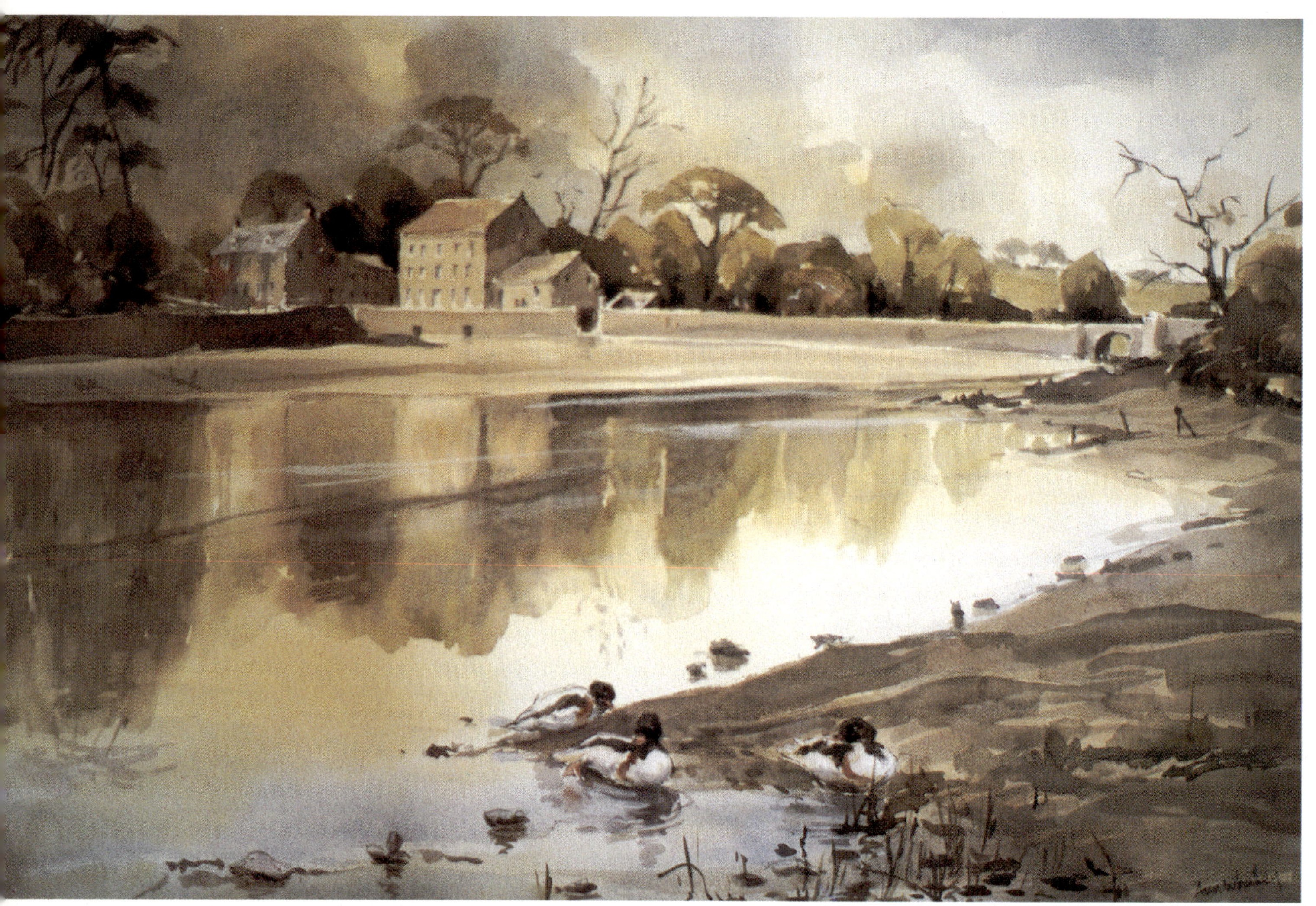

With increasing experience, one becomes able to draw while at the same time envisaging the painting which will result. One becomes instinctively aware of what must be recorded and what is irrelevant; and at the same time one begins to develop what I can only call an artistic shorthand. If we accept that good painting results from a painter's ability to react to a subject and then exercise his powers of selection and rejection, then all preliminary work on the spot assumes great importance. I prefer to work in monochrome for the most part, carrying the colours in my head. I come back again and again to an interesting drawing, and, by imposing different colours and atmospheric effects, I am able to make a number of different interpretations. A good drawing is far too valuable to be used only once!

CREATING INTEREST

I have covered reflections in some detail in Chapter 3, and still waters afford the perfect opportunity to put it all into practice. There are times, however, when there is a dearth of reflective possibilities, such as on a calm, clear day by the sea. Look for the odd passing cloud to cast a shadow across the water, or the sparkle of sunlight, and if it is nowhere to be seen, then invent it!

Clouds banking above a calm lake appear as long lines of shadow across the water, ranging in colour from delicate grey to deep purple. Always try to find a colour rather than resorting to dull grey, and use a large brush, plenty of water and the simplest and most direct of brushstrokes. Keep the shadow to a fairly narrow band,

Carew Mill. *The water here is tidal, and was almost in when I was painting, much to the taste of the mallards. I allowed the pinkish-sand colour of the mill and wall to permeate the painting, and played down the green of the trees to give a harmonious feel.*

remembering the compressing effect of perspective. This sort of reflection is most effective where the mass of water is kept to a pale, pure colour.

High cumulus lit by full sunlight makes a wonderful excuse for colour in still water. The cloud can assume tints of gold and pink, and shadows range from lavender to indigo, all mirrored in the water below. This sort of subject relies on simplicity and economy. Don't attempt to put in every detail, but concentrate on producing a well-understood, direct statement, keeping everything clean and fresh.

Aerial perspective is another good technique for bringing life to still-water paintings, and refers to the influence which atmosphere has on the colour and clarity of the landscape as it recedes. Some of the misting is due to particles of dust and debris suspended in the air, but a much greater effect is caused by particles of water vapour which hang suspended like a blue gauze just above the landscape. This is the reason why distant objects are almost invariably bluer and cooler, less colourful and less distinct than those close at hand. The tonal values are much closer too. It is an easy mistake to put in too much definition and colour, extending right to the horizon, which destroys the feeling of space. Try using a glaze of pure cobalt or lavender washed over the whole distant area. This serves both to mute the colours and to soften and merge any over-definition.

Put all this knowledge to good use, and vary the colour and tone from close up to the horizon. Introduce boats or the odd passing bird, placed strategically to direct the eye. There really is no excuse for 'concrete' water – it suggests either a poor imagination or lack of observation, neither of which is much of a recommendation for the watercolourist.

Rather than being completely still, water is more usually found to be a little disturbed, perhaps by a breeze or small currents, causing the surface to become textured and any reflections to be distorted. All this is fascinating, but is also immensely complex.

The name of the game here is simplification. There is no way that you could render every nuance and subtlety of colour and detail that your eye can see. This is when the importance of sitting and looking comes in again. You may be sure that, if you look long enough, all that complexity of colour and movement will eventually resolve itself into an endlessly repeating pattern. Then all that remains is to get it all down in the most economical way possible!

It is often a good idea to start by treating the sky and the water as one where the first wet washes are concerned. After all, the two are closely related and their colours dependent on each other. Consider the mood you wish to convey, and choose your colours accordingly. Then wash colour on to your paper as freely as possible, allowing colours to merge and mingle as they run down, letting things go to a large extent rather than directing them too much. Don't worry if a few unexpected things happen – these come as a bonus! As the paper dries you can begin to block in features such as hills, trees and buildings, putting in a few sharp, detailed touches to finish.

This of course is easy to say in theory, but the reality is so often very different. Washes go wrong, paper dries unevenly, paint runs

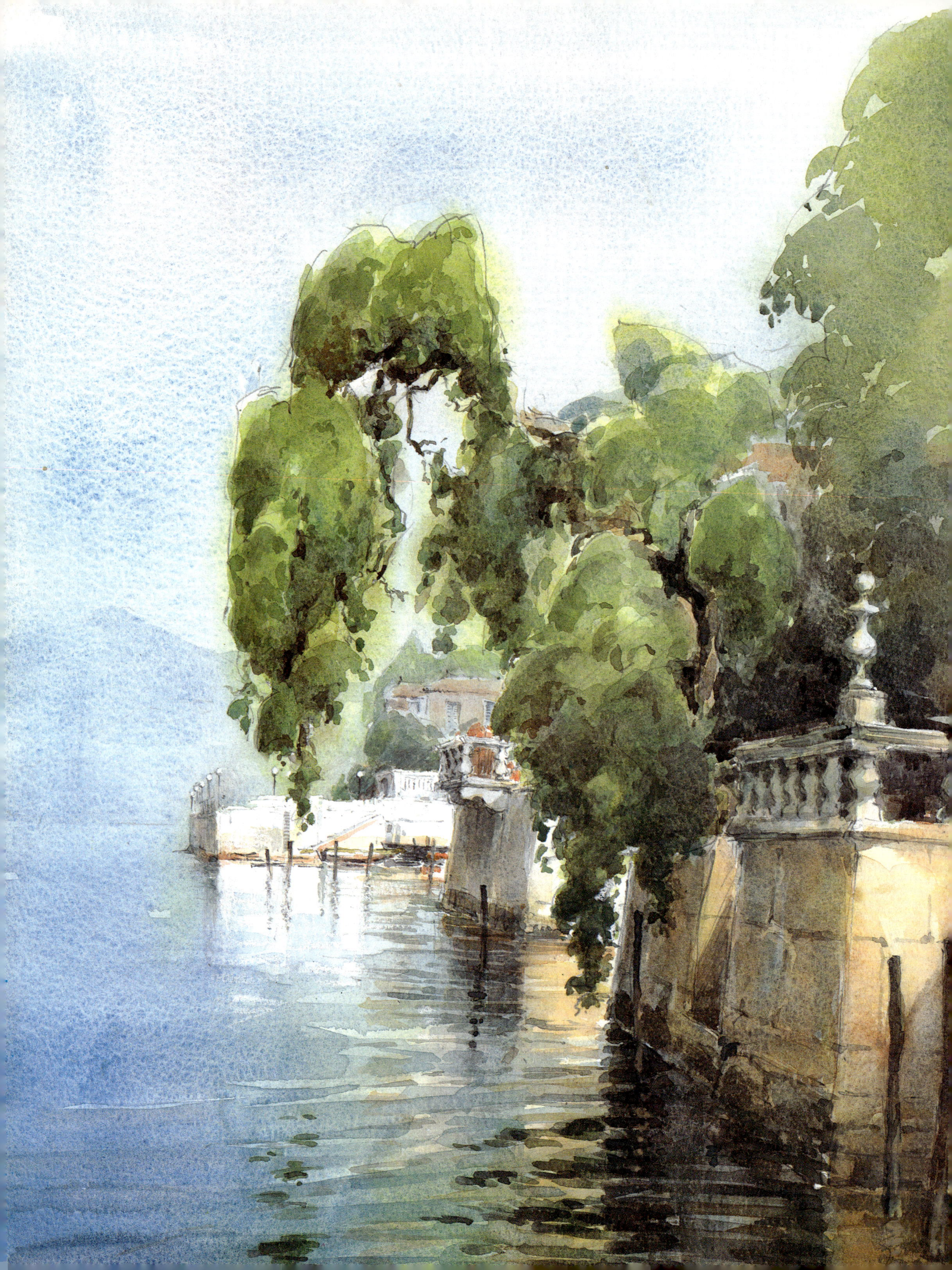

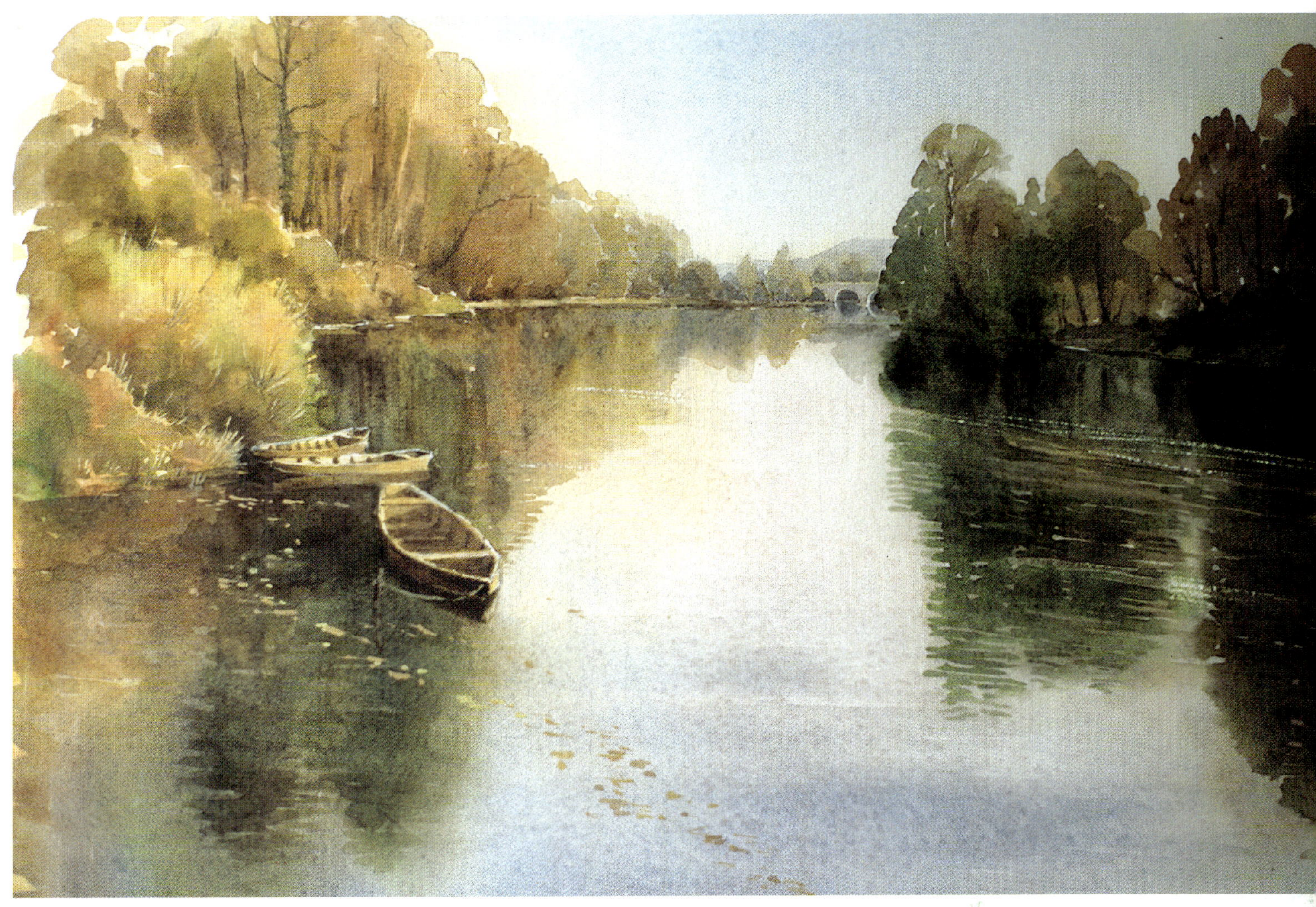

where it shouldn't and develops hard edges where they are not wanted, and even at the end a clumsy movement can ruin everything. This is not to advise caution or timidity, but rather the need to practise boldly over and over again and joyously throw paint on to paper until things begin to respond and work well, and you begin to gain confidence and feel in control.

Hanging trees over Lake Orta. *With barely moving water, you must look carefully at the relationship between object and reflection, both in shape and colour. You will see that the reflection is often two or three shades darker than the object, although this does not imply a dulling or greying of colour – normally the reverse is true, and the colour is actually enriched.*

USING THE BRUSH

Part of this new-found control concerns the way you use your brush to describe aspects of a scene. One brushstroke can speak volumes, and it is worth considering the actual strokes you might use – should they be long, swirling curves or quick flips with the tip? Always remember that the less 'going over' you do the better.

Practise using your brush so that the marks themselves become ripples. I advise standing up for this (a good way to work at any time), and dangle your brush full of watery paint above the paper, letting your arm move back and forth with what I can only call gently controlled, random arcs. This method allows for great fluidity of movement and amazingly varied and subtle gyrating reflections.

The Dordogne River. *Sun and shade in the south of France.*

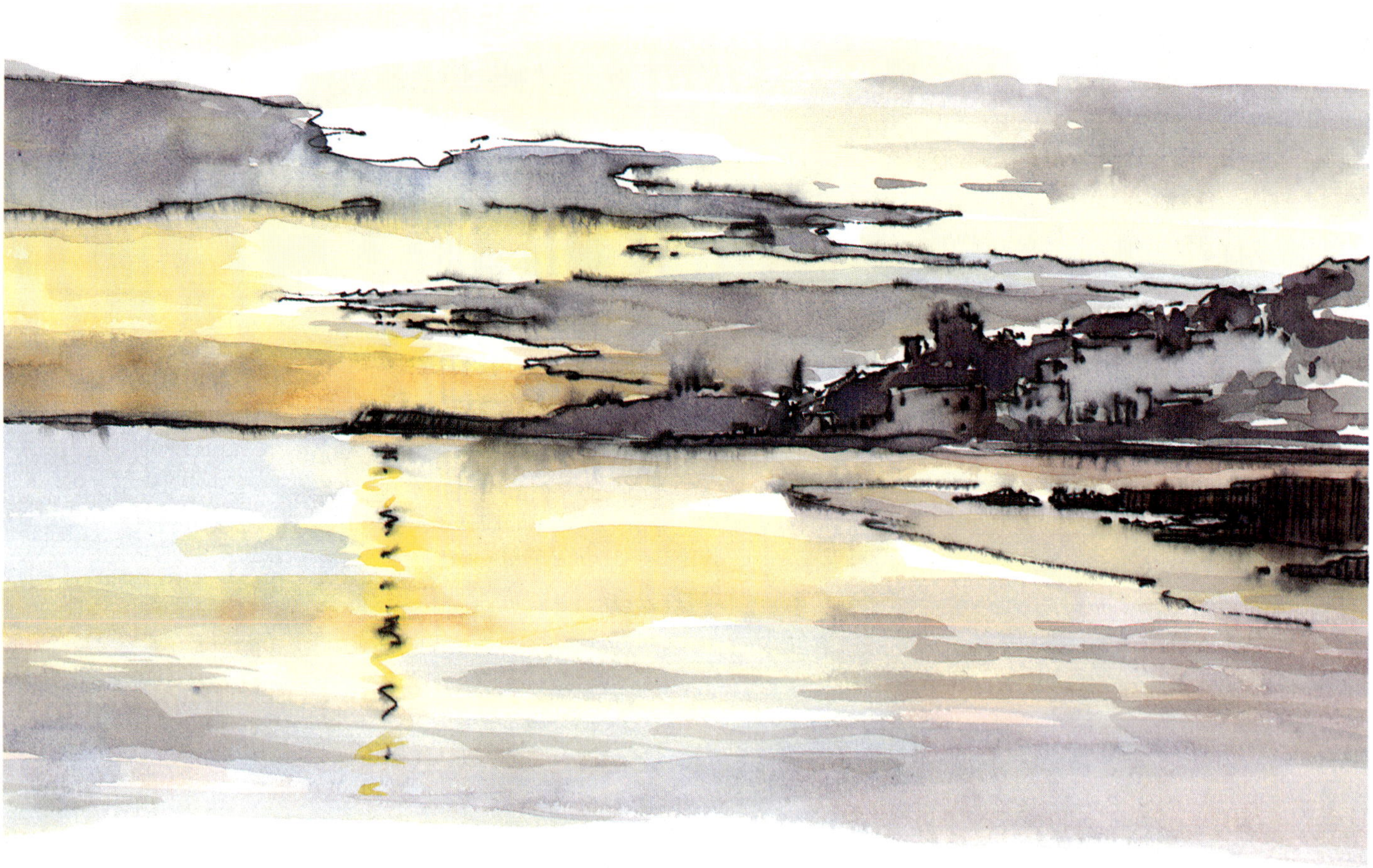

Sunset, Rovinj. *This is essentially a silhouette painting, but to create interest I used colour combined with pen-and-ink drawing. The light on the water makes this painting come alive.*

I suppose the most common fault of the watercolourist is that of hesitancy, usually combined with the compulsion to 'correct'. Try spending some time waving a brush over scraps of paper, or use it to describe single-stroke leaves or waves; try different pressures and angles, and different liquidities. Don't attempt a preconceived shape at first, but just play around and make a few discoveries. As well as being fun, this is all part of learning your trade. Great paintings are not often created by artists who cannot wield a brush competently. The more you practise, the more confident you will become and the more painterly your work will be. This won't happen overnight, of course, but it won't happen at all if you don't persevere with it.

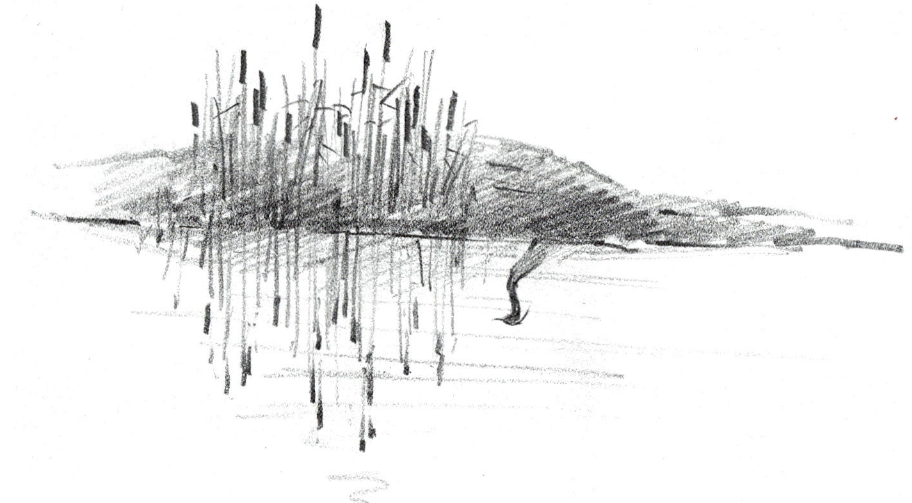

Reflection of hunting heron.

I saw something interesting the other day by the river near my home. There in the still water was the perfect reflected image of a hunting heron, but of the actual

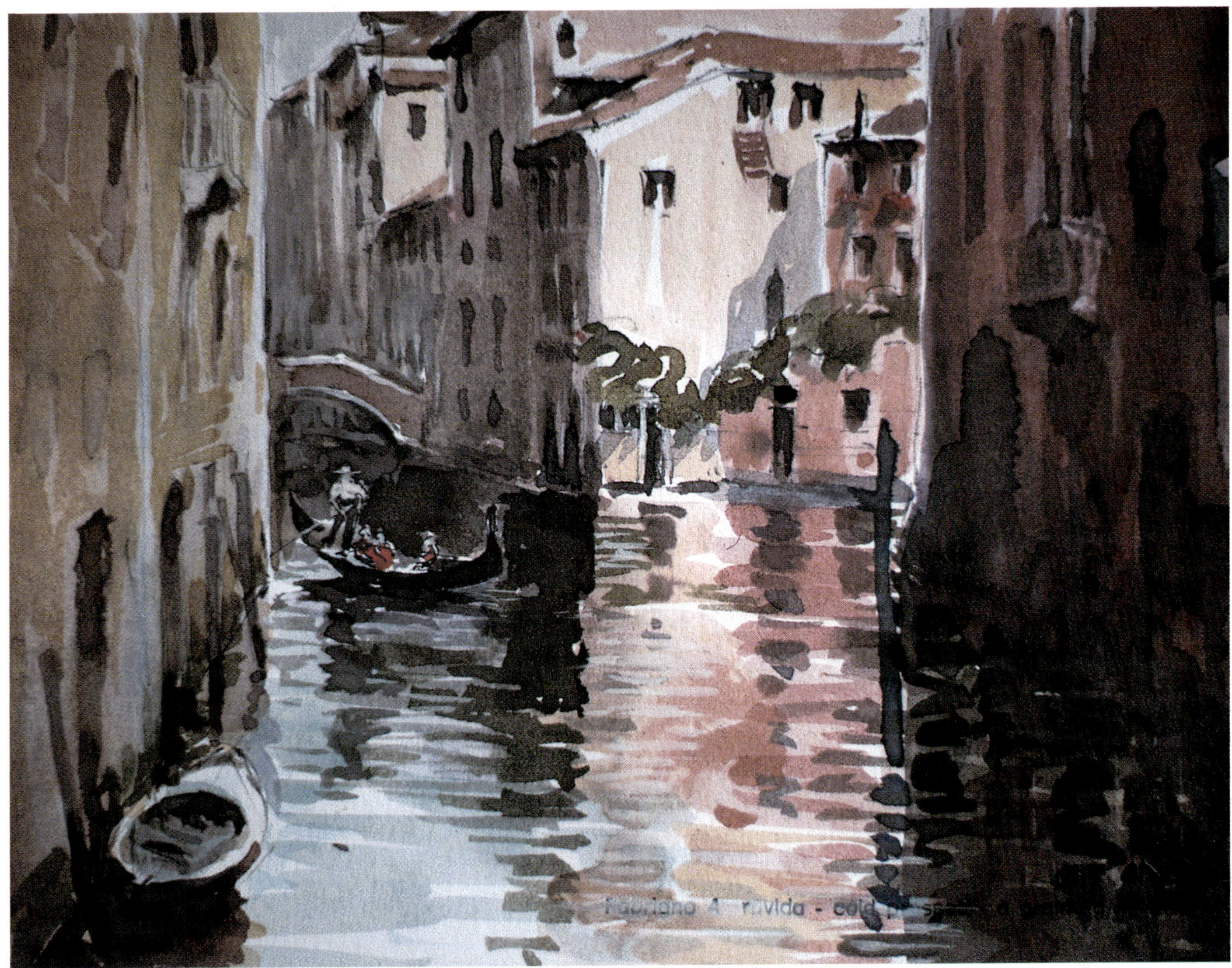

Small canal, Venice. *A typically Venetian scene, with its colour-washed walls, gondola and tall buildings reflected in rippling water.*

bird there was no sign, as it stood quite invisibly camouflaged against the reeds. There are always signs of wildlife along a riverbank or beside a lake, and it is good to try to include them in your scenes.

VENICE

Venice must be the perfect hunting ground for any aspiring painter of water. Exquisitely ornate buildings crowd the canal banks, casting rich patterns of red and sienna into the water. Gondolas with their elegant prows and boater-hatted oarsmen glide by, or moor among a forest of black and striped poles, and every canal is crossed by countless small arched bridges.

If at first scenes such as this seem too much to cope with, take your time and wander round, absorbing the style and proportions of the buildings, and the importance of sunlight and shadow. Study the way in which these are reproduced in the water. See how little sky is reflected in still water, and observe the distortions and dark tones. Plan the way in which you will set about the painting, making drawings and colour notes. I find a small viewfinder useful when dealing with tall buildings seen close at hand and in exaggerated perspective (an empty slide frame is perfect), and often it works well to let the nearest buildings run out of the top of the picture. One usually sees only snippets of sky above a fascinating roofline of chimneys, campaniles and old tiles all set at crazy angles. When

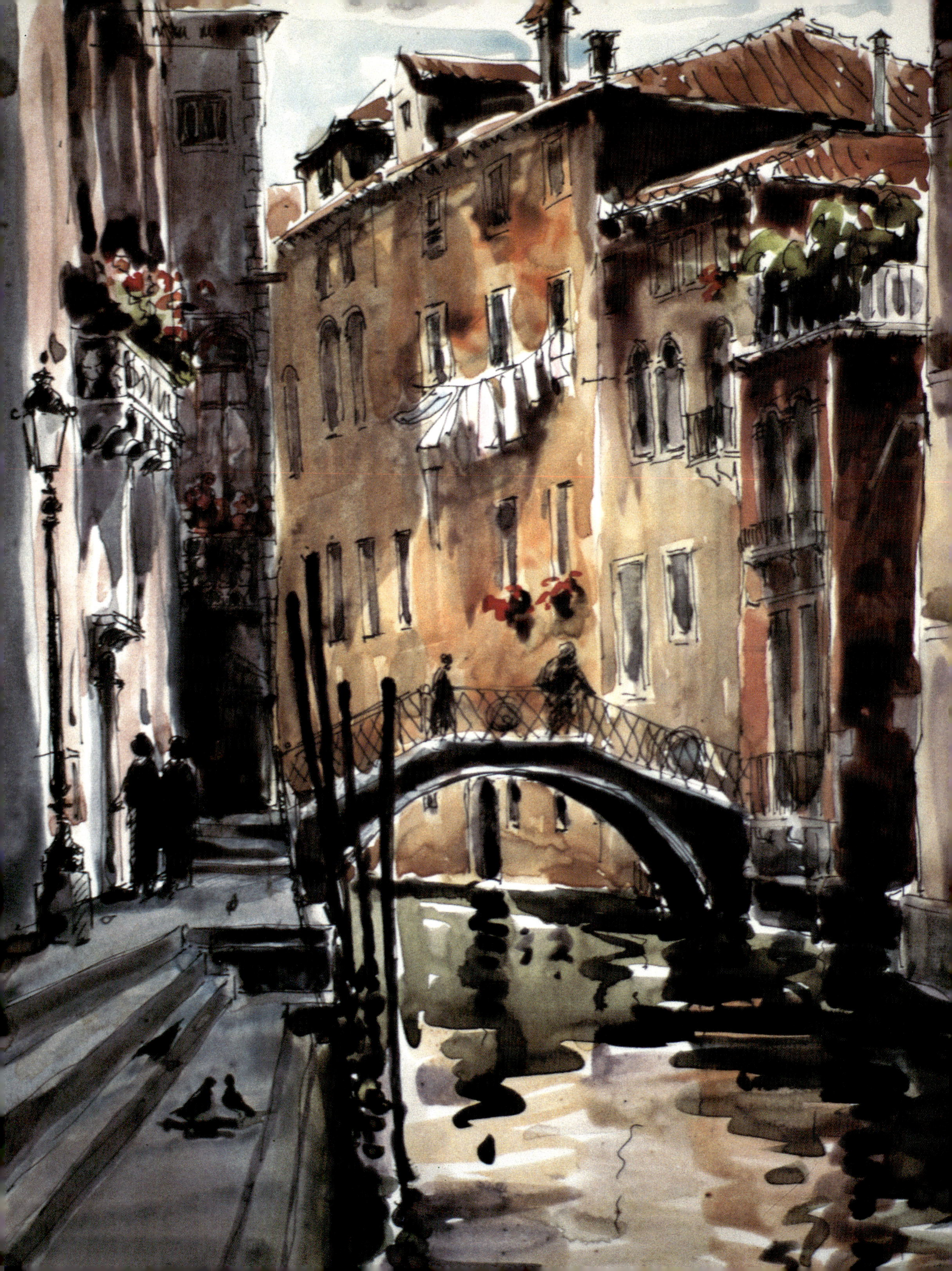

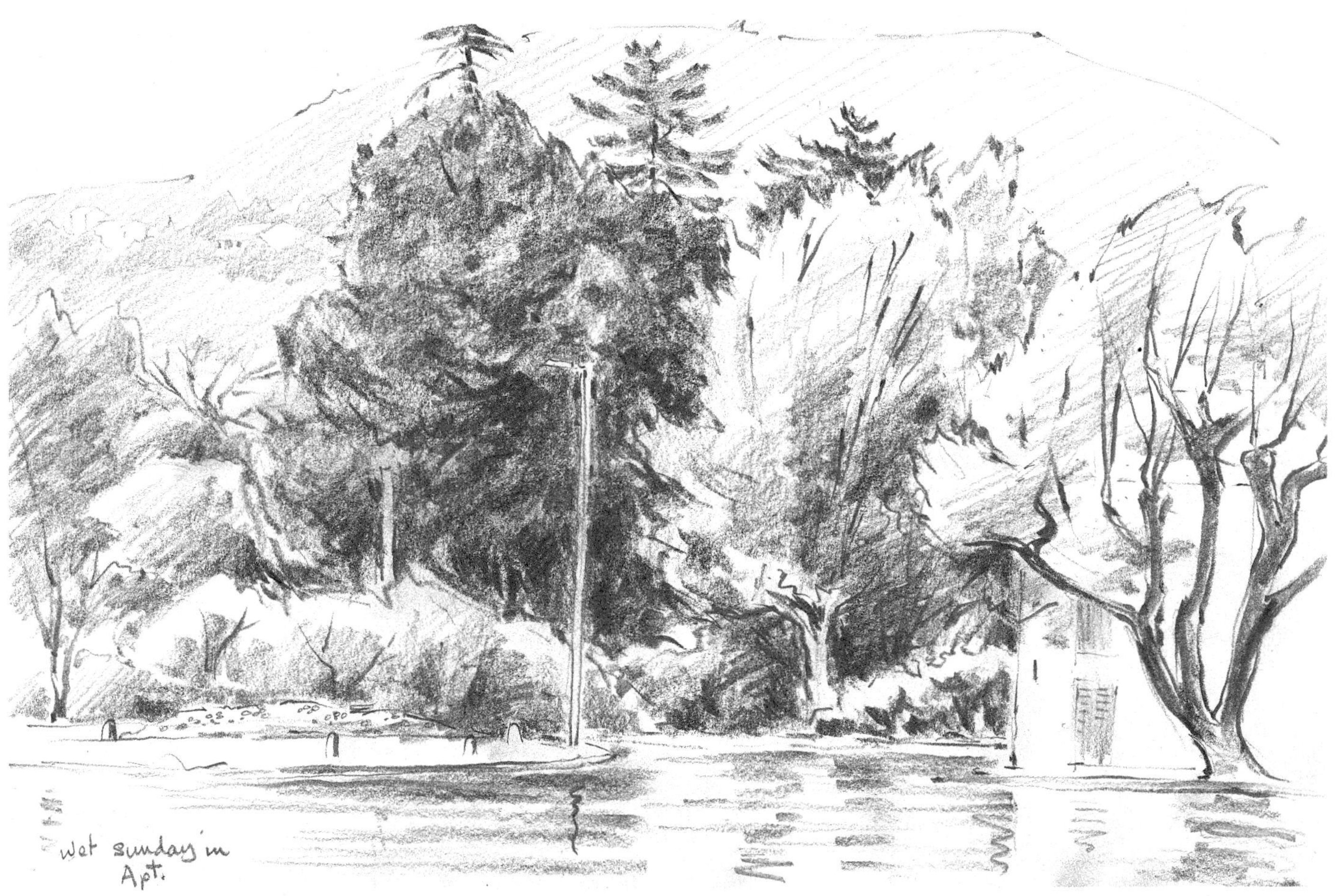

A wet Sunday in Apt, France.

planning your painting, consider reflections not as a separate afterthought, but as an integral element in the design. Look for repeated shapes, and the way in which they snake across the water.

Canal, Venice. *The answer to the problem of complex reflections, preventing them from turning into a formless muddle, is to simplify. Look carefully until you can explain what is causing the seeming confusion, discard everything that is not essential, and put in what is left as directly and economically as possible. Let the brush do most of it for you, and leave the strokes showing. Don't forget characteristic touches such as flower-filled balconies and washing hanging out to dry.*

SUBDUED LIGHT

Still water takes many forms other than the more obvious ones. A wet city street, puddles in a field, floodwaters or a garden pond are all very different, yet all make interesting subjects. It isn't every scene which looks its best on a sunny day. Limited contrasts and subtle colours can lead to interesting work full of mood and involvement – one just has to look a little harder. Take a trip to your nearest canal or to the docklands of a large city to see what I mean. On a dull, wet day shapes merge with their reflections, colours are more suggested than actual and the tonal range is much reduced.

When this is the case, imbue the scene with a feeling of *implied* colour while flooding the whole with the dimming effect of reduced light – almost a monochrome, but not quite. At the risk of being tedious, I repeat the need to make many tonal sketches, because with only a restricted tonal range to work with, the need to get it right becomes critical.

The effect of cloud cover or mists is to reduce the tonal contrasts even for objects quite close to you, while at the same time muting the intensity of colour overall. The

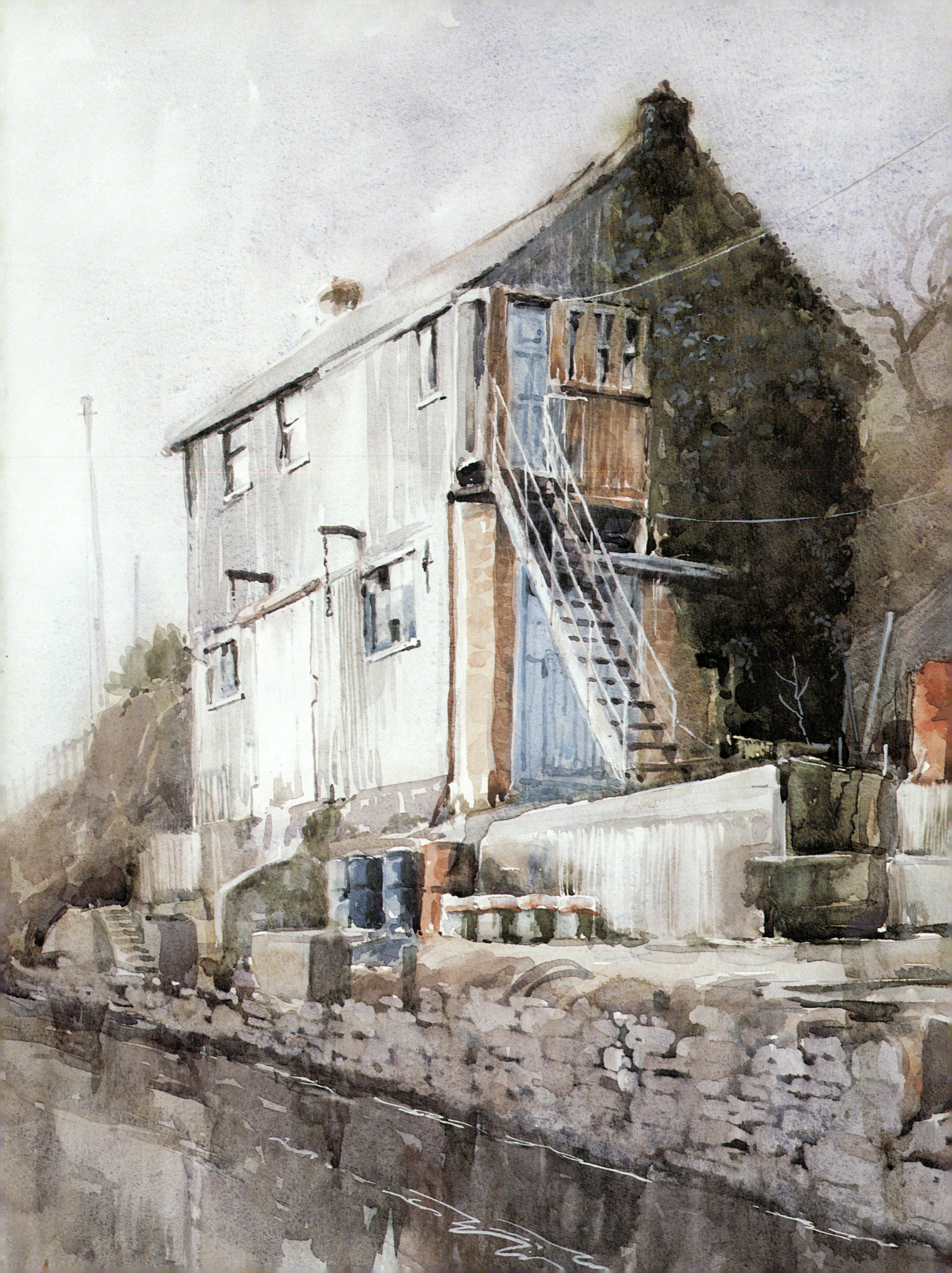

Tertiary warm and cool greys created by blending blues, reds and yellows.

combined effect creates a scene where shapes merge one into another and colours become more suggested than defined.

This does not mean that everything must be painted a uniform grey, or be dull and lifeless. In fact, it is rather the reverse. It is true that dark and light tones move towards the middle ground, but at the same time all the colours become more subtle and intriguing. You are now into the world of colourful greys: warm greys containing raw sienna; cobalt and rose madder; deep greys made with burnt sienna; burnt umber mixed with cerulean and perhaps a touch of indigo to add intensity; or delicate lavender greys of rose madder, cerulean and perhaps the merest amount of lemon to tone down the obvious. You will notice that I advocate the use of tertiary colour mixing for greys: that is, colours obtained from a mix of three pigments. This has the immediate effect of toning down the colour into a more subtle shade. (I would not advise the use of more than three pigments as the colour will then become lifeless.)

Deciding on exactly what subtle blend of colour you are looking at is not easy, but it helps to have previously experimented with colour mixing just to discover how many luscious and unusual shades are possible. The vast range of greys which occur naturally in the landscape are some of the most interesting colours you can use, and there really is no excuse for the dreary blue-grey monsters I see so often. Once you consciously begin to look for colour in the landscape, it will show in your work immediately. The dark water swirling beneath an old barge may appear black at first glance, but look closely and you will see that it is full of purple-browns, olive greens and rusty reds, all lurking there in the depths.

Colours always have more impact when a cool colour is laid alongside a warm one, so get into the habit of creating opportunities for this to happen. A muted pink mooring buoy set in a sea of blues and greens will make a welcome accent and bring a rather dull area to life. Try a little experiment using only three pigments. By using one in greater strength than the other two in rotation, see how many different warm and cool greys you can make. The choice of cerulean, light red and aureolin would be a good place to start.

This kind of subject is not easy to paint because everything is seen as if behind a veil. Only think of the paintings of the Thames by Whistler, or along the Seine by Monet, to see what lovely, evocative work can result.

You will often find that your colours tend to be over-stated and lack the hoped-for subtlety, but this can be a good fault. By washing over a glaze or series of glazes in pure blue or lavender, the tones and colours will immediately be reduced and brought closer together, while the formerly over-bright colour will show through as a subtle glow. Where the colours are about right but you have a lot of hard-edged shapes, destroying the hope of a misty effect, take a large brush full of clean water and gently wash over the whole painting, pressing slightly harder where you require the least definition.

Old shed, Milford Docks. *If you think that the buildings near your home are too dull to make an appealing painting, look again: it is not just thatched cottages that merit attention. I found this lovely old shed just before these docks were 'improved', and immediately fell for its rather seedy appearance and mish-mash of building materials, old tin cans and broken wall. I made no effort to change it but painted it just as it was.*

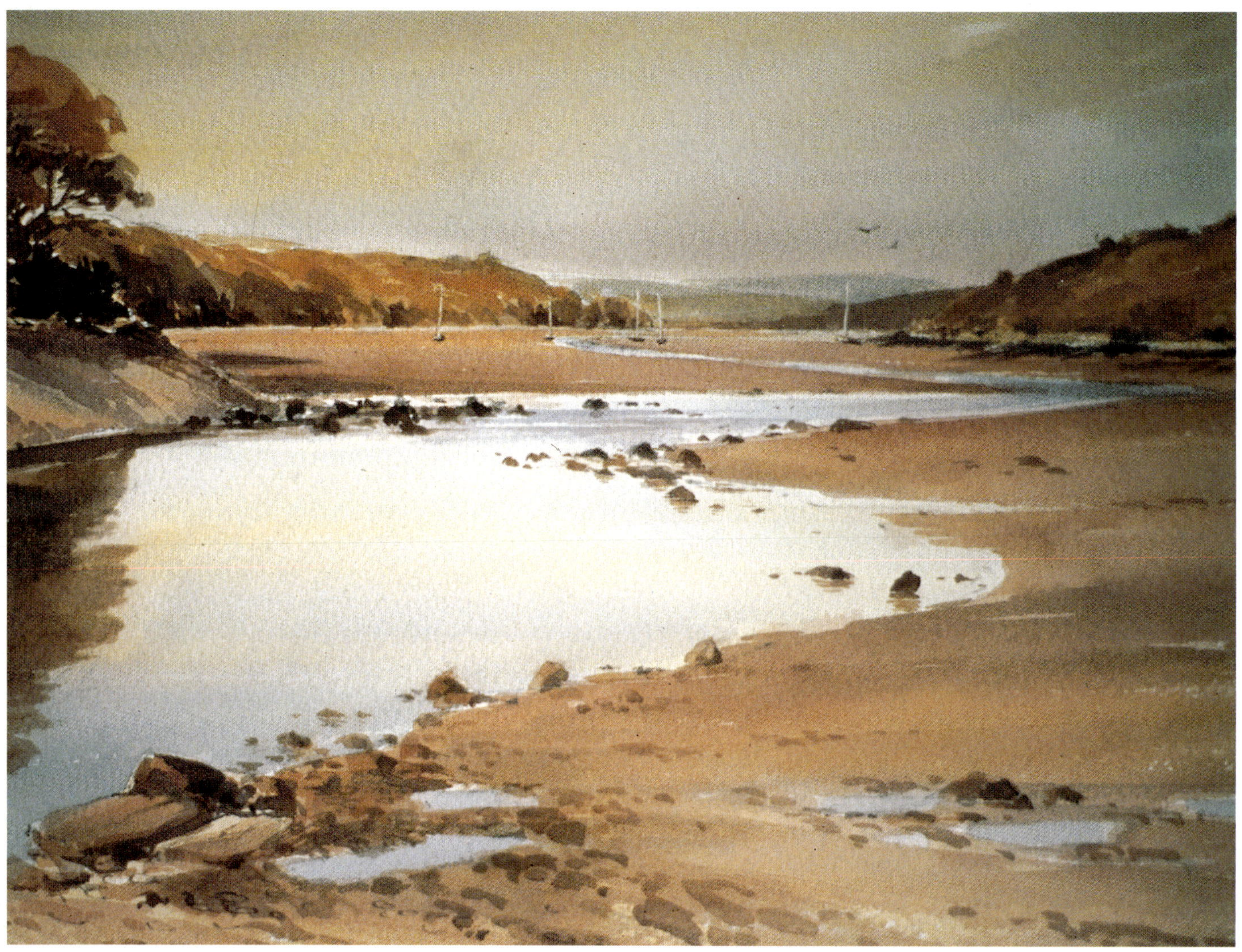

Perhaps the most still water you will ever find is in a freezing pond. A thin skin of ice creeps out over black water, and merges into frosted reeds at the edge. Nothing moves, there is no sound, and all is held in a ridged, icy grip. Snow pictures are always of great interest to the artist, chiefly because of the total reversal of values. The heavy sky is darker than the land and so the water appears dark too, while the snow assumes an unnatural luminosity.

As an experiment, try my suggestion of transforming a rather uninteresting sketch into a snow picture and see what happens. It could be a revelation!

Transforming a scene from memory and imagination into paint is tremendous fun. Take a familiar river scene and then imagine spring with the leaves newly green and the grass bright in the sun; or turn it into autumn and clothe it all in lovely russets and reds. Or perhaps it is winter, with the trees stripped bare and the riverbank a tangle of bleached, dead grasses. The possibilities are endless.

Just a brief word on foregrounds. Where feasible, it is better to allow at least some part of the water to extend right to the bottom of the picture, so that the viewer is 'invited in' and not confronted by a fringe of vegetation extending across the lower edge. This may look as if you had run out of paper too soon, and you would have to draw reeds and grasses like an angel to get away with it.

Sandy Haven. *I painted this at low tide – you can see the beached boats in the distance. I used only burnt and raw sienna and cobalt, and concentrated on getting the tonal values right.*

While I abhor rules, which in my opinion are only made to be broken, I offer for what they are worth some maxims I have found useful. Try to work as broadly as you can for as long as you can, with as large a brush as is

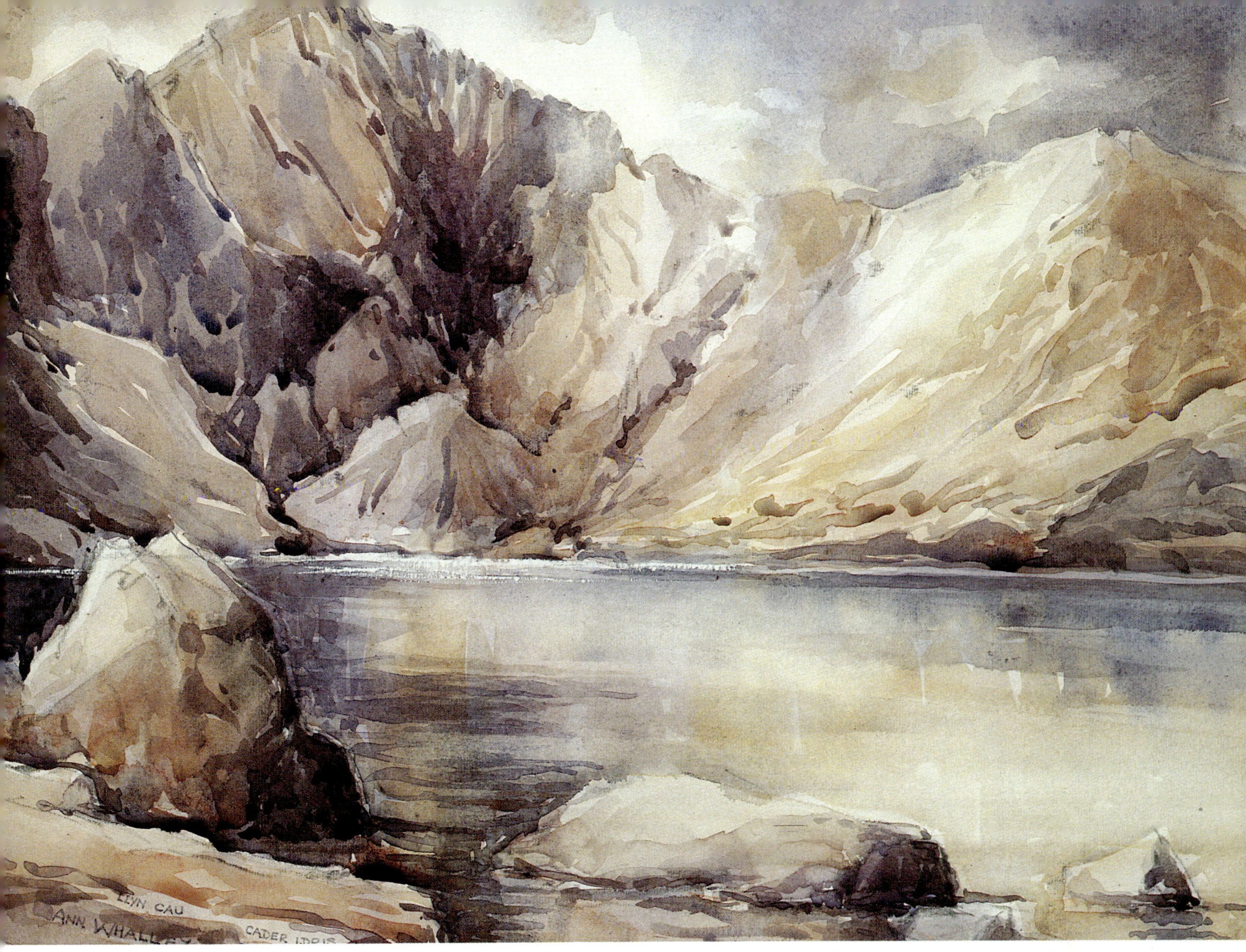

reasonable, and as wet as you can. Work from far away to near, from large to small, from soft to sharp, from pale to dark, from cool to warm and from wet to dry. Write this out and stick it up where you can see it when you start your next painting – you may find it helpful. Reserve any detail until last, for it may be that, if the painting has gone well at every stage and is reading as you had intended, further work will not be necessary. Many a painting has been terminally damaged by misguided, last-minute 'improvements'.

Ask yourself where the attraction of still water lies for you. Is it the sense of open space and distance that you love, and the opportunity to experiment with the effects of atmospheric changes? Perhaps you are excited by the upside-down world of reflections swaying gently. Wherever your interests lie, your greatest friend will be a big brush with good water-holding capacity and a decent point. One of the worst things that can happen when laying in the broad washes is to run out of paint halfway through, for the last thing you want is a hard line or a dried-up mess where a flowing expanse should be.

Before you start, make up a number of different colour washes. The main colour will probably reflect the sky, but also have to hand washes for cloud shadows,

Cadre Idris cauldron. *This rather dramatic and Turneresque view was stunning. It was like being on another planet, and so full of 'presence' that it made me quite apprehensive. I hope something of that feeling has come through in the painting.*

wind flurries and the beginnings of the colours of reflections, which may all be used either as wet-into-wet soft-edged colour, or into damp paper as firmer lines. The tones at this stage should be quite light, but this need not result in insipid greys. Look for pinks, greens and blues, and try more than one blue to create the effect of recession. As the sky above your head is a deeper, richer blue than

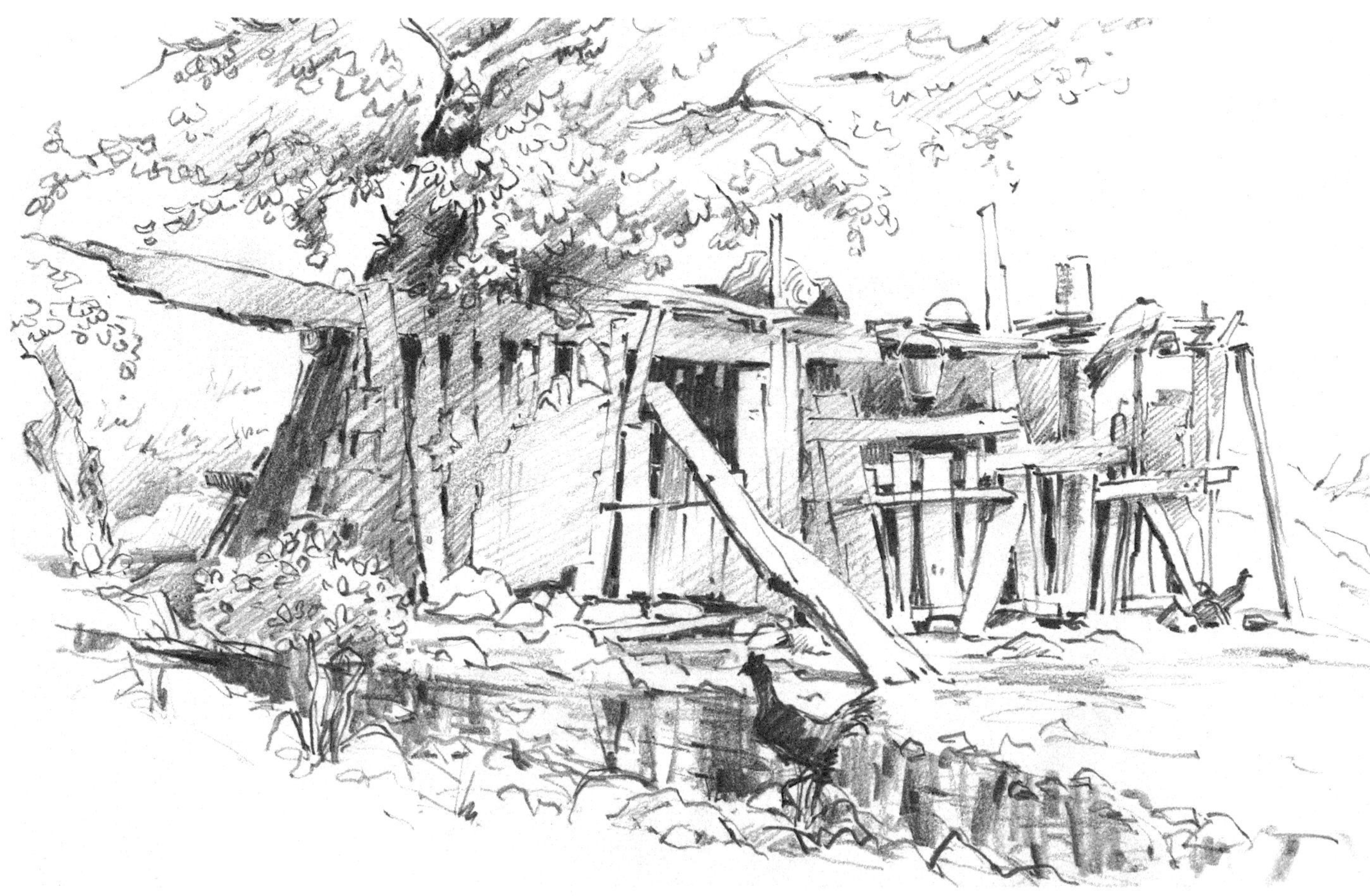

The chicken house, Turkey.

that at the horizon, you will find the deepest sky reflection in the water nearest to you, while the distant water will echo the more delicate hues of the sky at the horizon. Always make up more colour than you think you will need, and err on the generous side with the pigment. You can always add more water to the wet paint on the paper, but it is more difficult to get a flowing result if layers of colour have to be superimposed.

Depending on the nature of your subject and the effect you require, you may decide to add the colours of the reflections into wet paper, thus arriving at a diffuse mass. Be careful to keep the amount of wetness much the same, for if the new paint is much wetter than the first wash there will be a danger of blooming. This is why it is so important to have all your colours mixed in advance, so that you can progress from one stage to the next without a break.

When the reflections are close to you, they probably have far more shape and definition, and, because you will be looking down into the water, will have much more of a pattern quality echoing the ripples on the surface. As with all close objects, the colours will also be stronger.

An easy confidence in controlling your brush and the marks you make comes only with practice. When you are faced with an area of snaking, rippling colours, spend time trying out a few strokes, blending colours on the page and getting to the happy position when you know what will happen. Try various brushes and note the different marks they make. Work sitting down and standing up, and practise holding the brush right at the end and letting it wander across the paper – some very exciting results may happen. The greatest mistake is to attempt to dictate too rigidly and carefully where every mark must go. The way to achieve a free-flowing, water-like impression is to practise until you have the confidence to let things happen and the expertise to leave well alone.

As always, look for opportunities to introduce interesting colours, and try not to be so involved in the exact form of the reflection that you lose spontaneity by turgid over-painting. Remember that you are painting a generalization which sums up your attraction to the subject, not an exact copy.

CHAPTER SIX

RUNNING WATERS

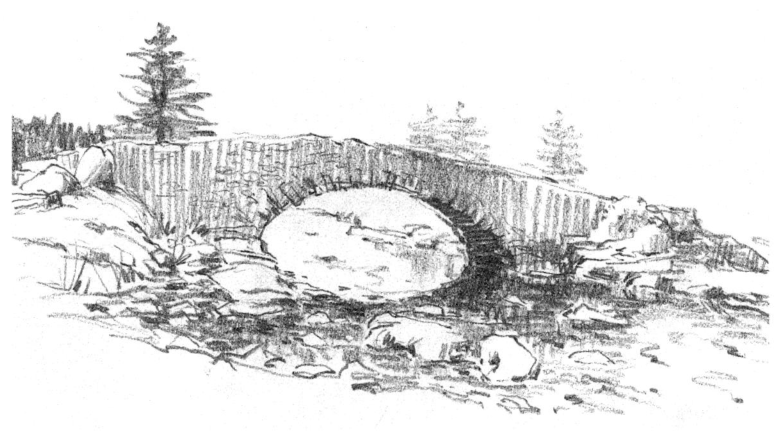

Bubbling streams, swift-flowing rivers and broad estuaries each have their own special character and appeal. As this is caused largely by the varied landscapes through which they flow, the study of rivers is as much the study of all landscape as the water itself.

It is a curious thing, but except when one is standing on a bridge or at the water's edge, one really sees very little of a river as it flows through the landscape, and even less of a lowly stream. For the most part they are concealed by bushes and reeds or the lie of the land, and appear only as a distant flash of silver. So great is a river's influence on our lives, however, that we frequently attempt to overstate its scale in a painting. The next time you approach a stream, make a point of noting just how near you have to be before being able to see much of the water. We know that the stream is there, but often only because the line of the bank is visible as a darker shadow.

I think of a fast-flowing river as a living force, busy and purposeful and going somewhere. It is not enough just to look and record, there has to be involvement and feeling about it all too. When you wander on a summer's day through sunlit watermeadows beside a gurgling stream, breathe it all in, and let it enter your soul. Your total involvement will surely show in your work. The same goes for a day of wind and rain and general awfulness. Unless you have physically experienced all the discomfort, how can you convey what it felt like to others?

A sketchbook and pencil are really all you need to carry on an initial fact-finding stroll along a riverbank. Quick line and tone drawings will give you all the information you need to make a painting. Draw some general views showing the river in its setting, trying some possible compositions and arrangements. Concentrate on broad tonal areas and experiment with possible centres of interest.

In addition, make some more detailed studies of individual subjects and groupings: different aspects of a farmhouse and its outbuildings; farm machinery; a copse of trees; reeds or wet mud at the water's edge; and the pattern of eddies and flow in the river. Trees which actually have their roots in the water or hang their branches low to touch its surface are always exciting. Study the way the water flows around obstructions, and practise using your pencil to render the changing texture of the water. Studies of herons, swans and other wildlife all add interest. Intimate studies of small riverside happenings are delightful to do, and make your work far more personal.

You may feel that pencil drawings alone do not give you quite enough to work from, and that some colour studies would be useful. If this is the case, do not hesitate to supplement your pencil studies with some fairly broad colour-wash sketches. As you will already have sufficient detailed pencil work, these should be made primarily to record specific colour effects that you will want to include in the eventual painting. For a scene of sunlight dappling through leaves, use pure lemon yellow or aureolin for the sunlit leaves and grasses, and then add deep greeny-purple for the shadows, maximizing the sunny effect. Keep the statement simple and uncluttered and the colours clean. If there is a reddish tree, then paint it red; if the grass is lemon and the water indigo, then paint them so. It is your immediate response that is important here.

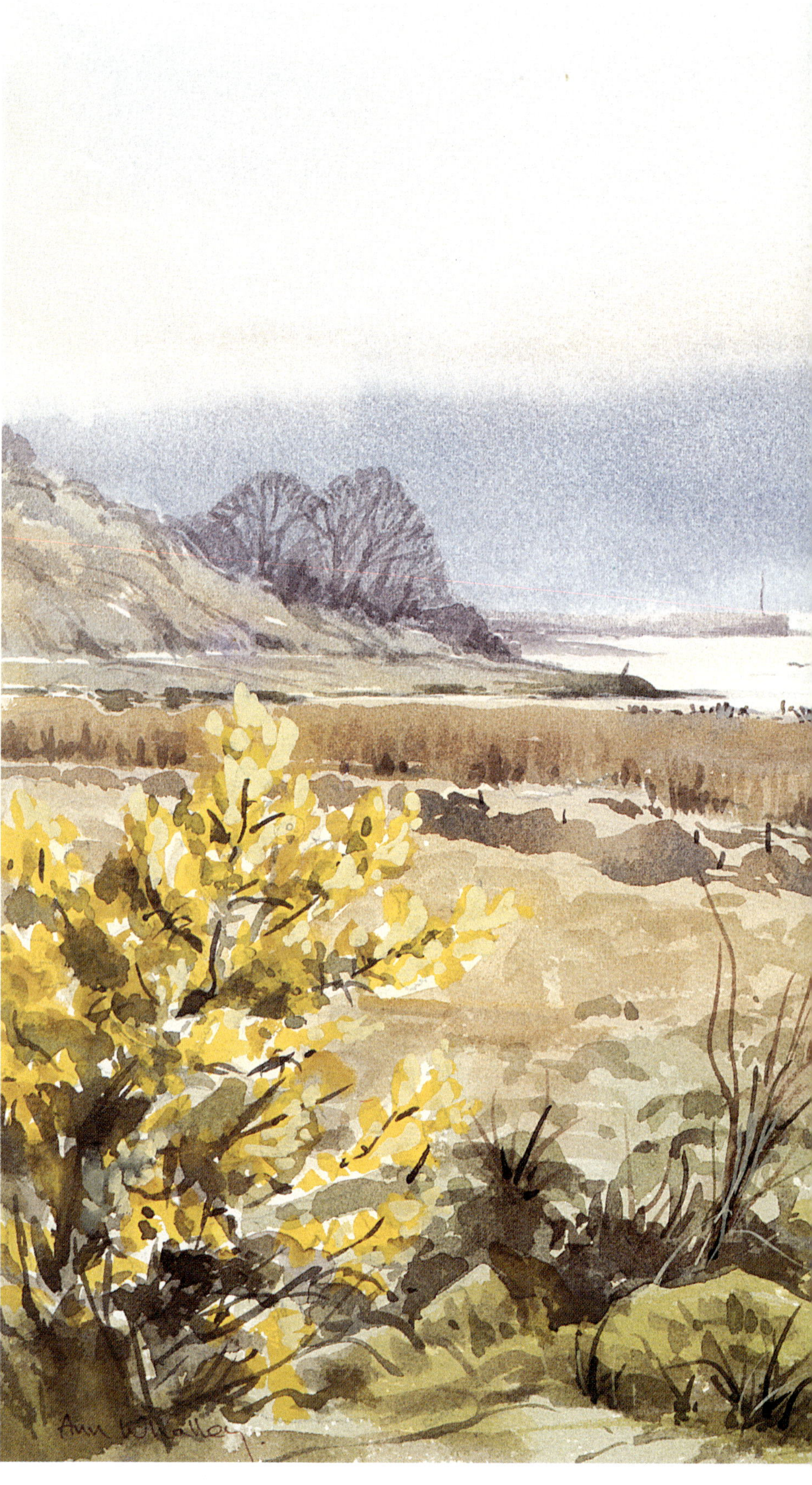

Spring gorse. *This painting of the path and stile down to the Cleddau from my house is another instance of how little one sees of a river.*

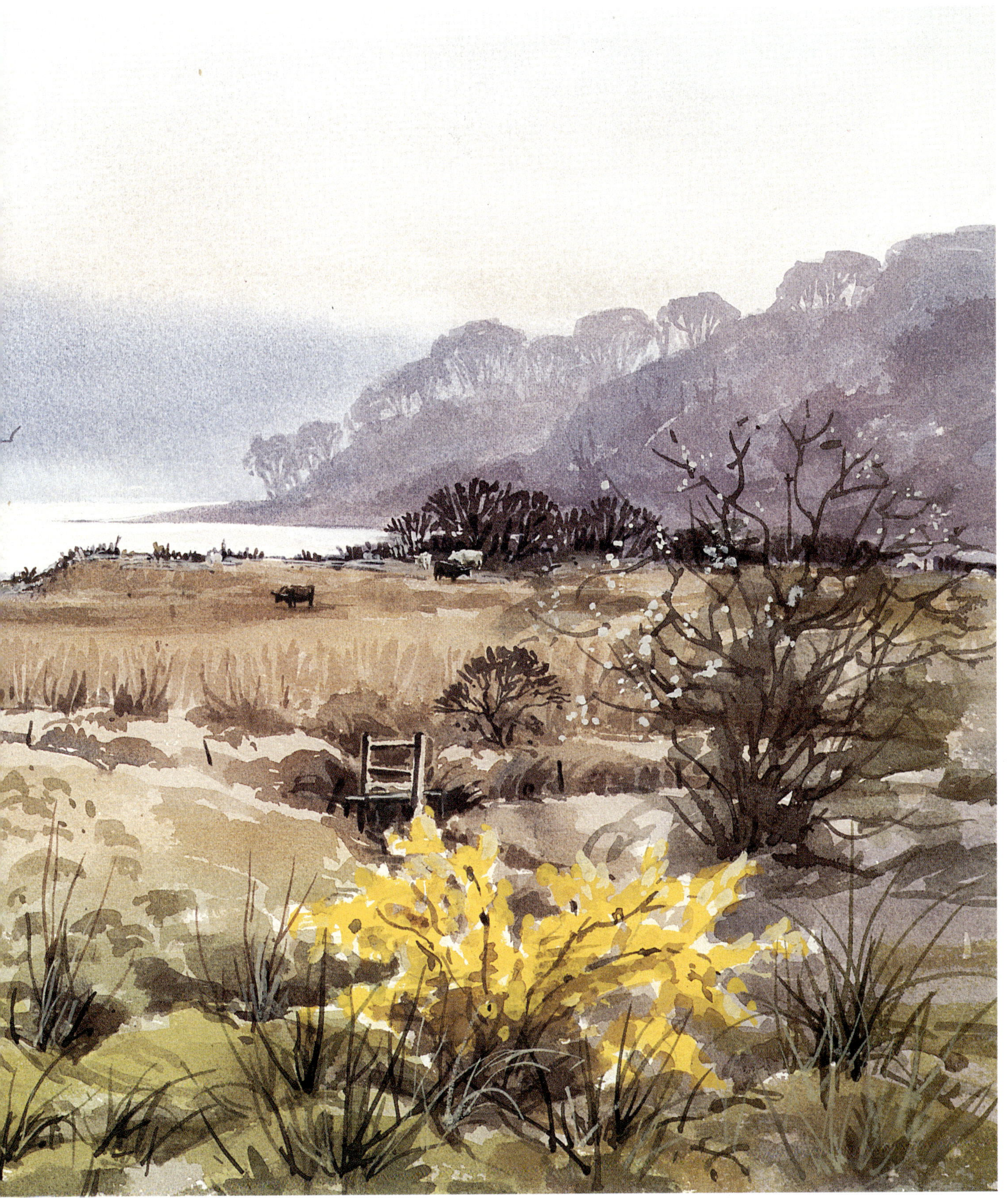

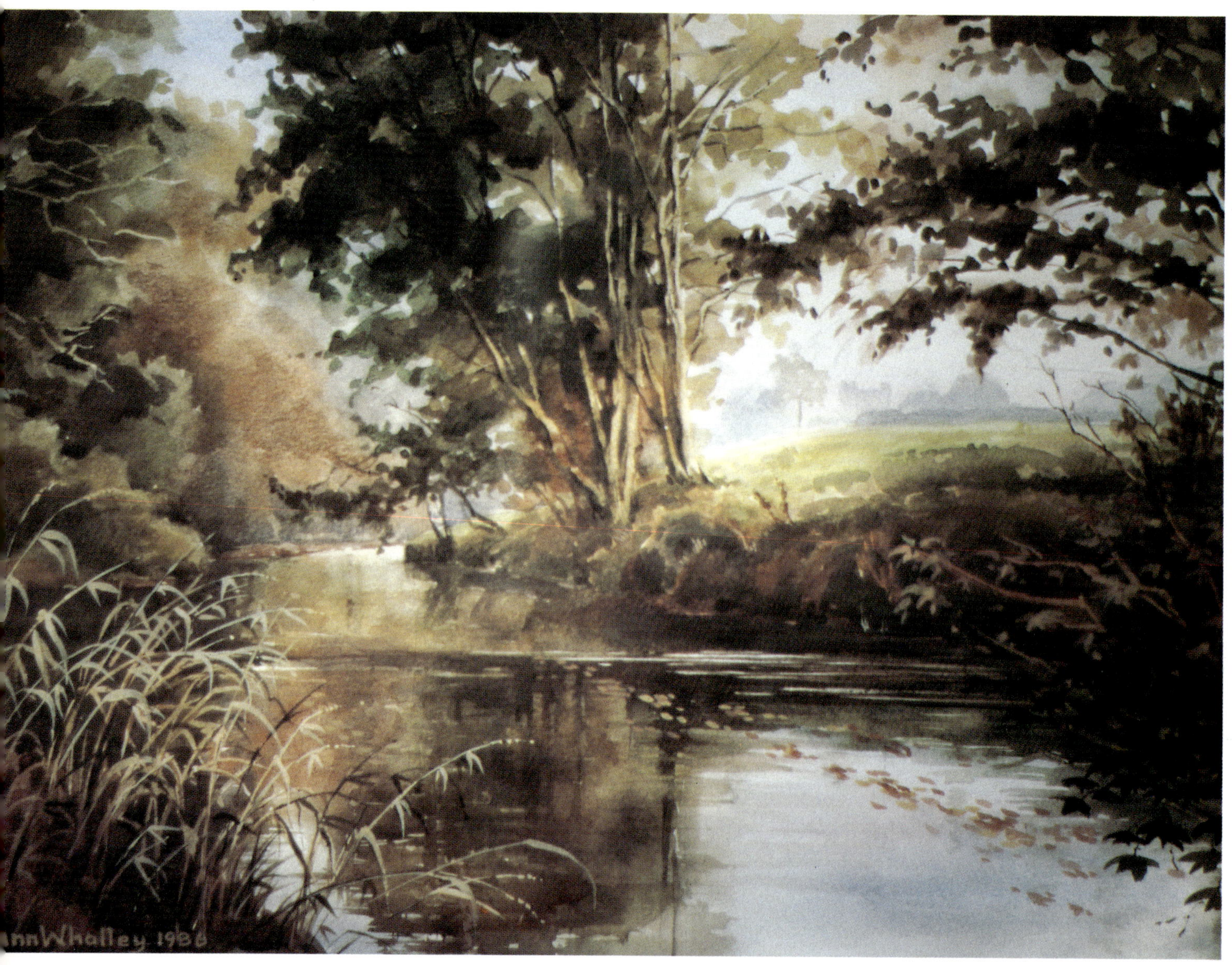

Trees by the river. *Painted in the summer, this was a lazy, slow-moving stretch of water basking in the afternoon sunshine and making a very tranquil scene (see also the painting on page 88).*

Sometimes one sets out intending to complete a painting *in situ* in one sitting. Ideally you will have visited the site on previous occasions and made a few studies, but whether you have done so or not, having decided on your view, do take a little time just to look, absorb and make a few decisions. Consider the boundaries of the painting, the placing of the various elements and what is to be prominent. Decide on the four or five pigments which will combine to give you the colour and tonal range required. This takes only a few minutes but may save you hours of wasted effort in the long run.

When washing in the palest colours for the sky and water, there is no need to paint round trees, etc. The succeeding washes of colour will cover these first washes with ease, and at the same time the underlying tint will act as a useful harmonizing aid. Gradually build up the deeper tones, either painting in already mixed colours or glazing one over another (see pages 27–9). Take great care to reserve any areas of bright sunlight – these can never be retrieved satisfactorily. Pay particular attention to the bright blobs of sky where these are reflected.

Where a painting contains a lot of greens (as is frequently the case on a riverside) add a degree of purple or reddish-brown to the shadows. This acts as a much-needed foil to the green, which can be very boring. Never just use a darker shade of green for the shadow, but look closely and seek out exciting combinations that bring out the best in each other.

It is impossible to advise on a palette for painting rivers, but I can suggest a few groups of colours which might be used in different circumstances. For a crisp winter's day with a smattering of snow on the ground and a cool blue sky, I might choose raw sienna for the dead grasses and bare trunks of the near trees, cobalt for the sky and the river, and a mixture of cobalt and madder brown for the warm purple trees in the background. I could complete a colourful painting quite satisfactorily using just these three colours, reserving the white paper for the snow, washed blue where any shadows fell.

For the same scene in May, I would use aureolin for the new grass, mix this with cobalt for shaded leaves, and mix the cobalt with light red for the underside of the clouds and the muddy riverbank. Use more cobalt with the red for the cool colour of tree reflections.

With the coming of autumn all the colours will change again. Alizarin combined with either raw sienna or burnt sienna makes wonderful shades of russet and gold. Against this almost any blue will sing, but either cobalt or ultramarine will combine well with the warm colours to produce deep, rich darks. The possibilities are endless, and, ultimately, it all boils down to your own powers of observation and invention.

A river encompasses all life and all landscapes, from mountains down to the sea, and during its long journey it changes character from a sparkling thing bouncing down over the rocks to become a smoother, deeper, swift-flowing mass, before eventually widening out between banks of sand as it finally reaches the sea.

It is not only the river that changes its character – so too do the surrounding landscape and the people who live on its banks. Open countryside gives way to villages, towns and even smoking industry and cities as a river runs it course. The way in which the water is depicted must reflect this. In your

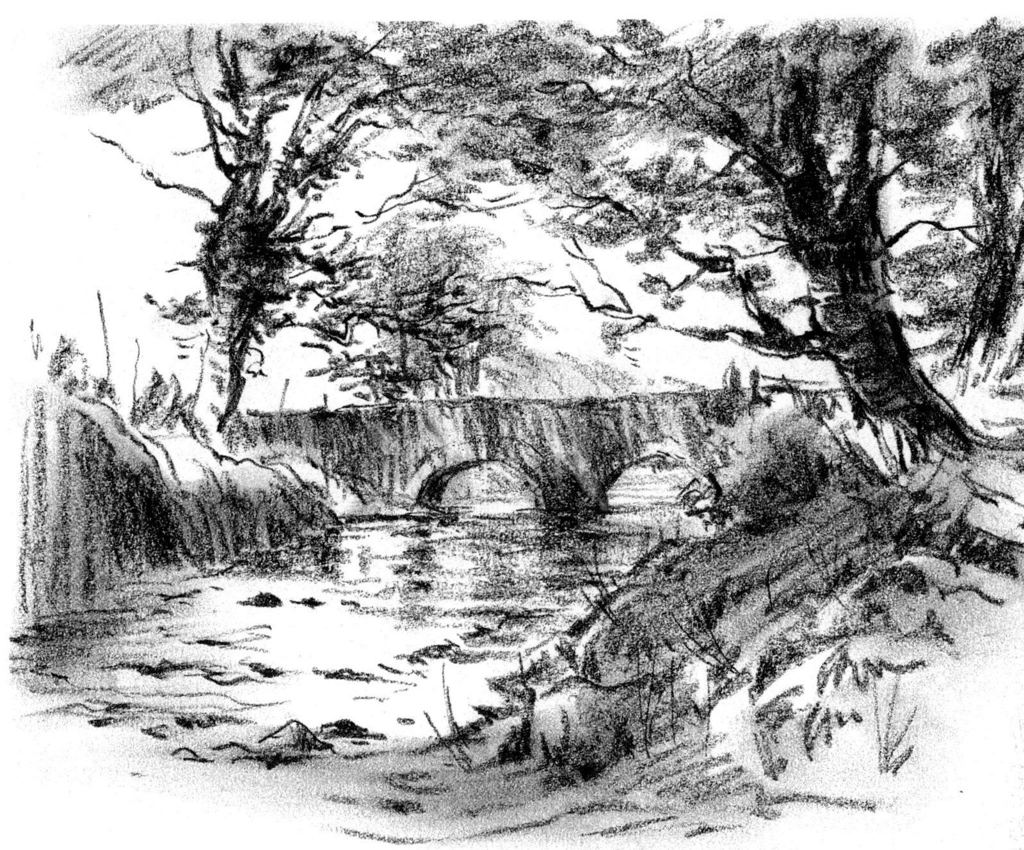

Shafts of sunlight *(see finished painting on page 89).*

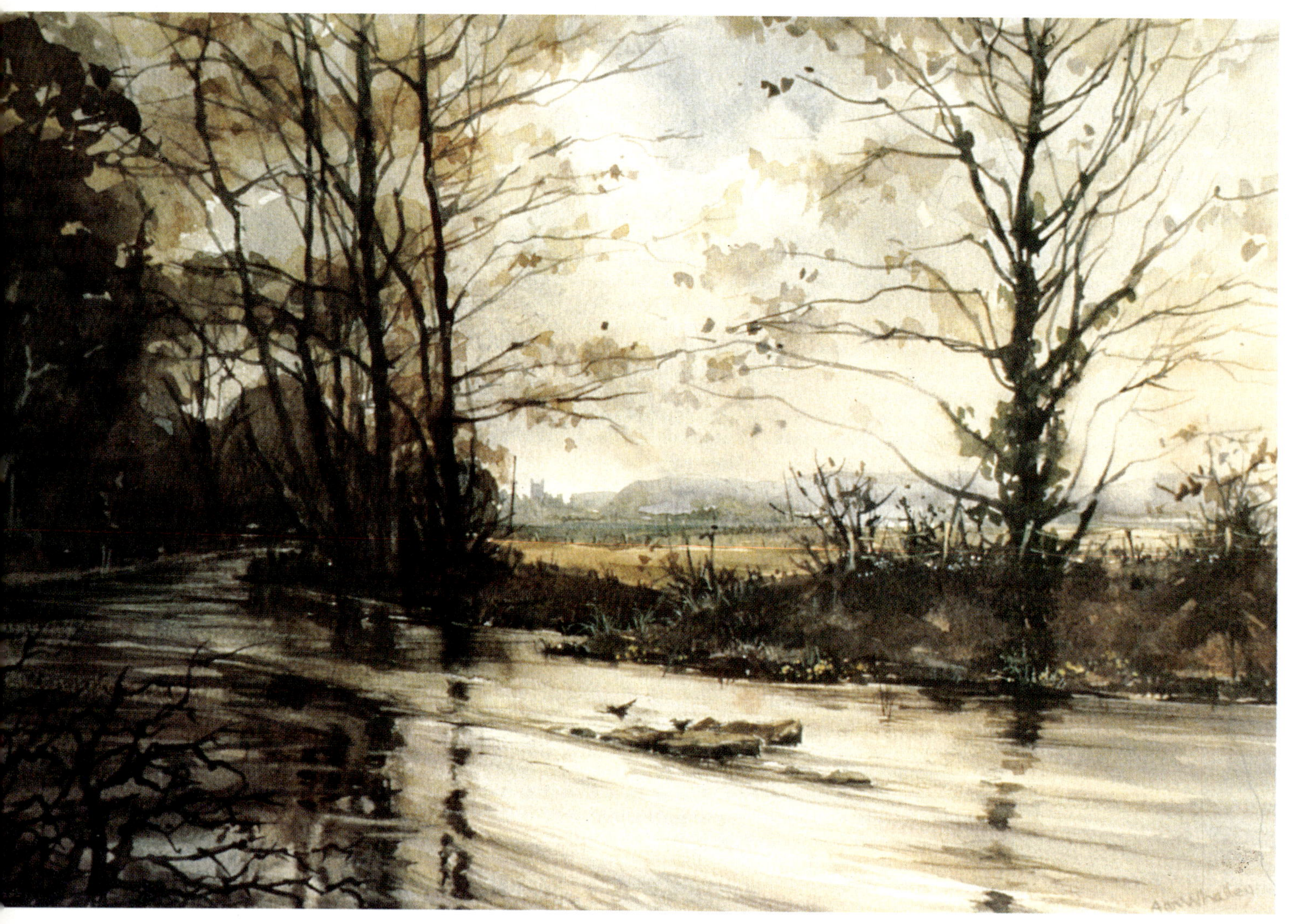

sketches, try to show the varying textures of moving water and the effect of any impediments within it. Actually *draw* the changes in the surface texture, using marks which describe flow and direction. Try to define currents and eddies, and note what it was that caused them. Observe how reflections are broken and distorted: they are usually clearly visible only where the water is still, whereas more agitated areas are influenced largely by the sky, and show as paler streaks. Practise the ways in which you will tackle all these problems, using odd scraps of paper and trying out different brushstrokes.

To tackle a river scene, select only the most significant lines of motion and then try to simplify them. This requires a conscious effort of analysis on your part and will take time, but the importance of looking and thinking can never be overstated.

On-the-spot studies of flowing water – or anything else, for that matter – need not be very large. In fact it is often better to keep them small and to make a lot of them. In this way one can work more quickly, and of course there isn't room in a small sketchbook for too many niggling and unnecessary details. Have you ever seen any of Turner's sketchbooks? Many of them are no more than seven by five inches, and they are literally *crammed* with drawings of every conceivable object he found interesting, drawn from all angles and even overlapping at times.

Trees by the river, January. *What a difference six months make (see page 86). Now the water has risen and is flowing swiftly, and the trees stand out stark and bare. I used a completely different set of colours here – mainly cobalt and raw sienna – to convey the harsh feel of winter.*

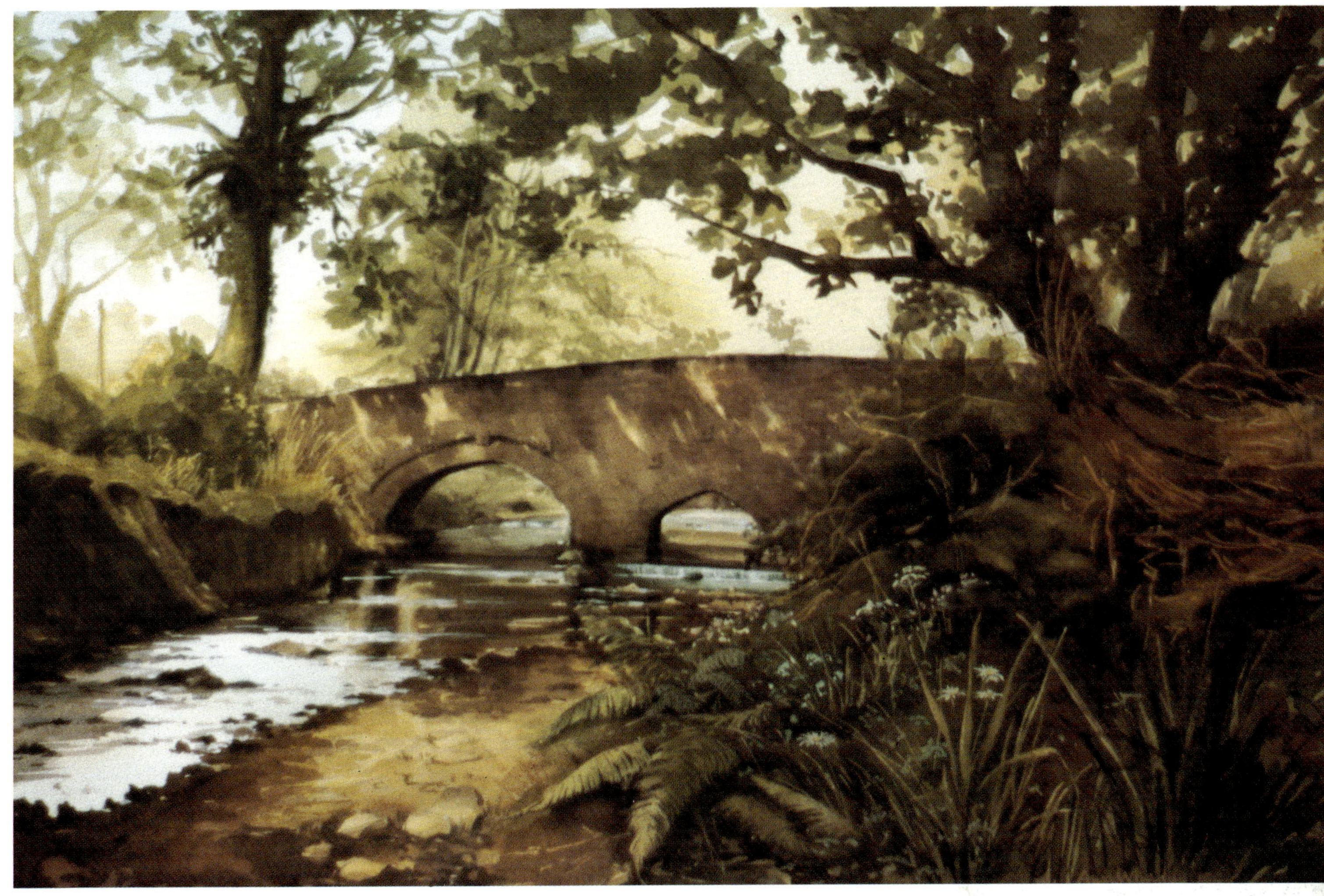

After a day out sketching one comes home brimming with new ideas and eager to transform them into a more complete statement. Somehow that initial excitement of discovery has to be retained. It may have been a strange light on a familiar subject; a particular combination of shadows and highlights; or an interesting conjunction of colours – and at the time, the impact was stupendous. Later, beset by problems of composition, colour mixing, perspective and so on, this can so easily be forgotten. You may well find it useful, as I do, to make notes at the time of making the sketch, stating exactly what it was that engaged your attention, and why you chose to draw it in the first place.

Shafts of sunlight. *This painting grew out of the sketch on page 87. I was particularly interested in the slanting bars of sunlight on the bridge, and in the different-sized arches – well worth the scramble through the undergrowth!*

CROSSINGS

One of the most attractive features of streams and rivers is their bridges. In Pembrokeshire we have a wealth of old stone pack bridges, hump-backed and often with two or three arches of different sizes. While a bridge is an ideal place from which to view a river, the best way to see the bridge itself is by climbing down the bank and looking back. This can be a revelation: what seemed from the road to be an unremarkable crossing may be shown from a new perspective as a quite unique structure well worth studying.

The hidden aspect is always exciting. Stone bridges lost in overhanging trees and undergrowth, with shafts of light bouncing back off the water to light up the undersides of the

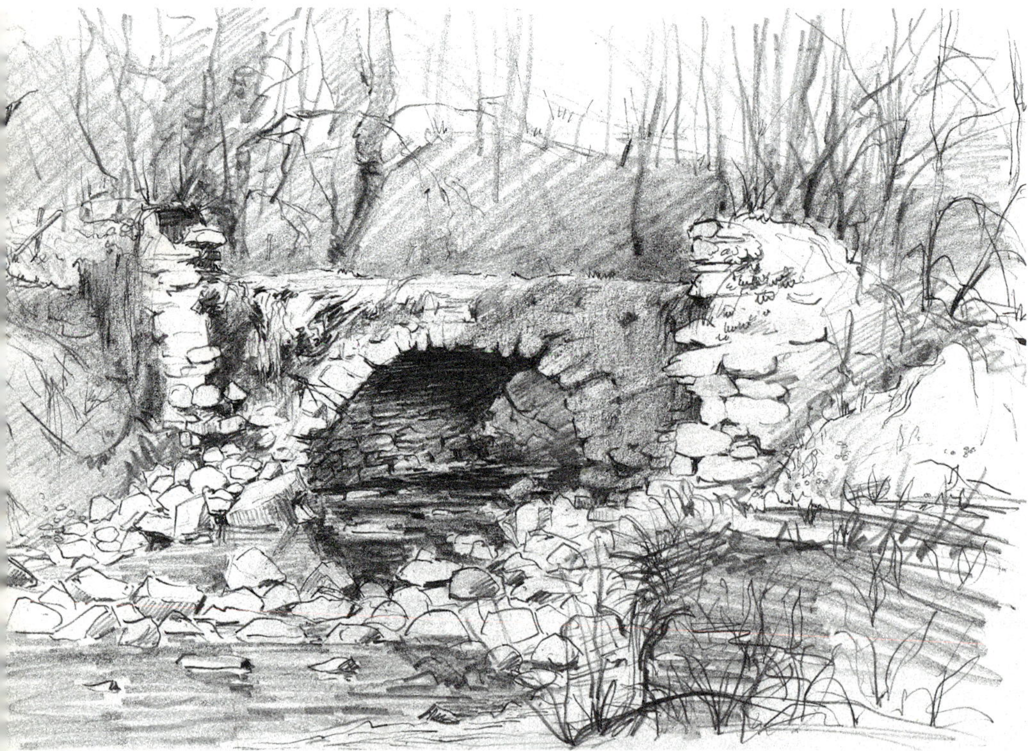

The broken bridge, Blackpool mill.

arches, can be fascinating. Look at the way that dappled light flickers over old stones, and at the colours of small plants and lichens clinging to the crevices.

There is a great logic in the way that landscape exists, and how the world works is something every artist should study and understand, so that in time one is able to construct quite complex scenes from memory and experience. If something looks awkward or uneasy, the chances are that the drawing is at fault, not nature.

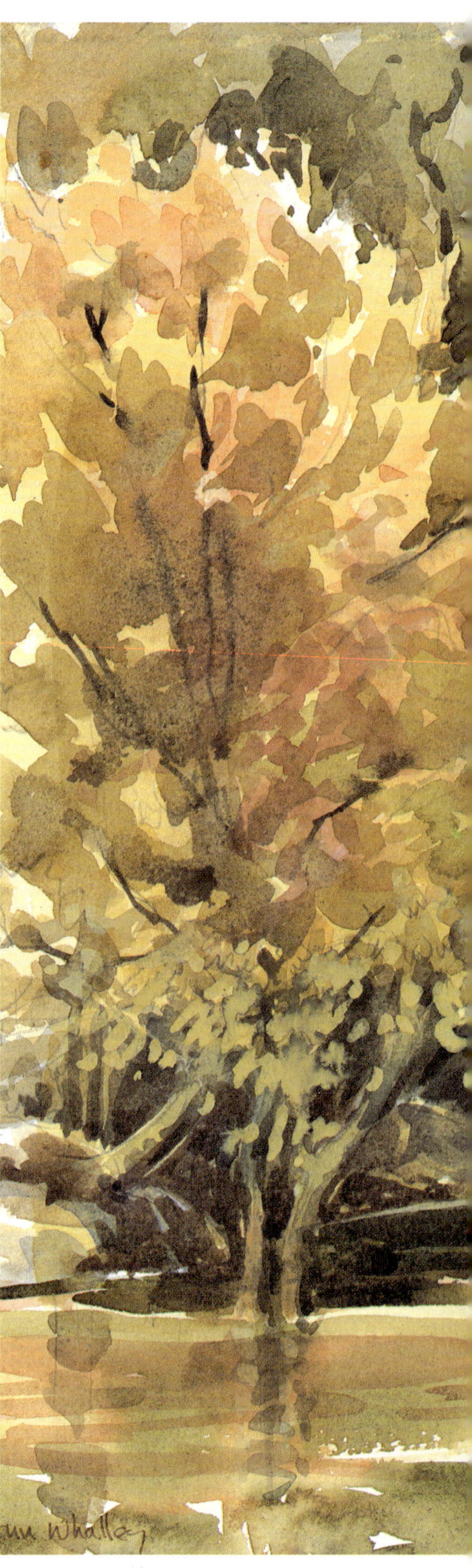

Llawhaddon bridge.

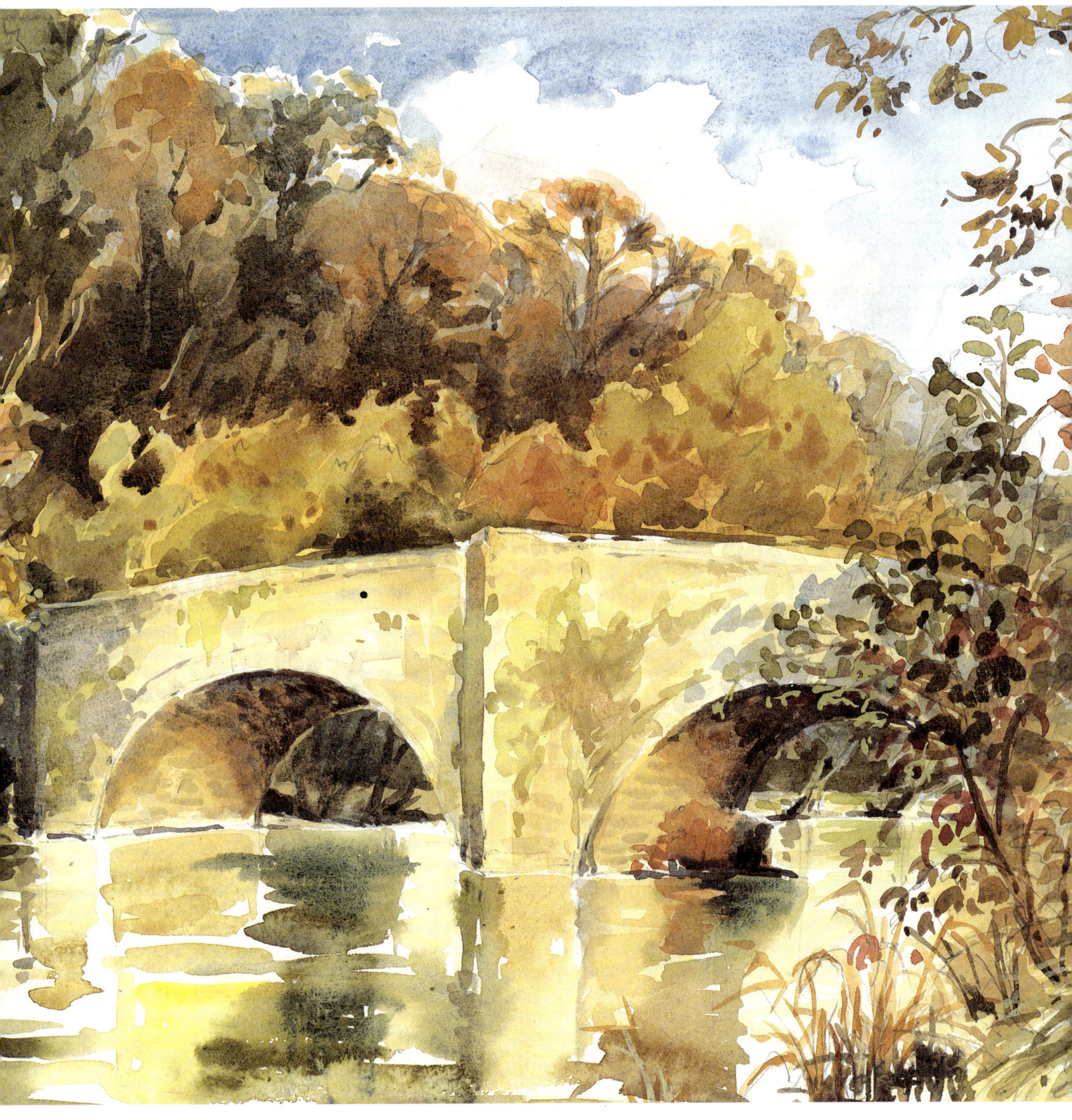

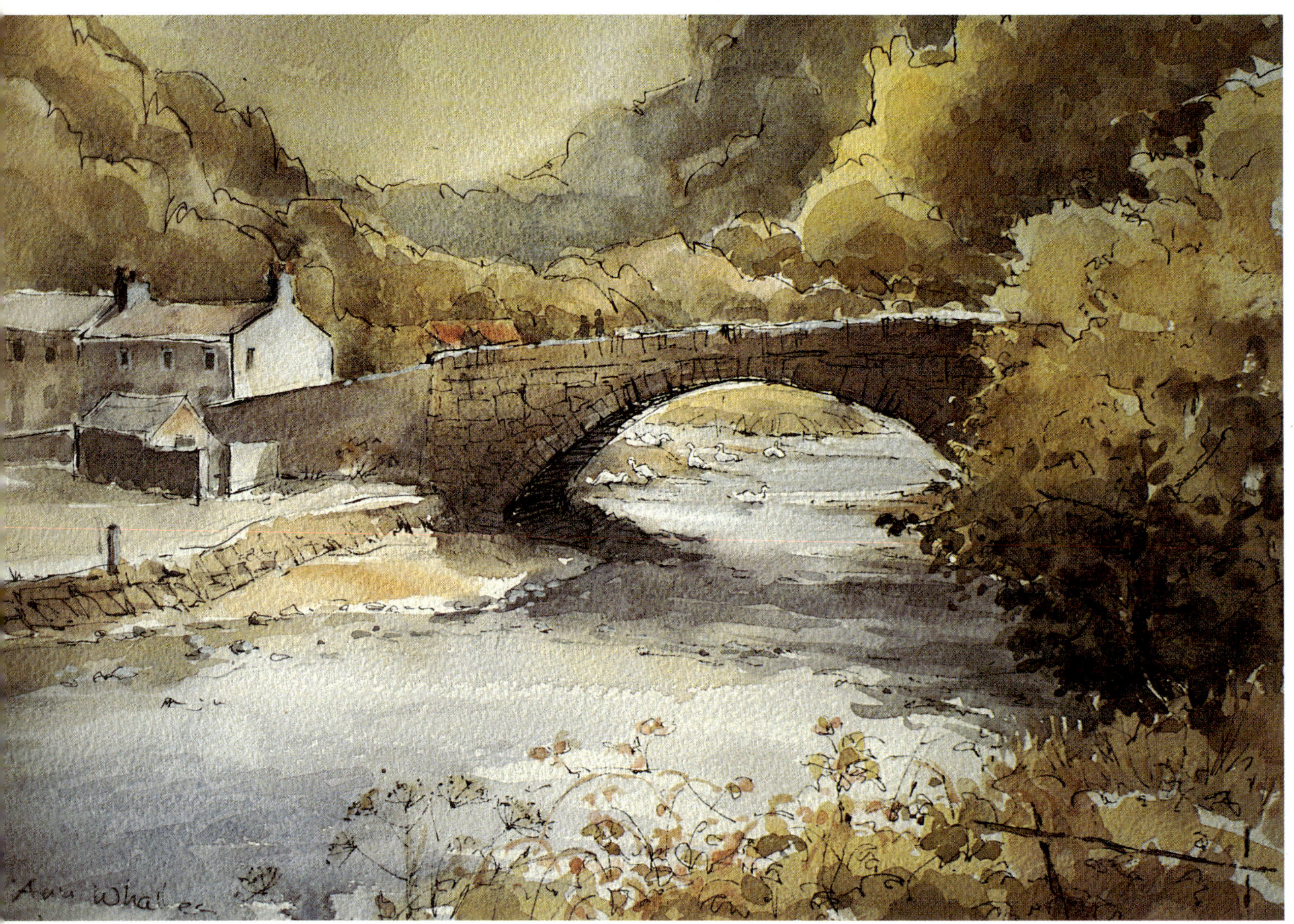

Every part of the world has devised its own way of crossing water, and the more I travel, the more I enjoy the novel and ingenious methods used. Do not spurn industrial scenes – they have a lot to offer, not least in their intriguing shapes, skyline and smoky atmosphere. The world does not have to be pretty to make it worth your attention, and there is something special to be found in the most unlikely places.

Lowertown, Fishguard.

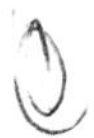

BOATS

Rivercraft have a completely different appearance from sea-going boats. They are not designed to surmount huge waves or gale-force winds, but exist in far more sheltered conditions. This is the reason for the shape of their hulls and the angle of their bows and sterns. Think of the jobs that boats are built to do and the conditions in which they function. Barges are for carrying bulk cargoes, motor boats are for hurrying about and rowing boats are for short journeys, fishing or just pottering about. This is obviously an over-simplification, but you will appreciate the point I am trying to make.

When studying boats, set off early in the day and be prepared to spend a good deal of time at it. Look carefully at the boats, at their grouping and the way they overlap, at the reflections they cast and, very importantly, at how they sit in the water (there should be a sense of the boat's hull below the water line as well as above it).

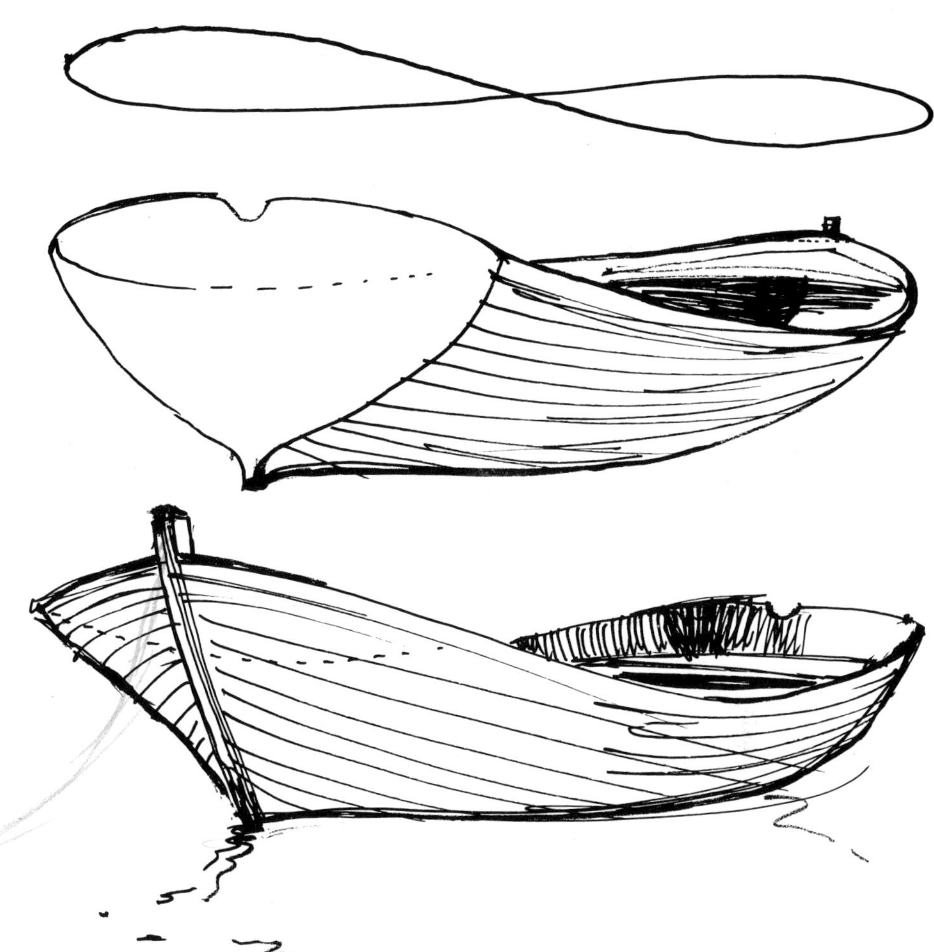

Figure 14. The lazy figure of eight.

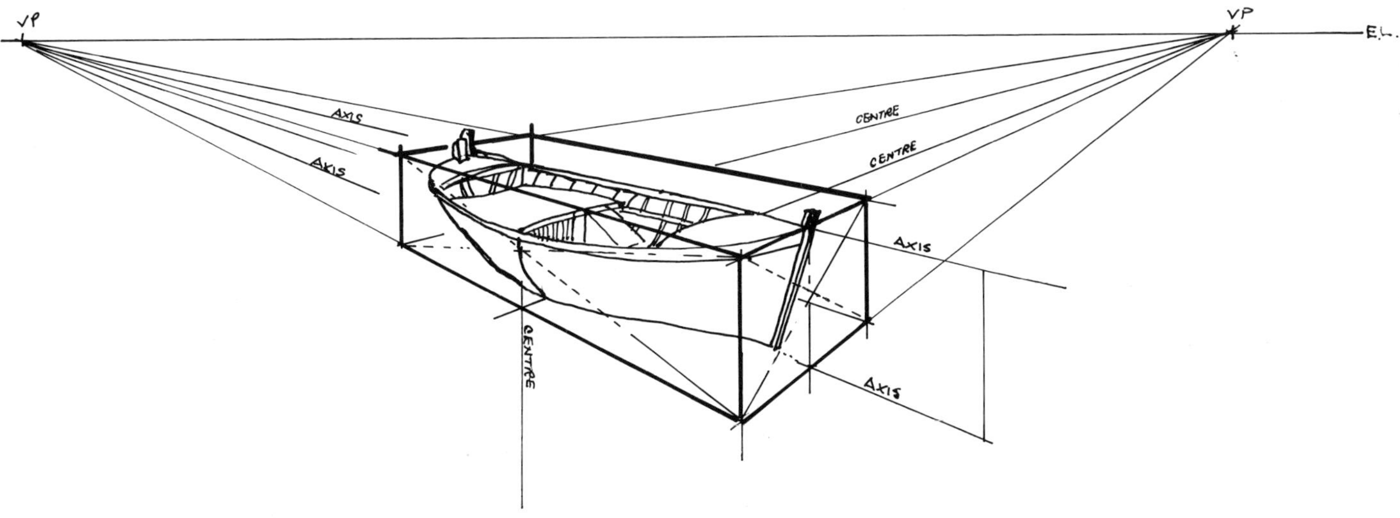

Figure 15. The boat in a box approach.

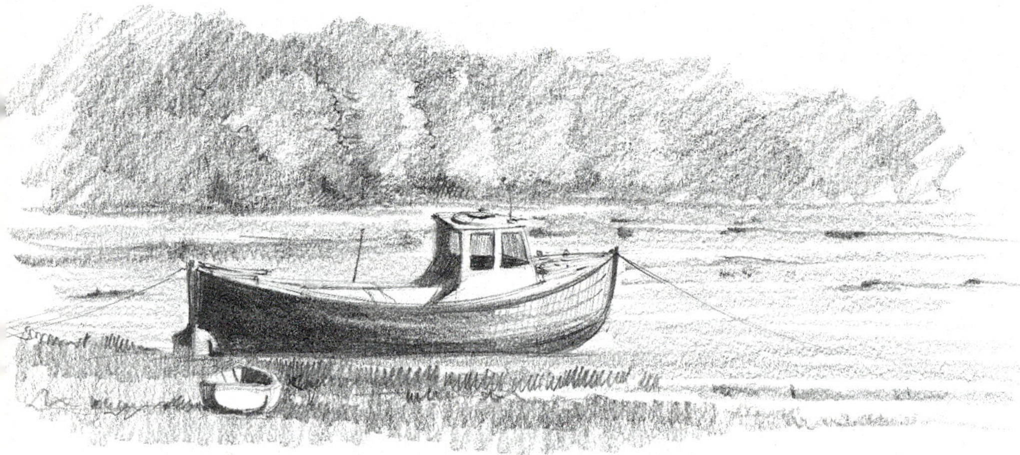

River boat.

will be transformed into glowing russet and gold by October. Keep going back to promising spots again and again over the year, just to see what changes have occurred. That bridge swamped into invisibility in summer may well have emerged in all its beauty to delight you in December.

This close familiarity with an environment is very necessary to the artist. Over a period of time one develops an intimacy akin to love for regularly frequented places. Each visit reveals something new in a well-trodden spot – a gentle re-awakening among friends, as it were. Artists must constantly respond to stimuli of one kind or another, and the ability to be excited by small features as well as great ones is an important quality.

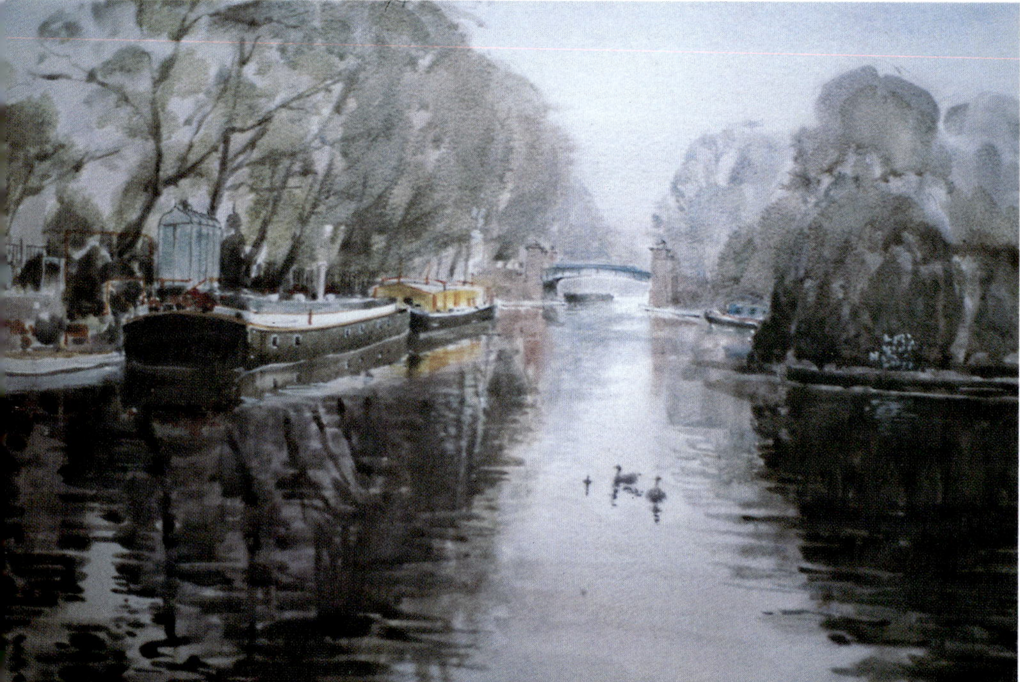

Little Venice, London. *Even in winter this is a fascinating place in which to work, with constant activity on the water and canal bank.*

Make sketches, and take photographs to use as further reference. One rarely sees the whole outline and shape of a boat clearly; it is far more likely that some parts will merge in with the general clutter that always seems to surround boating activities.

Sailing boats and small dinghies add charm to a river scene and are a useful focus of attention. White sails scudding along against a dark background give a sense of movement and also suggest the blowing of a breeze, but remember to tilt the mast in the right direction!

The changing seasons are much in evidence along a riverbank. What may be wall-to-wall green in July

(Opposite) **Quiet stream.** *I used only raw sienna and ultramarine here, which shows what can be achieved with a restricted palette. As I wanted a warm, autumnal feel the sienna predominates, allowing the blue to give depth to the shadows without degenerating into dull grey.*

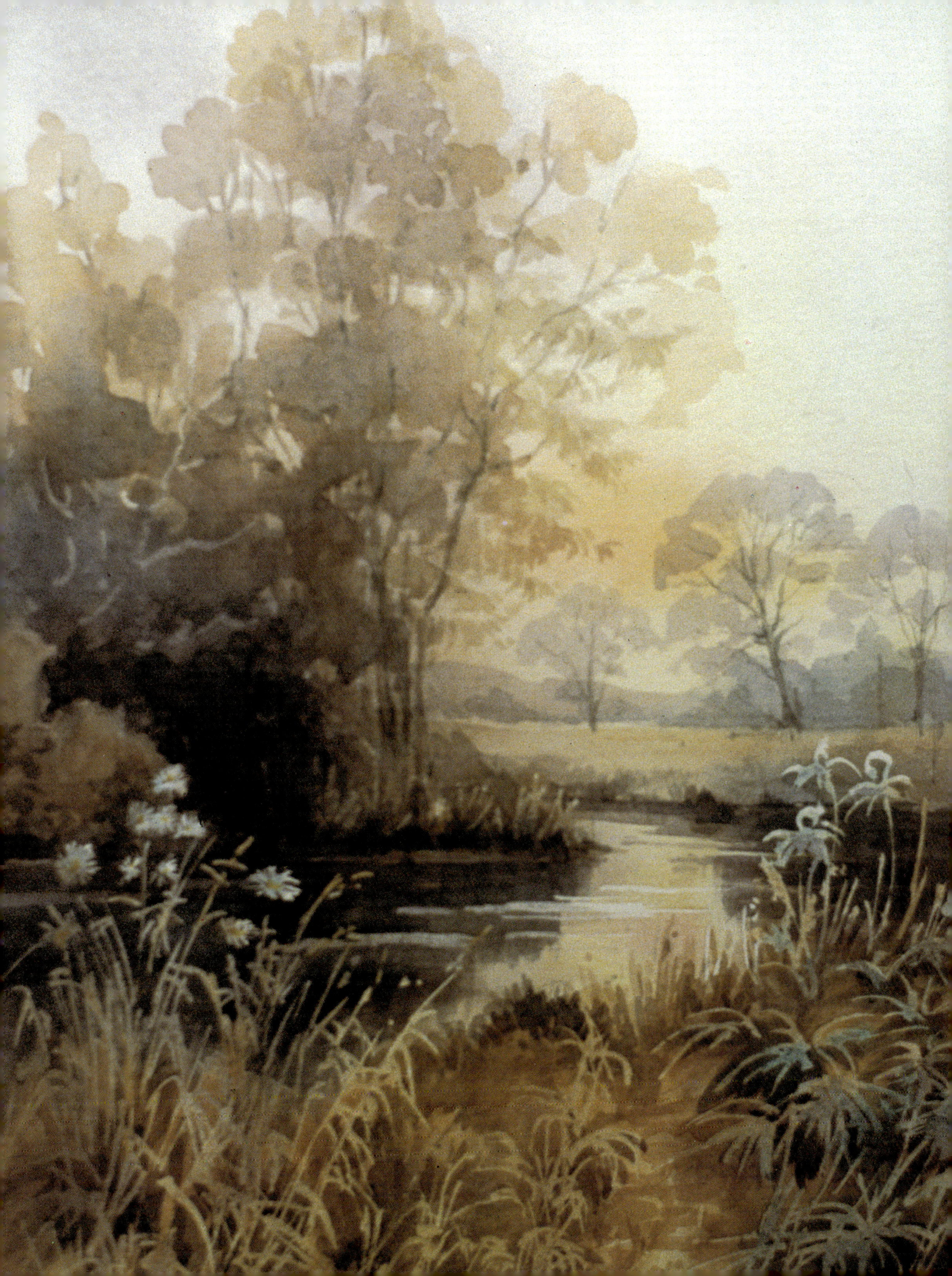

CHAPTER SEVEN

FALLING WATERS

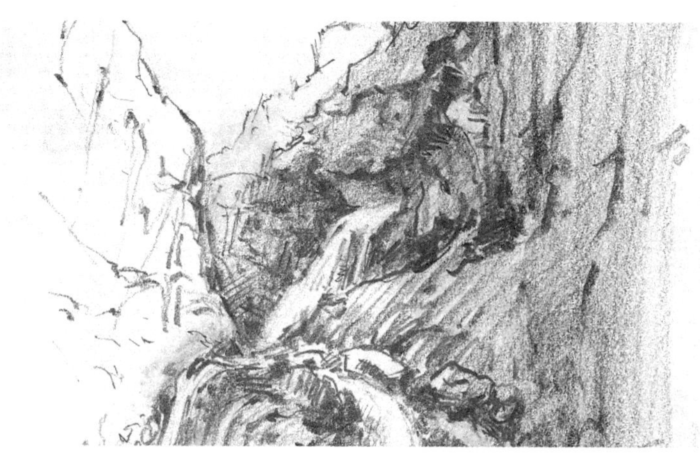

When I was young I lived in the Yorkshire Dales, in a land bubbling over with waterfalls, cascades and rushing waters, and for sheer excitement it took some beating. All my holidays were spent walking and riding the fells until I became immersed in their presence, and this intense response to wild, lonely places has stayed with me ever since.

Now I live in Wales, another place of mountains and streams, but I have to admit that even after thirty years it is for the Dales that I yearn. Perhaps south Wales is too kind, too lovely, too spectacular, so that it lacks something of the harsh bleakness and dark power of the Pennines. Waterfalls, however, Wales has in abundance.

Wherever one happens to be, there is no denying that falling water is one of the most difficult subjects to paint. The surging energy of water tumbling down the mountain and roaring through a gorge over rocks and boulders, the foam bursting wildly until it sweeps into deeper, calmer places is awe-inspiring. Organizing all this drama into paintable form is also fairly awe-inspiring! Do I hear you saying 'Oh, no! That's not for me – I'll find something easier'? I'm sure not, for think what you would be throwing away, remembering too that we cannot move on unless we attempt more than we think we are capable of doing. I know that it takes a degree of courage to risk failure, but failure is relative, and, although the first results may be less than you had hoped for, you are learning all the time and the more you try, the easier and better it will become.

ECONOMY AND SELECTION

Once again, this is the time for some hard thinking and hard looking. Try to pick out the main directions of movement of the water, and think of how best to place the lines of force on the paper. At the same time, work out the most economical ways of explaining this. The flow of water will be greatly influenced by immovable objects blocking its path, so note any rocks, fallen trees or other impediments and observe the way in which the water is blocked and diverted around them. See also how the activity constantly repeats itself. Above all, from the start, isolate the areas of white foam and spray, and make a pledge not to 'muddy the waters'.

At the same time, try to develop a form of visual shorthand. Use

(Right) **Waterfall, Yorkshire Dales.**

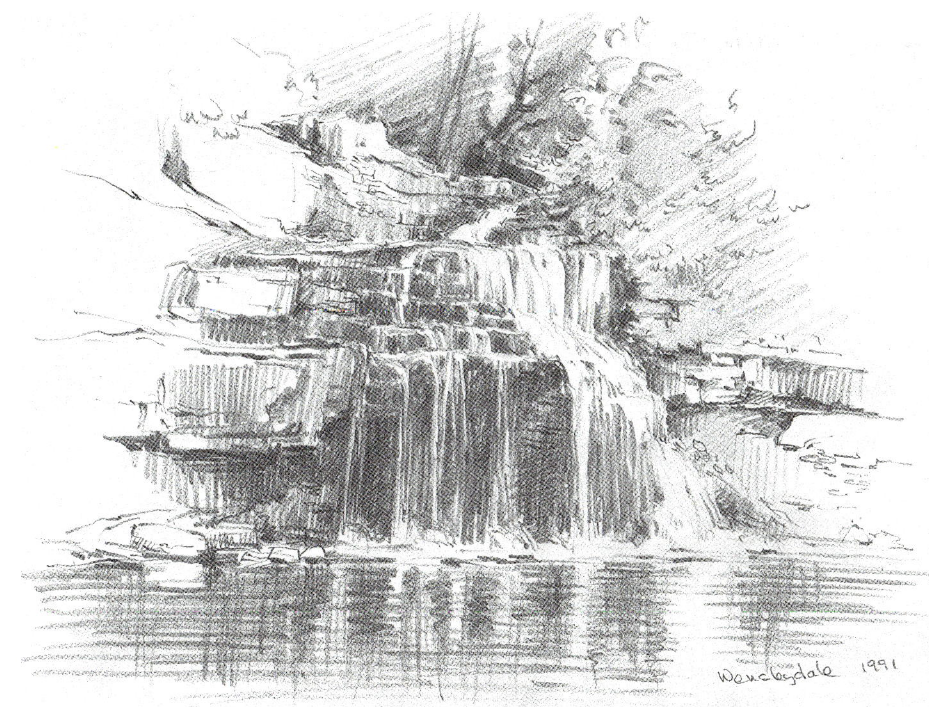

(Below) **Cenarth falls.** *The excitement of a waterfall is often outweighed by the fear that it is all too complicated to paint. Contrary to what may at first appear, however, not everything is moving. Look for the static objects, place them well and strongly, and then let the water flow around them. It is the contrast that is so interesting here.*

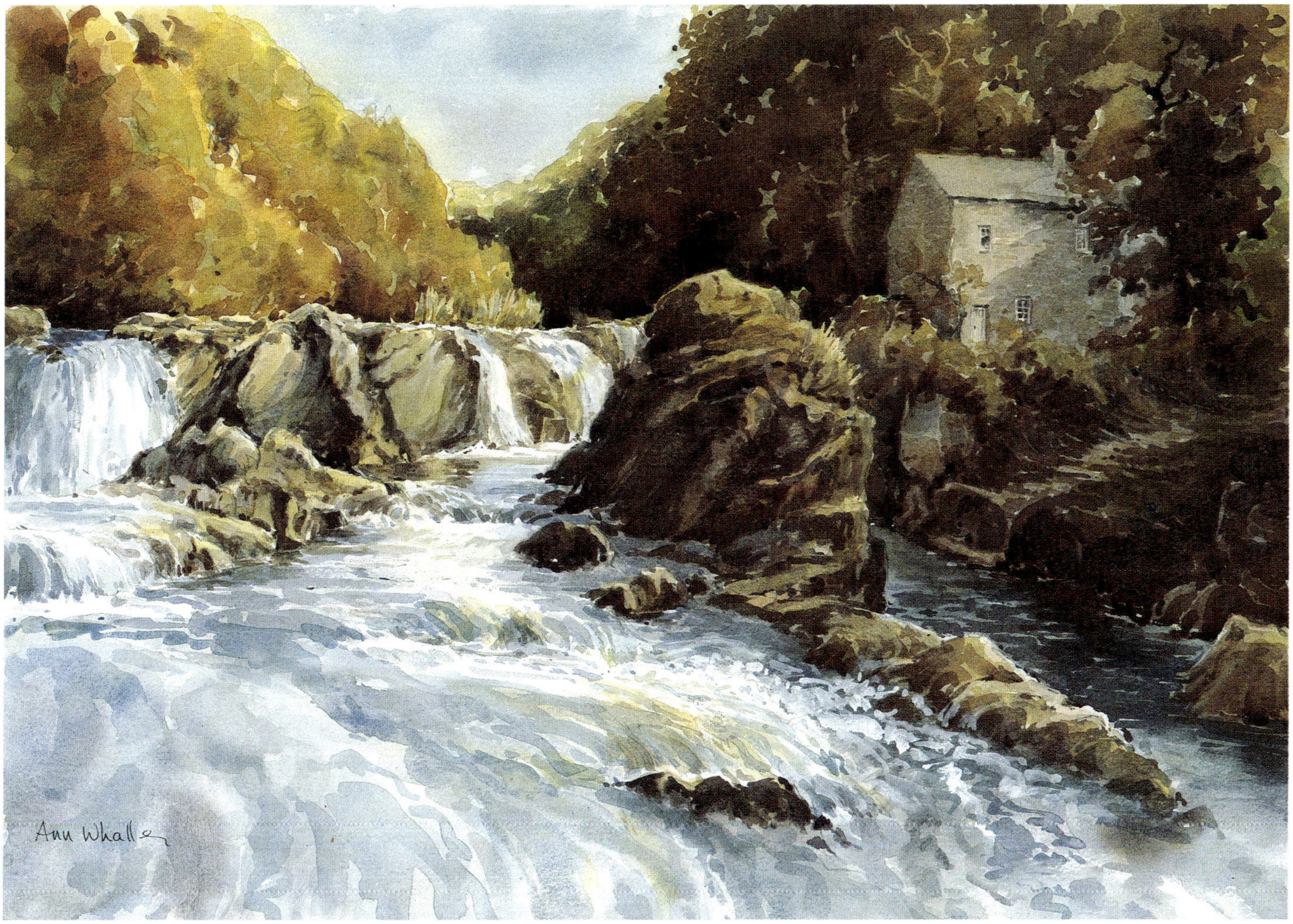

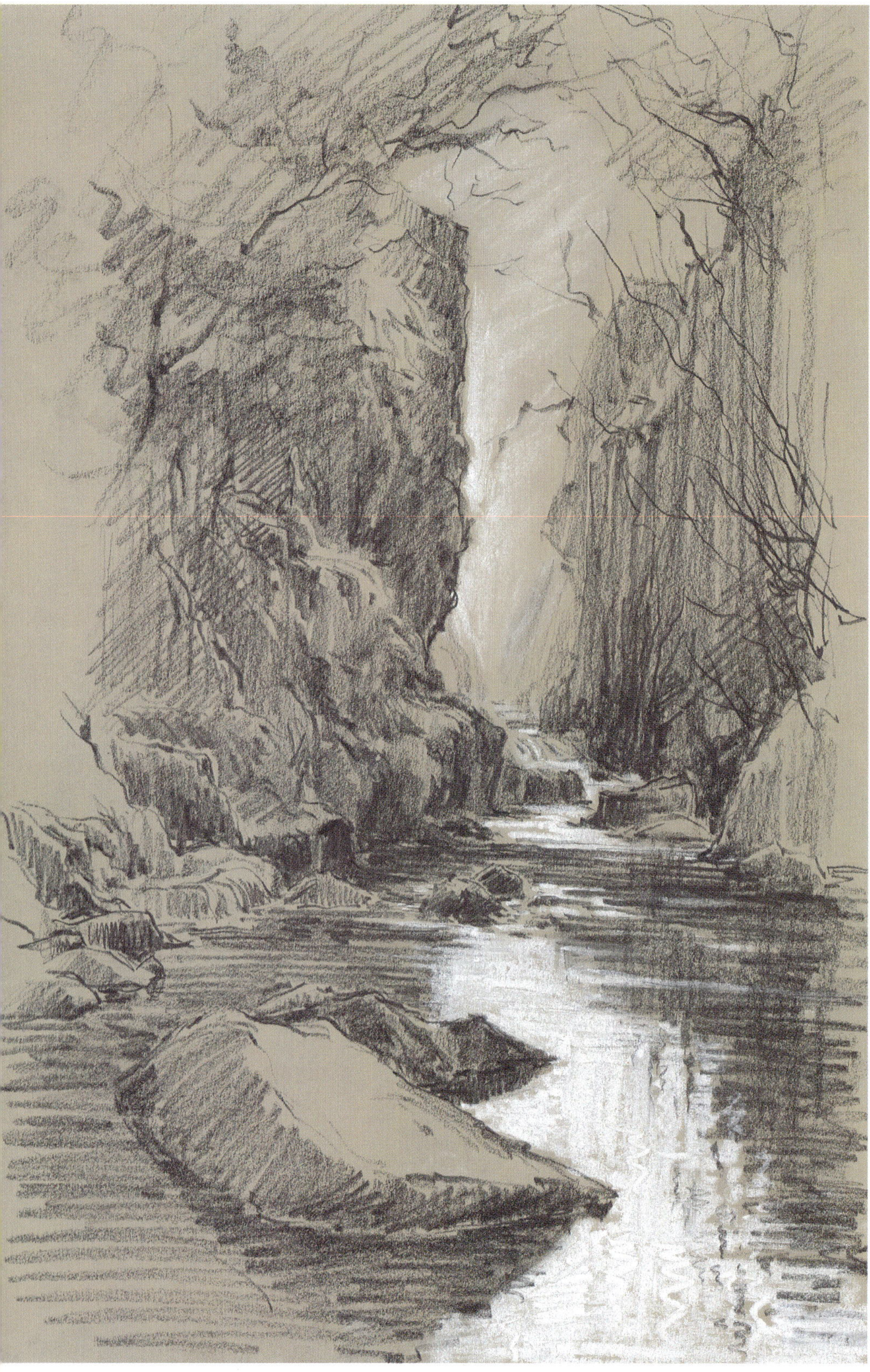

one line instead of half-a-dozen near misses, and make a definite statement, even if it is wrong. Anything is better than an indeterminate apology of a drawing, where the intention has somehow got lost along the way. Make your marks as expressive as possible: long, vertical lines to represent the falling water; short jerks for the tumbled part beneath; and smooth horizontals where the torrent slows and widens. Never stop looking for new ways in which you can explain movement and form, such as varying the intensity of tone and the thickness of the lines.

Do everything you can to convey your own excitement to the viewer – the marks you make should possess a quality of sensitivity which has nothing to do with the objects they are intended to portray. There is something magical in the way a master works which far transcends accuracy.

Ravine. *This is part of the wild Snowdonia range. I used white pastel, charcoal and soft pencil to achieve the effect of solid rock and moving water.*

USING PHOTOGRAPHS

Painting falling water is one time when I would certainly back up my sketches with slides or photographs. Note, however, that I say 'back up' and not 'substitute', as nothing can replace your sketches as a personal response. Slides are often better than photographs because they can be blown up big on a wall and are the nearest you will get to re-living the experience of actually being there. For this reason, you must use only your *own* slides, and not those taken by somebody else, or you will lose this vital intimacy with the subject. By this method I am able to recall almost exactly how I felt at the time: the roar of the falls, my sense of vertigo, the struggle to get there and how insecure my footing was!

Failing slides, photographs (preferably in black and white) are a useful recall aid to detail, texture and the frozen moment. Colour photographs have certain dangers which you can avoid once you are aware of them, the most frequent being the great temptation to copy. How many times do I catch my students glued to a photograph, intent on slavishly copying it on to paper, ignoring any consideration of the placing of features, the tonal values or how much to leave out of the composition.

The problem is that nature rarely presents a perfect picture, and invariably needs some help from the artist. I have already mentioned the importance of selection and rejection, the placing of emphasis, and creating centres of interest. Just because something appears in a photograph, it doesn't mean that you must accept and

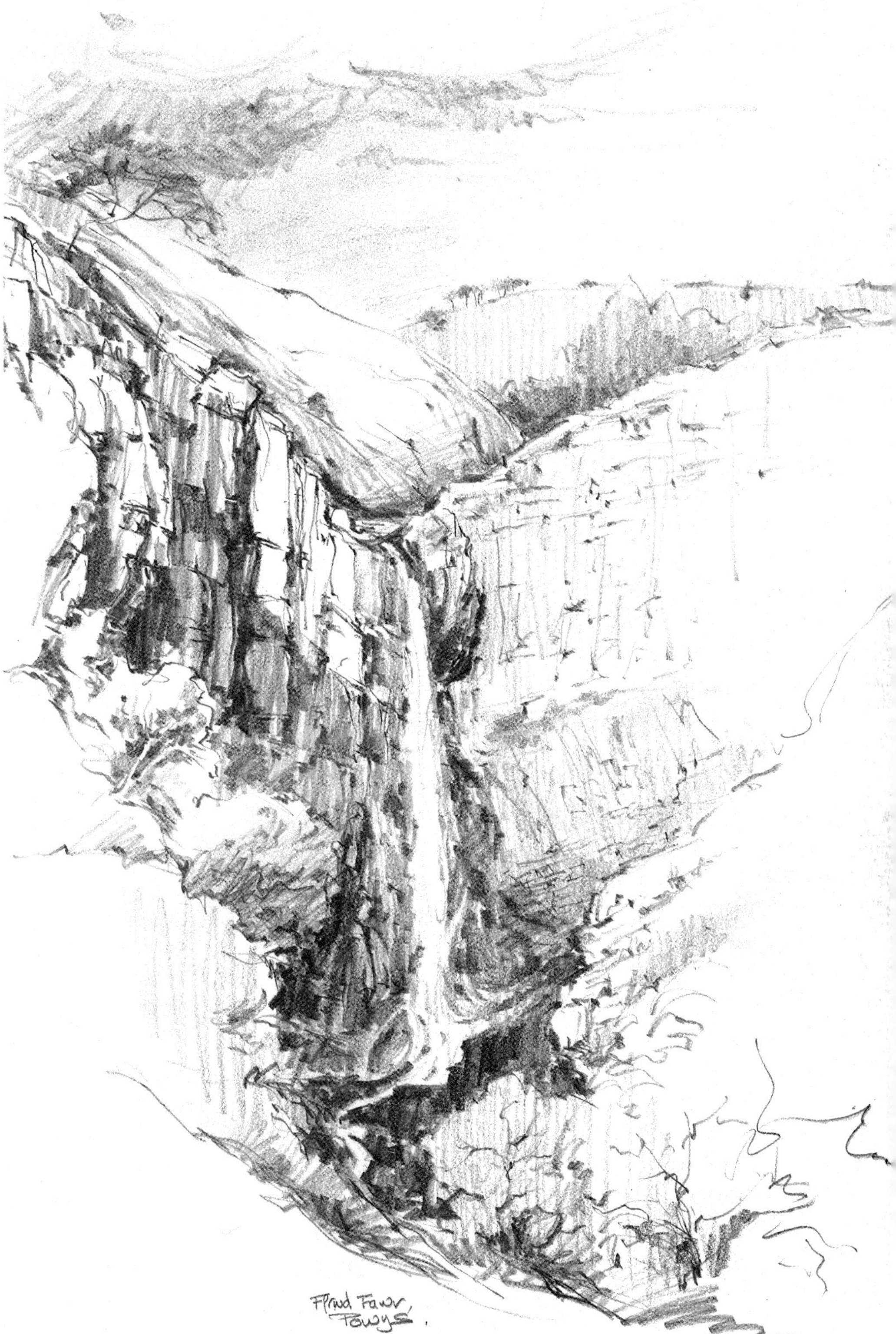

High Falls, north Wales.

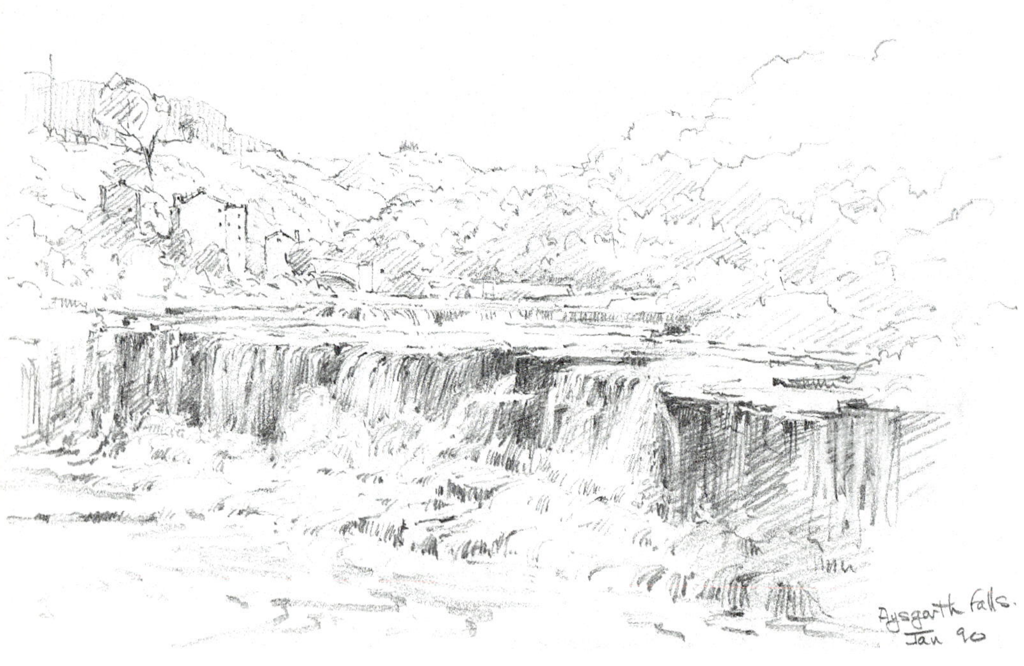

include it in your painting. All paintings contain a greater or lesser degree of distortion.

Another drawback to the use of colour photographs as reference is their colour, as this will vary enormously depending on the quality of the printing. I had some scenes taken at the height of a Greek summer returned to me in sad shades of blue/grey, but when I sent them to another firm they came back much nearer to the vivid colours I remembered. The problem is that it is difficult to ignore the colours in a photograph and impose your own instead, in the way that one does when working from sketches.

I have evolved a method of avoiding many of these problems. Set up the chosen photograph so that it is at least four feet away from you – if you can't see it clearly, so much the better. From this, make a few sketches – some for possible compositions, some to decide tonal arrangements – until you arrive at something which seems to express your feelings and

Aysgarth falls.

which also makes the most interesting arrangement on the paper.

Once you have done this, put the photograph away! Using your sketches, draw and work up the painting just as you would if you had made the sketches on the spot, referring to the photograph only towards the finish if you need to check up on details.

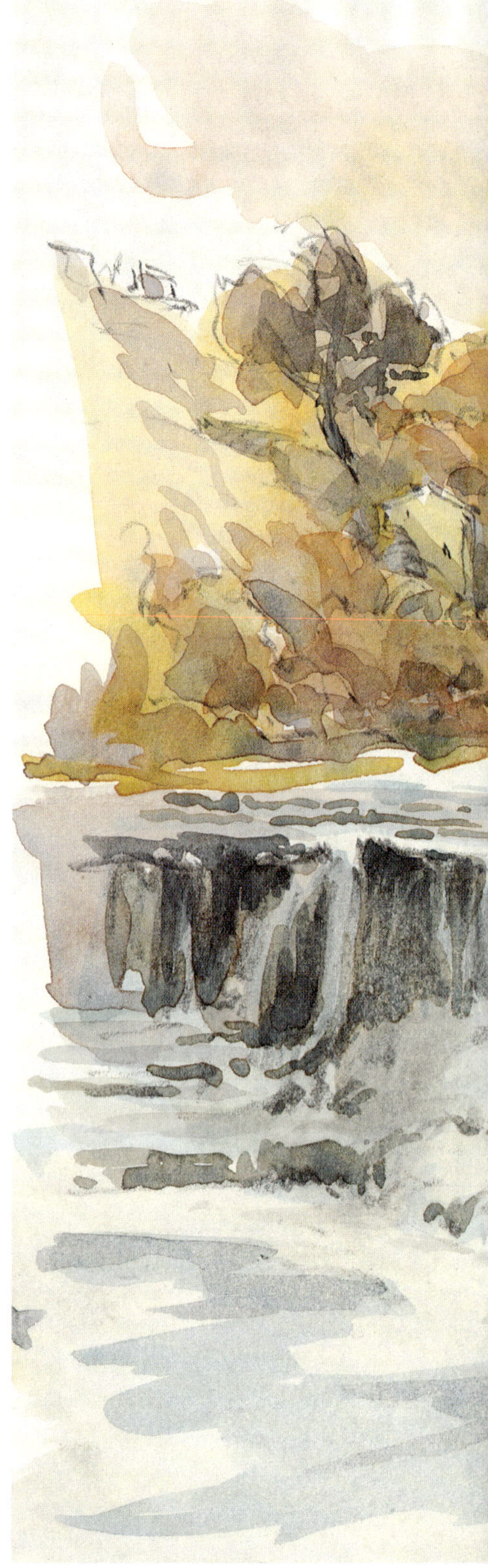

Aysgarth falls. *I did this as an on-the-spot sketch to back up my drawing of the same subject (above). Both have been set aside for the moment, waiting until I feel ready to make a more considered painting.*

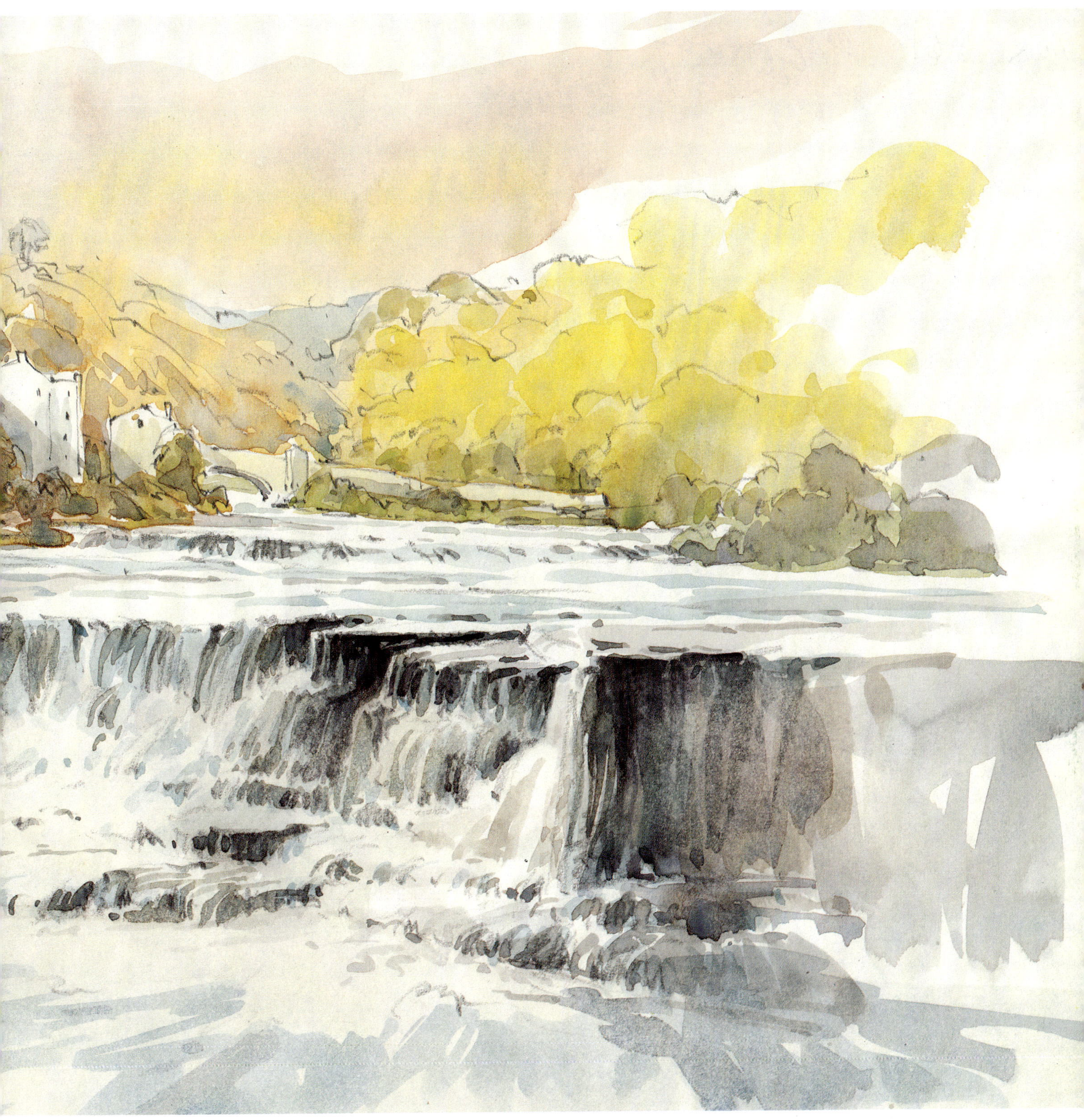

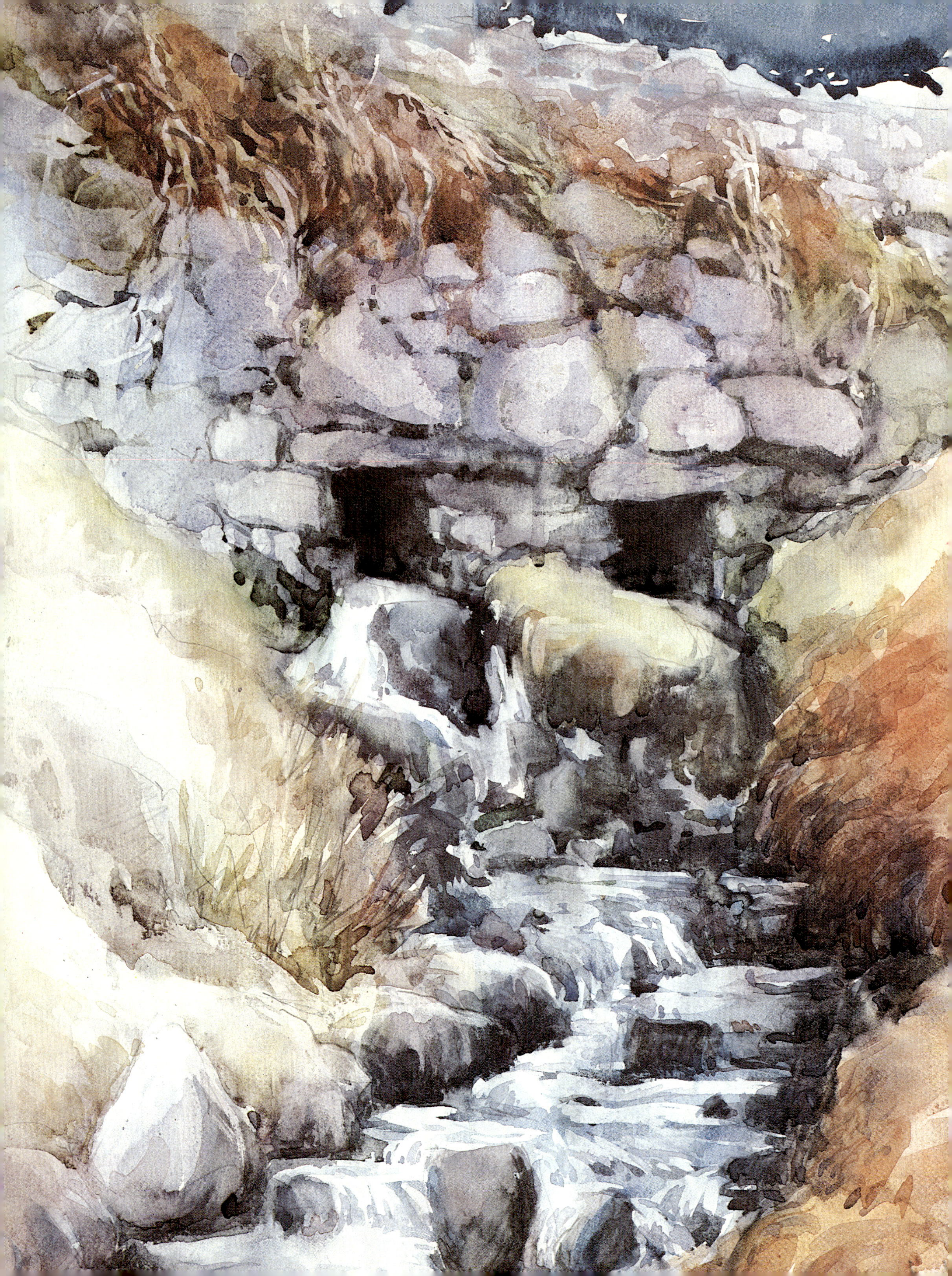

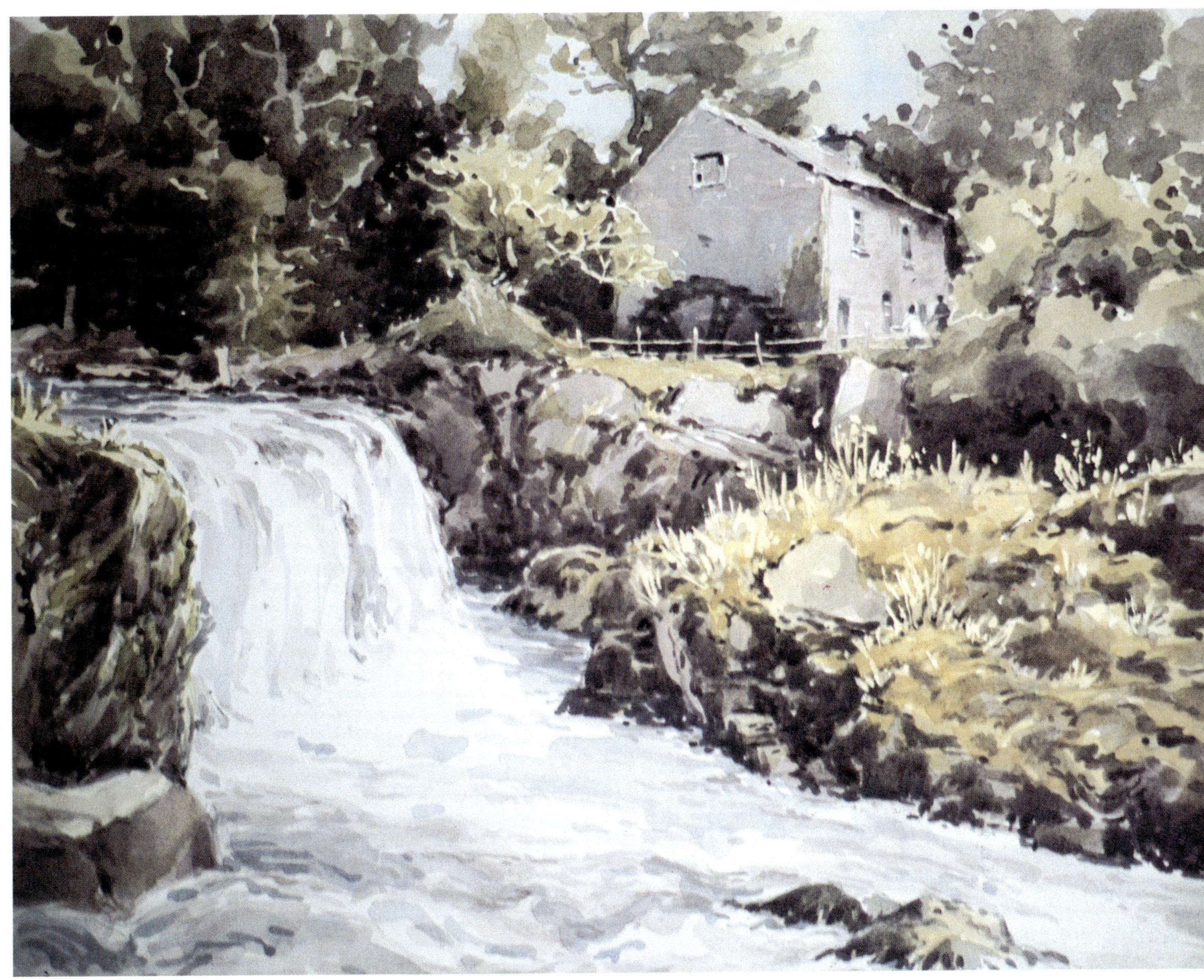

Cenarth falls and mill. *The almost totally white water attests to the speed of its flow.*

I often prefer a bad photograph of falling water to a good one. The blurred, out-of-focus effect of rapidly moving water seems to express its nature better than a more professional, sharp version. Under- or over-exposure may also be assets, causing you to put more of your own interpretation into the work. Never assume that a photograph depicts an inviolable truth, as the truth lies with you, and with your own unique values and vision.

What we hope to express in scenes of falling water is velocity and great force, and very possibly the insignificance of man amid such natural magnificence. Look, for example, at the way in which Turner so often included tiny figures in his scenes of mountain grandeur, and at how unrepentantly he exaggerated the height of his mountains and the drop of his waterfalls.

In all such scenes there are bound to be immovable objects such as cliffs, boulders or bridges. Make good use of these as a means of holding the design together.

Carn Ingli water race. *This sort of water crossing is frequently found in the Preseli hills. It was almost unnoticeable from the road, but splendid from below.*

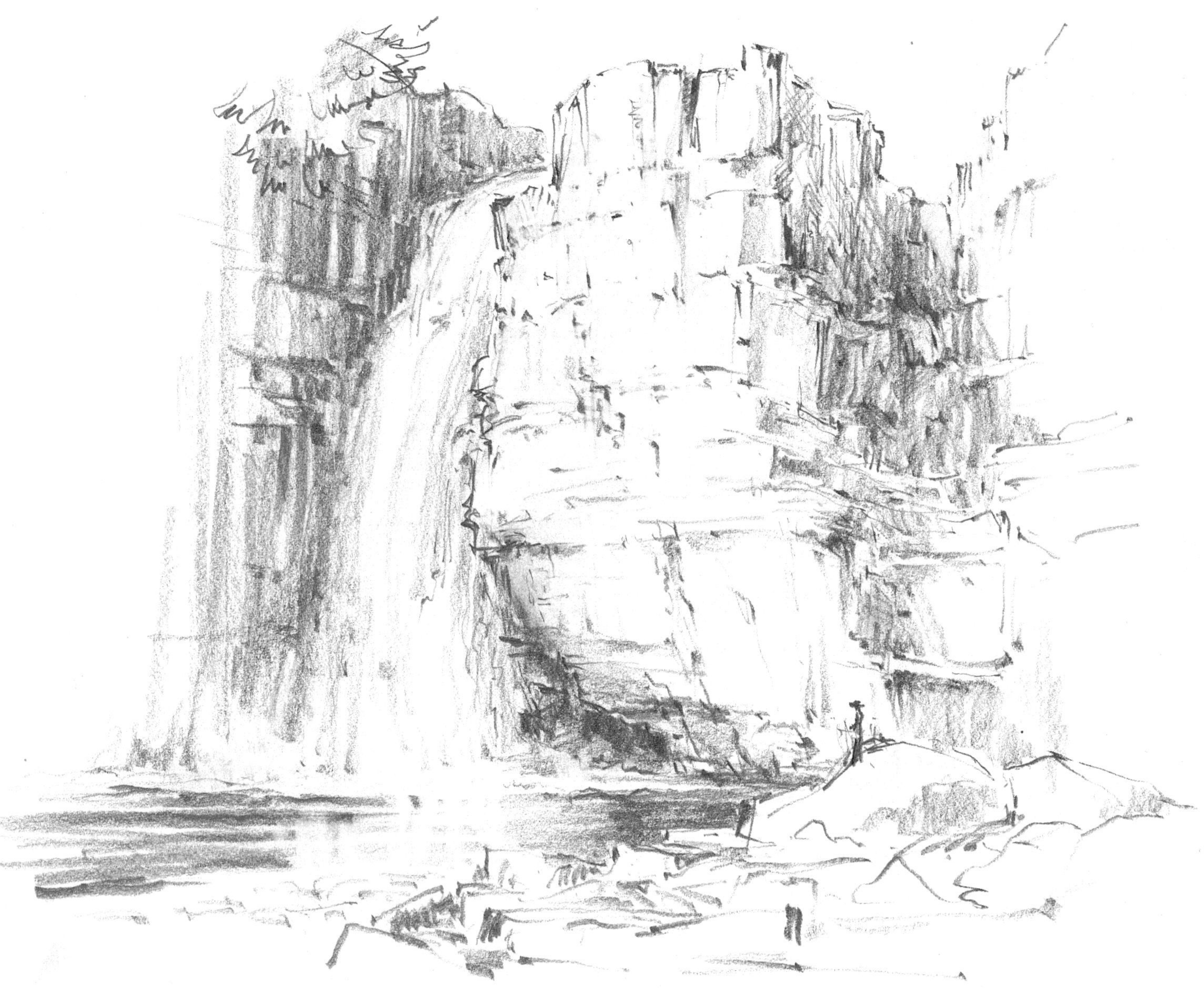

Usually they are darker in tone than the foam-flecked water, and this is a help. Emphasize their strength and hardness, and literally let the water flow and gush around them. You are involved in a never-ending battle between earth and water, and it is very exciting: try to get this feeling into your paintings. Make good use of the dramatic counterchange between fluid white water and dark immutable rock.

Look carefully at the changes in direction of the water at each drop or obstacle it meets. The way water finds and flows down crevices in the rocks is a great help in defining their shape. Make use of every device you can think of: mix media, scratch or sponge out, introduce inks, pastel, white gouache or wax. After all, a painting is no less acceptable because the artist has used a variety of means to achieve the finished result.

My best advice when tackling waterfalls is to stay calm, consider the scene before you at length, prepare yourself fully and then just have a go. It may work or it may not, but at least you tried, and in doing so learned many new things and gained great satisfaction – and tomorrow you can always try again.

Waterfall.

CHAPTER EIGHT

SECRET WATERS

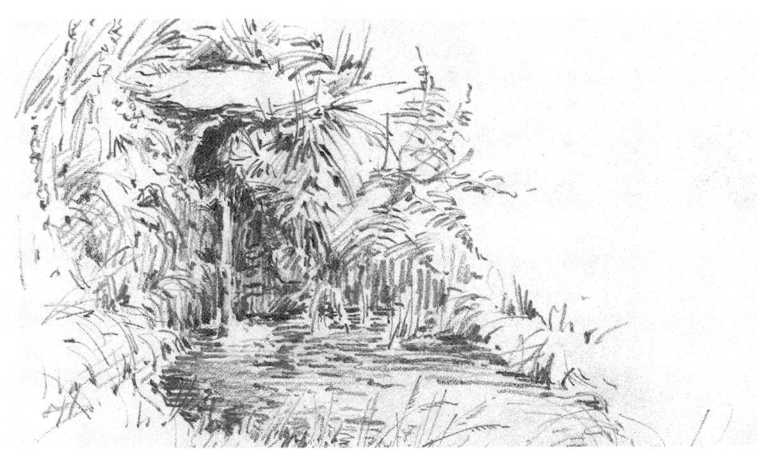

Of all the many conditions of water discussed so far, I think this is the one I love best. You do not have to live in a special place to find wonderfully quiet and enclosed places. They are all around us for those who are prepared to search – in the abandoned relics of small rural industries or still flourishing boatyards, great ports or overgrown streams – wherever you are, it is all there waiting to be painted.

I am particularly lucky, for all along my river and coast are the remains of old quarries, lime-burning kilns, fishing cottages sprouting small trees, small quays and sunken boats, mostly derelict now and gradually becoming submerged beneath fallen trees and scrub. Castles abound, perched high above the river or guarding the seashore. The river's bank is broken in places by strange indentations, the muddy remains of deserted quarry workings which now flood with every tide, and which can be approached only by struggling through swathes of reeds or by boat.

Not that secret places have to be decayed remnants of a bygone age. A shadowed corner of a busy town, a tidal pool beneath an overhanging cliff or a quiet spot by a stream all offer possibilities. These secluded places encourage wild things to feel safe, and one is well rewarded for a little discomfort and patience by seeing the shyer creatures venture out. There is a spot by my river where a family of otters sometimes plays; I see stalking herons, wild geese, mallard and small wrens, snipe and waders of all kinds, turquoise kingfishers poised to swoop down in brilliant flashes of colour, and one autumn evening a badger trotted past me to drink. Rabbits and foxes love the dusk, bats flutter overhead, and at night the owls fly. I am usually so mesmerized by just watching that I quite forget to draw!

If, like me, you enjoy these kinds of places, make a point of discovering some for yourself, and make them your own. These might be a rockpool at the edge of the tide where the water distorts the rocks and weeds into strange convolutions and where small fish dart; puddles in the mud at a farm gate; deep pools beneath an old bridge; a sad, sunken barge in an overgrown canal; even a pond in a park, with ducks resting head-under-wing beneath a sheltering willow. There are hidden places everywhere for those who stray beyond the obvious into the byeways of the world.

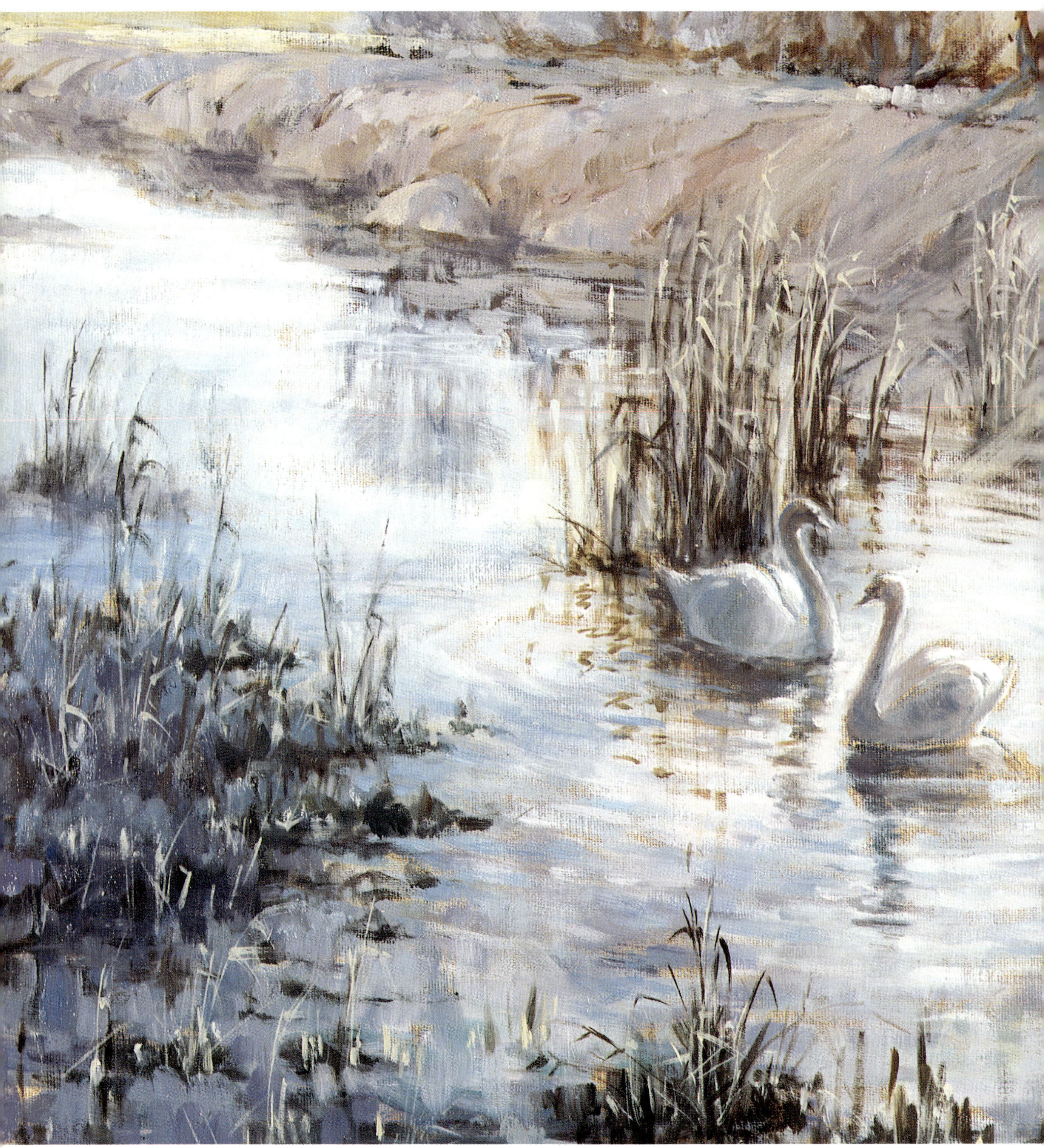

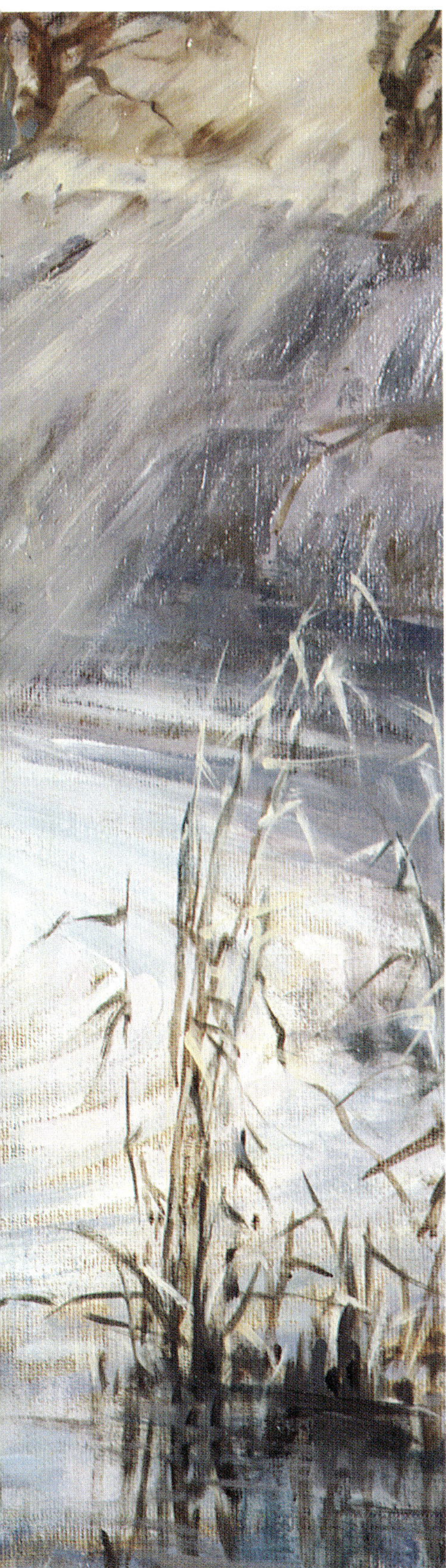

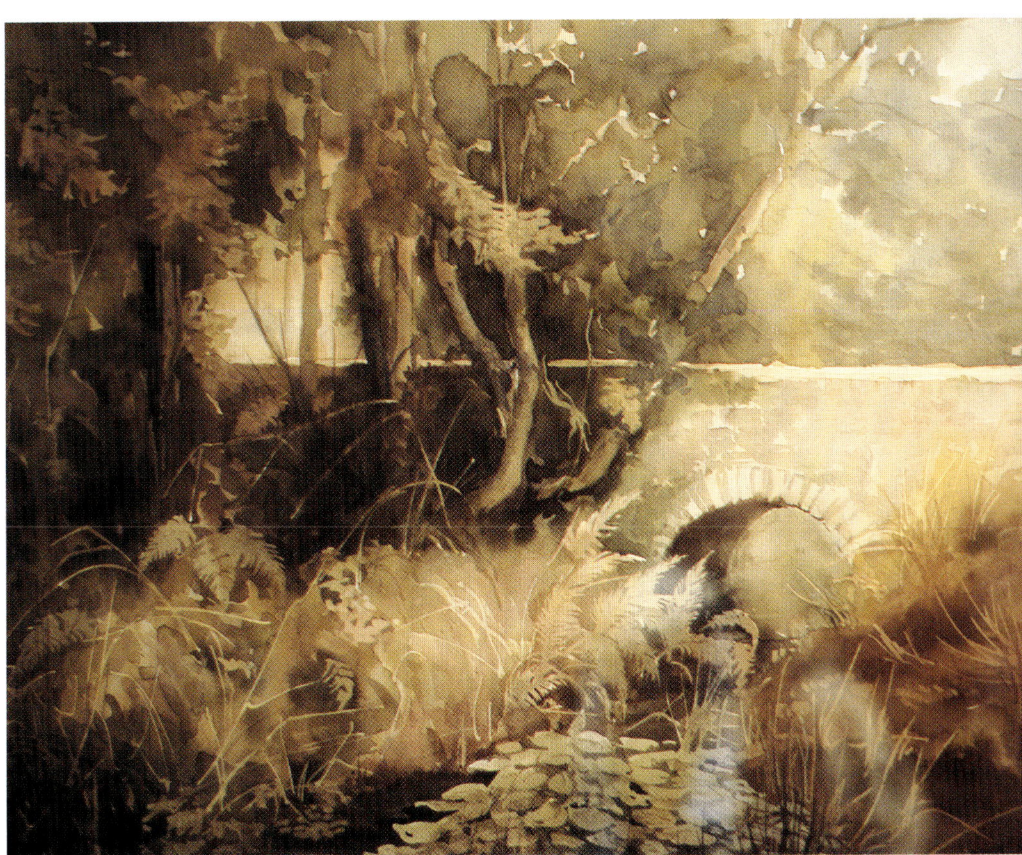

Lost bridge in the undergrowth. *This is an enchanted spot where almost anything might happen! There always seems to be a special quality to the light here, even on the dullest day.*

Swans at sunrise.

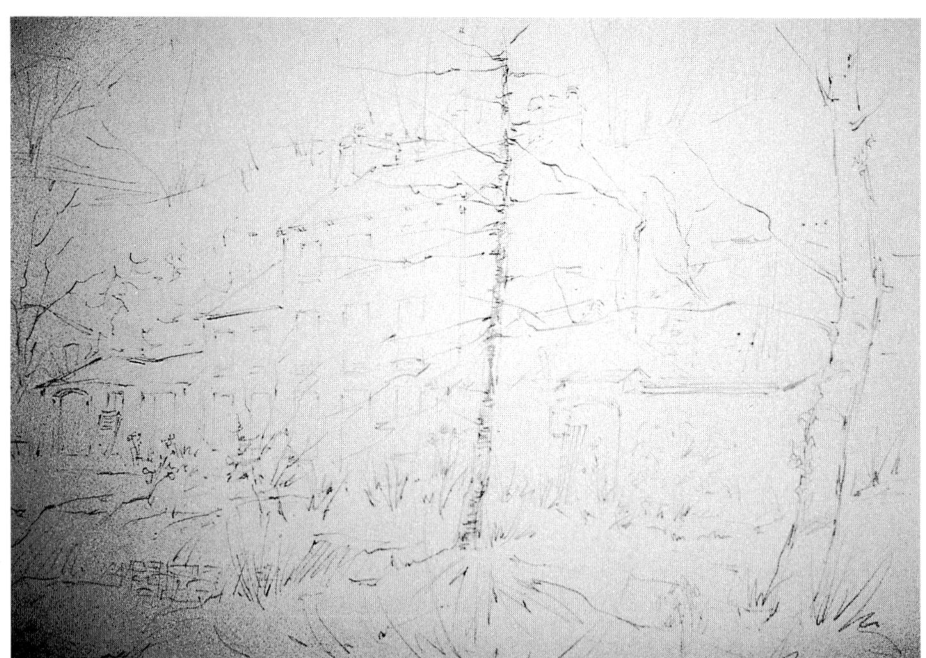

The mill-owner's house. *A preliminary outline sketch made on the spot.*

(Below) A more detailed sketch.

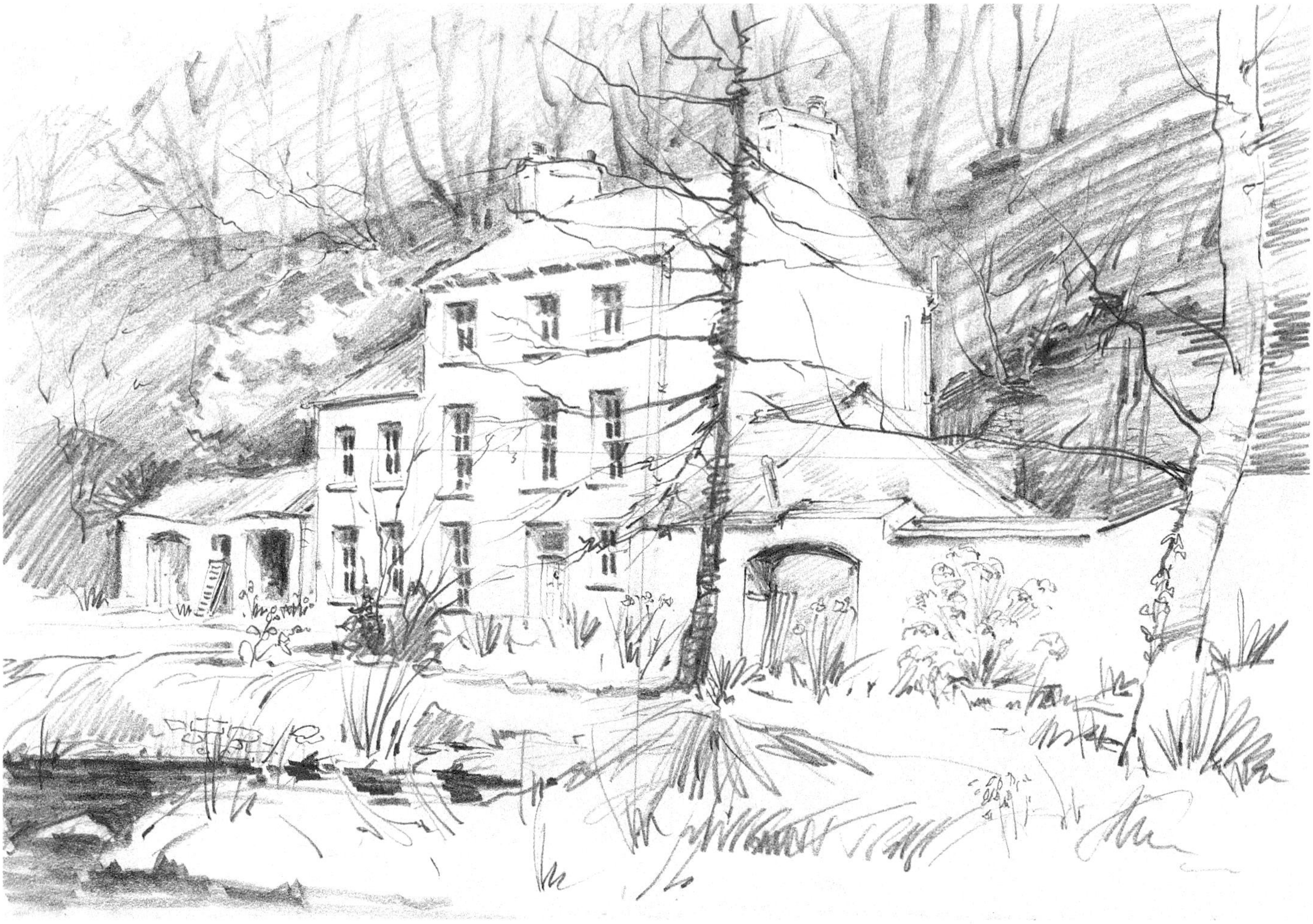

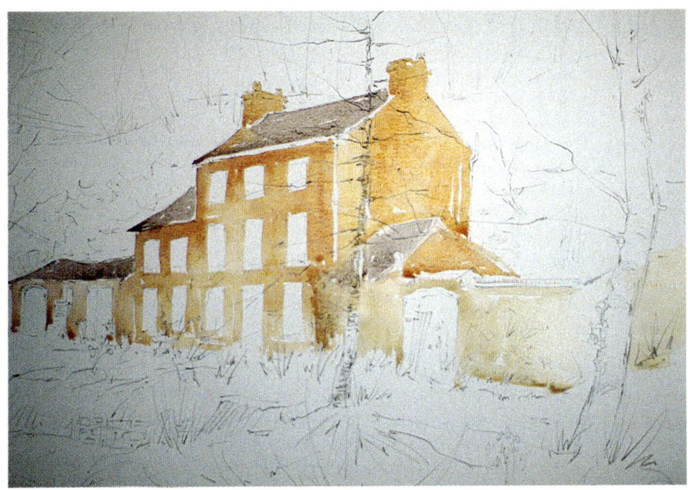

The mill-owner's house. Stage 1, *I began by washing in the warm colour of the house, leaving the window openings untouched for the moment.*

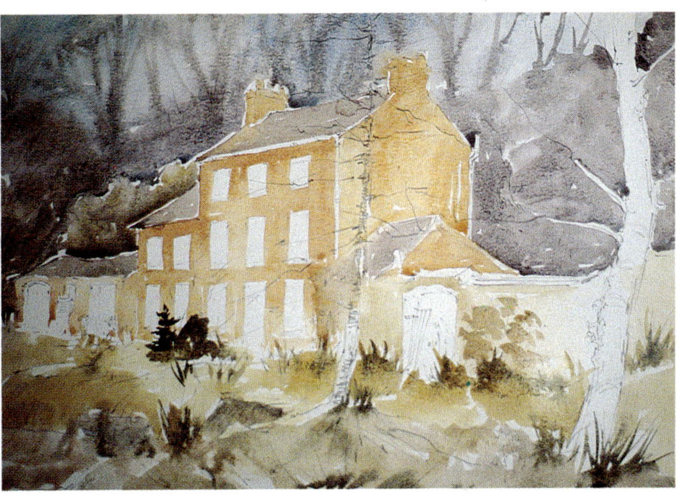

Stage 2. *I used a cool blue-purple for the background trees so that the warm house would stand out, and then introduced some muted warmth into the foreground. At this stage the work was kept very broad and understated. I did, however, set the tone of the dark foliage just in front of the house.*

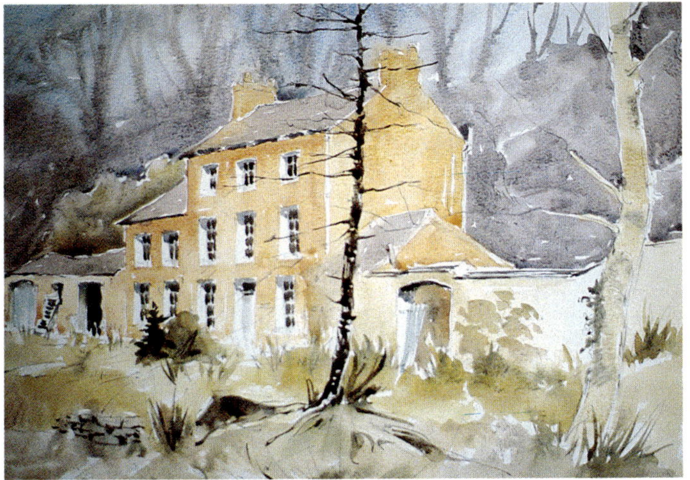

Stage 3. *It was then time to begin some detailed work around the windows and the foreground tree. I painted all these with a large, pointed brush and plenty of liquid to avoid becoming over-tight.*

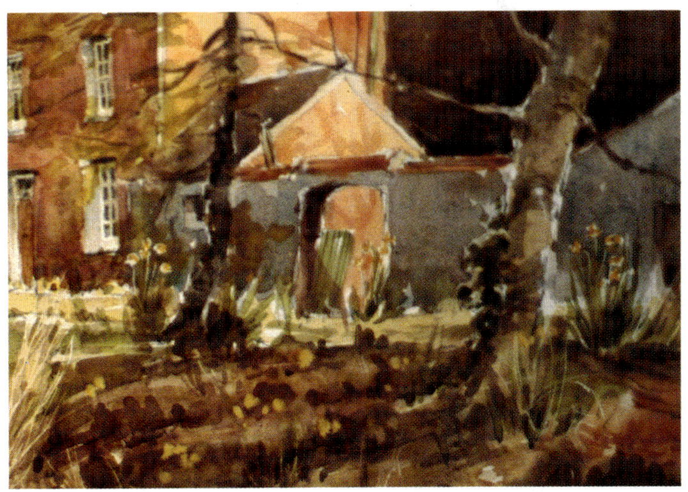

Detail of the finished painting (see overleaf).

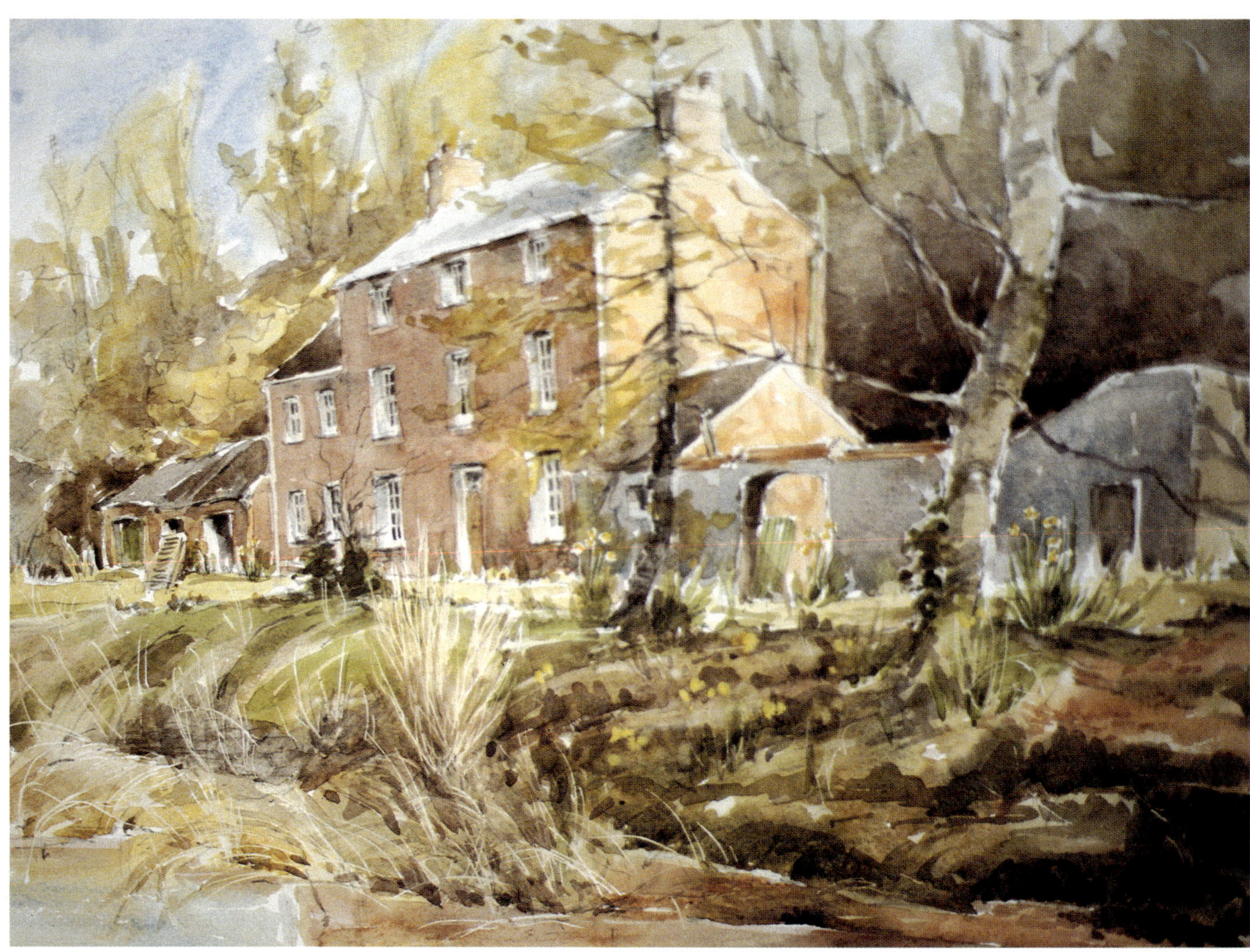

The finished painting. *I added a little warmth to the trees in the background, and brushed in some shadows across the foreground, where the passing stream is also now visible. This gave the impression of far more sunlight, especially after I had darkened the bank behind the wall. This house has been empty for years, and nobody goes there now.*

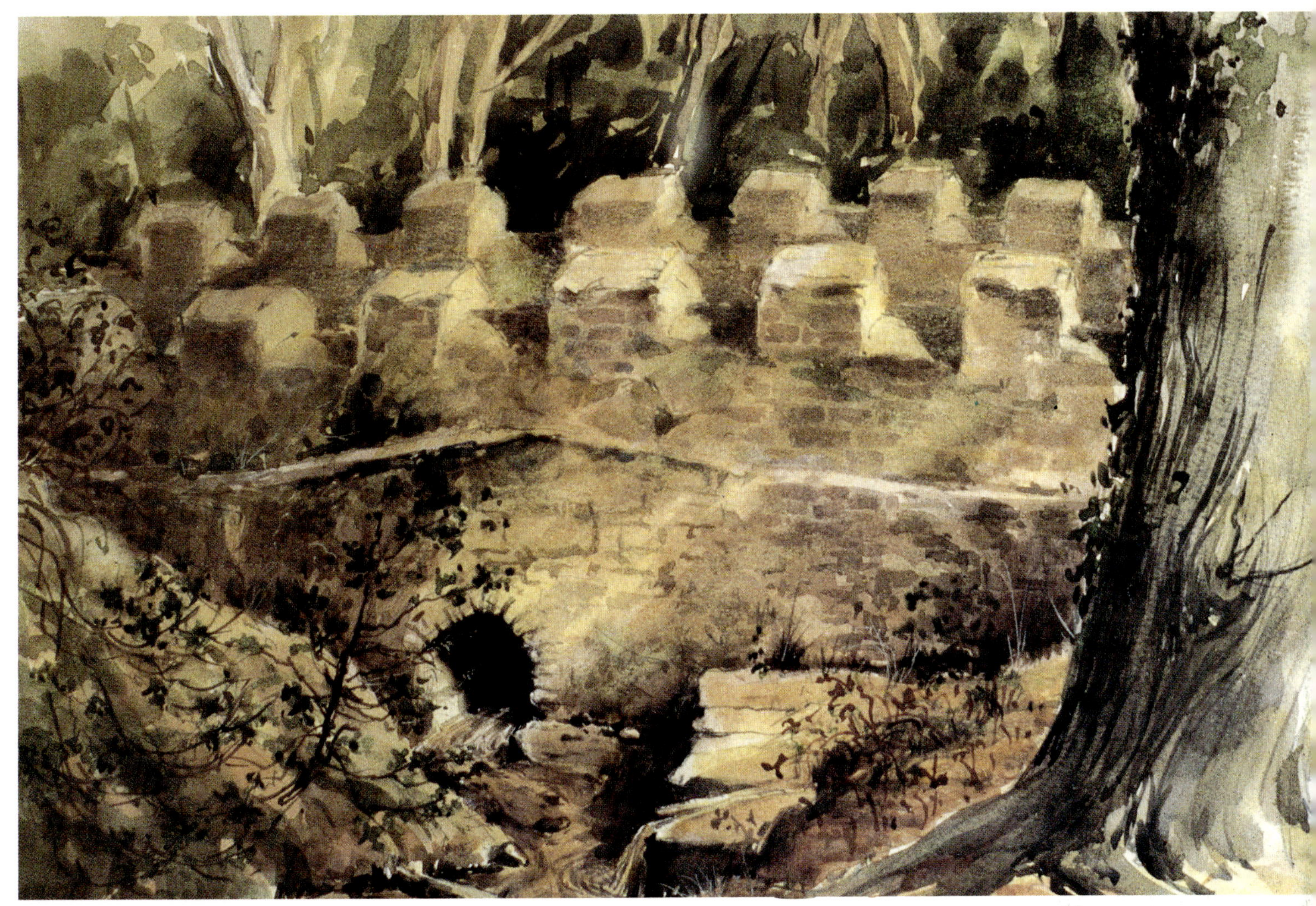

INTIMACY AND DETAIL

Clearly, these are not paintings dealing with broad vistas or great occasions. Rather, they concentrate the mind on the small, intimate details of life, where the excitement lies in discovering a private world of small mysteries. All this involves a certain adjustment in mental attitude. One must be very clear about what one is after, and the mood and atmosphere one seeks to convey. This is greatly helped by having an intimate familiarity with the subject. Spend time just looking, taking notes and experiencing the feel and sounds of the place until you gain some awareness of what its real meaning is for you. Prepare yourself well, and never try to get away with sloppy drawing or unconsidered colours, hoping for the best – this is one occasion when your fascination with detail can be indulged to the full!

Common to almost all of these secret places is the feeling of enclosure, of being in a small, private and slightly mysterious world. There is a delicious sense of being enveloped in something rather special and intimate. We are looking for small happenings: sunlight shafting down to form pools of light among shadows, or things half-seen or only glimpsed through foliage. One is all the time aware of the need to build up atmosphere and a 'sense of place', where you, the artist, play the part of a benign intruder looking in.

If at first the confusion of leaves, undergrowth, reflections and dappled sunlight makes you wonder how on earth it can ever be sorted out and then translated into paint, do what I do and sit quietly for a while as you let your eyes wander slowly over the scene.

Crenellated bridge. *I found this quite by accident on a cold day in February when I climbed down a bank to escape the wind. I was intrigued by the tiny opening in such a massive wall.*

Take your time, and let order appear out of chaos as details slowly assume their rightful importance. The more complex the scene, the more relaxed you should be.

Begin working in the broadest manner possible. The temptation will be to become involved in the minutiae from the start, and certainly it all needs to be carefully planned and possibly drawn in. However, the first washes should be very free, merely indicating warm and cool areas and hinting at final colours and tones. At this stage you may like to reserve certain details with masking fluid (see pages 114–5). Great care is required for this. So often clumsy masking brushwork can destroy the whole effect, and, instead of elegant tapering grasses or fine branches, crude and over-thick blobs are revealed at peel-off time. If a brush fails to give the desired sensitive line (masking fluid does a brush no good at all) try using a drawing pen or even a piece of sharpened stick. Always keep masking to a minimum.

Once the masking is dry, continue to build up tones and colours, perhaps using glazing (see pages 27–9), but be sure not to lose any of the bright spots of sunlight. You will find that you are working towards progressively finer details and deeper tones. Amid such complexity it is often helpful to keep the colour scheme almost to a monochrome, relying on tonal values to describe depth and form. As a final modification, a glaze of cool blue might help to define the shadows and emphasize the contrast between these and the sunlight.

Where the danger lies is in overworking features by building up layer upon layer of paint, until all delicacy of colour is lost in a muddy fog that bears no relation at all to your original intention. Remember that when one colour consisting of, perhaps, a mix of three pigments goes over another mixed colour, the result is a mix of half-a-dozen colours all cancelling each other out. Here there is a need to go back to evaluating light precisely amid shadow, and warm against cool colours, while all the time preserving glowing colour throughout.

GLAZING

I find that the technique of glazing, described earlier on pages 27–9, is particularly useful here. You will remember that this involves the application of pure, unmixed pigments in transparent washes one over the other to build up translucent darks full of colour. Each layer must be allowed to dry before applying the next, and be carried out with a very light and direct touch. Thomas Girtin was a master of the technique, and study of his work would be helpful – look particularly at his treatment of massed trees over dark water. As you become more skilled, allow for more flexibility of working. Let pure cobalt run and combine with pure lemon, for instance, or drop a touch of rose into the wet paint.

The pigments you choose for this type of painting depend on what has gone before, and on the atmosphere you are seeking to build. Be sure to allow for the effect of the underneath colours showing through the new ones, and carry out some 'dummy runs' first, as the results may come as quite a surprise. Employ colour deliberately to set the atmosphere: a wash of cobalt or cerulean over a passage that is too warm will cause it to recede or merge; while a wash of aureolin over a rather drab foreground will cause the sun to come out.

The technique of glazing encourages a slow build-up of mass and the subtle isolation of detail. There is no necessity to rush or to keep large areas wet, and any over-hard edges can always be softened with a clean, damp brush later on. If you can get to the stage of planning the layers in advance this is even better, because you will

Backwater in Venice. *My favourite method of freshening up dreary colours when painting a dull or rainy scene is to use washes of two or three colours only. Here I have used my favourite three – cobalt, aureolin and rose madder – to build up a feeling of rich colour in muted light. I included only minimal detail – just interesting abstract shapes.*

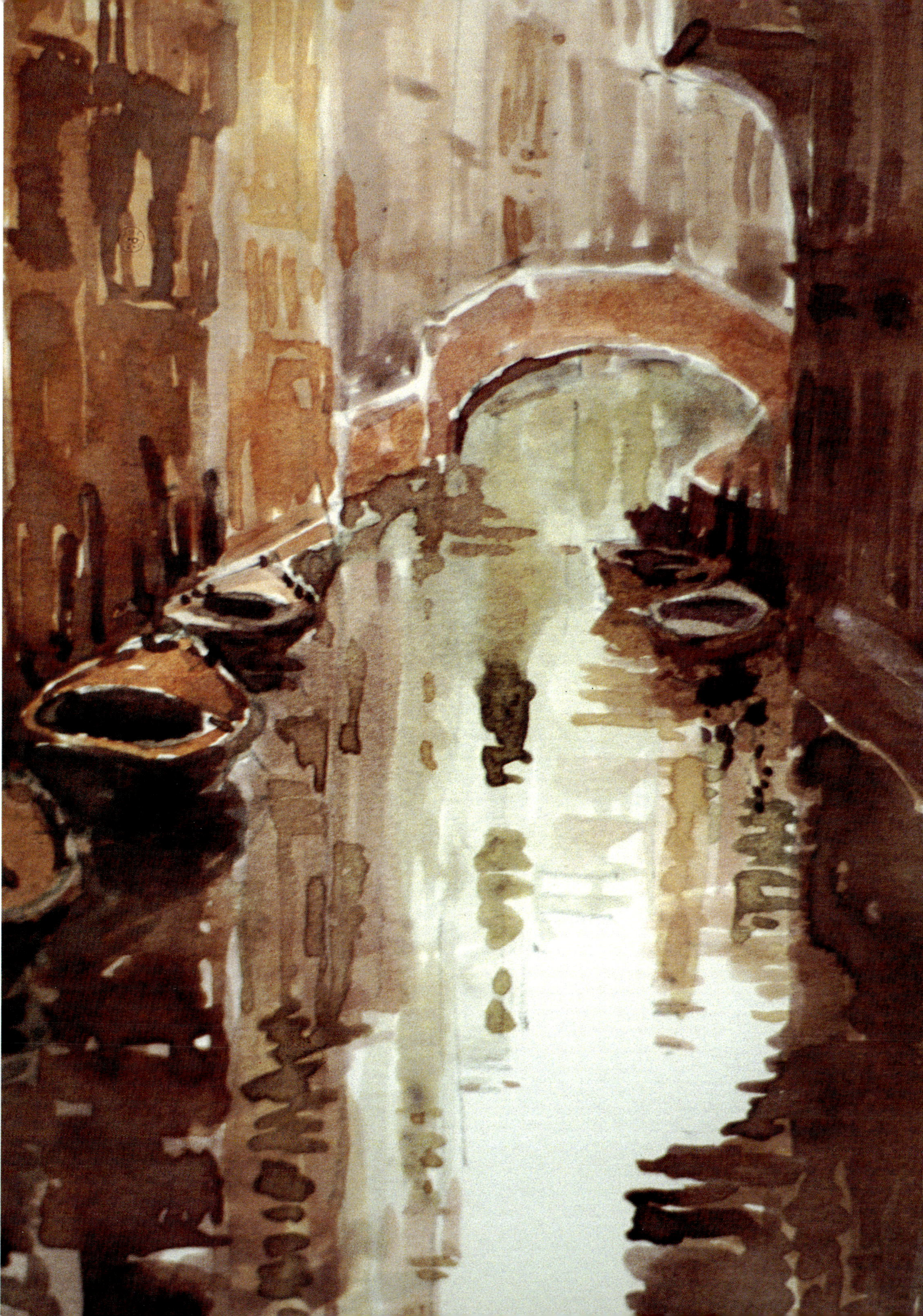

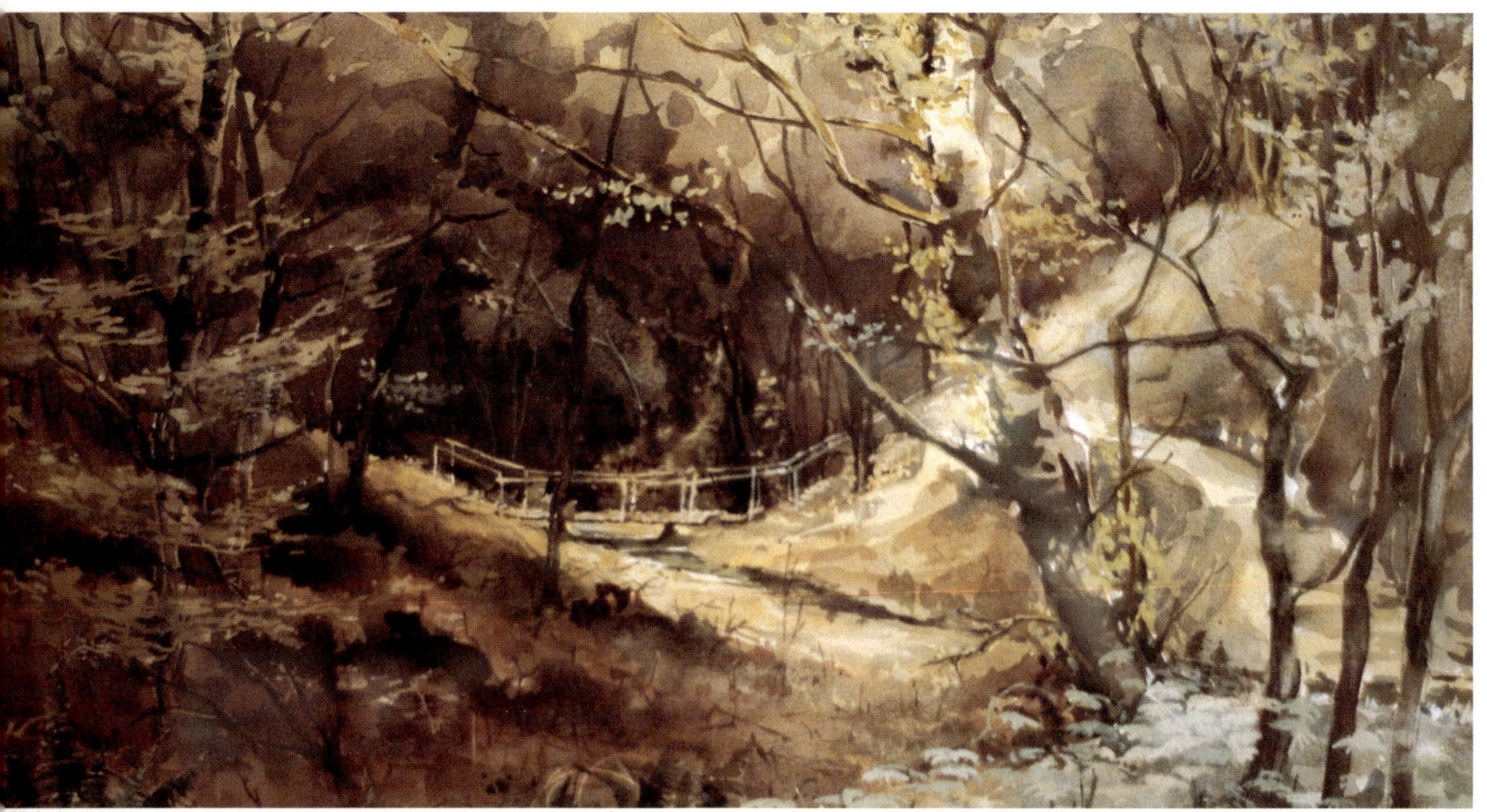

really be in control, with the final effect no longer a matter of chance or happy accident. Use the parts of the painting in shadow as an excuse for subdued yet exquisite effects, and really work hard to get the contrasts right.

MASKING OUT

Mastery of the technique of glazing will not, unfortunately, always be enough by itself to complete the painting. So often it is the sparkle of light on water which makes the scene, or the counterchange of bright grass or foliage against the shade. A technique used by many artists is to mask out certain areas either before beginning to paint, or at various stages during the painting. This can be very effective, but only where it is done with meticulous care and precision, with a fine applicator. Just as brush or pencil marks should have a quality in themselves, so the masking fluid should be applied with equal sensitivity. A clumsy line will ruin everything, as it is only such fine detail as is difficult to paint around that we are concerned with here.

Keep the masking to an absolute minimum to avoid the 'spotted-dick' impression. It is, of course, possible and even desirable to mask out at different stages of the work, as long as the paper is quite dry at the time. This enables marvellously subtle leaf and old-stone effects to be achieved, and makes it possible to isolate satisfactory areas while continuing the build-up of tone elsewhere.

After the masking has been removed, some of the revealed areas will need to be blended or softened in places. Never try to confine this to the exact area left

Woodland glade. *You almost expect to see the fairies dancing! I found this piece of unspoilt woodland while working for the Dyfed Conservation Society, and the painting is now a part of their exhibition.*

by masking, as this will leave you with a dark outline. Instead, wash faint colour softly over the whole section, varying the pressure depending on how much you want the details to stand out.

A candle rubbed over the paper provides a different form of masking, and again can be used at any stage of the painting. The result is more textured and broken-edged: lovely for a rough path or speckled light on water, but the waxed area cannot be painted over, so be careful.

Another way to simulate sparkle is to dry-brush colour across rough paper, leaving broken white paper showing. This technique demands a certain expertise, however, and therefore needs practice, as there can be no second chances.

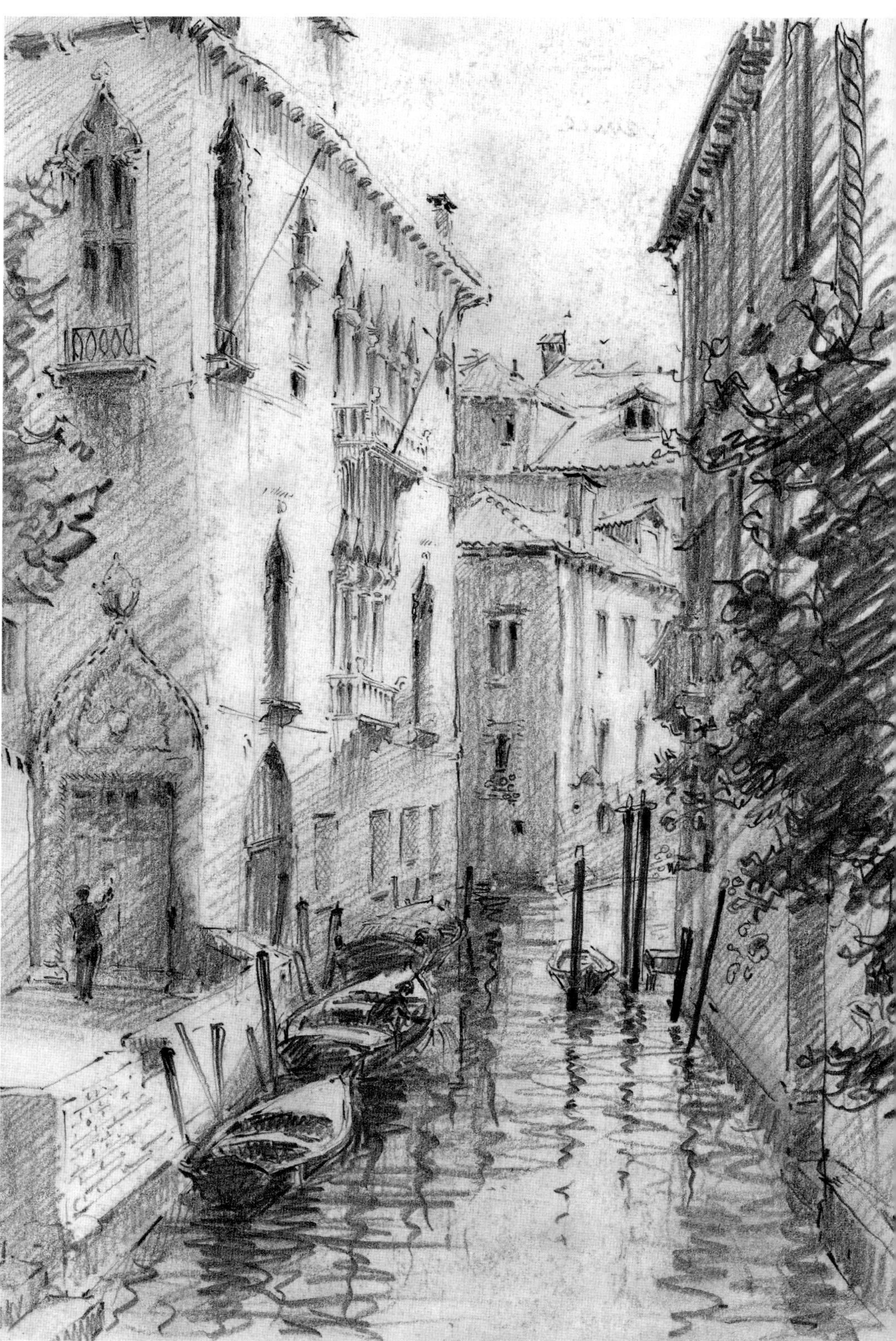

Canal in Venice.

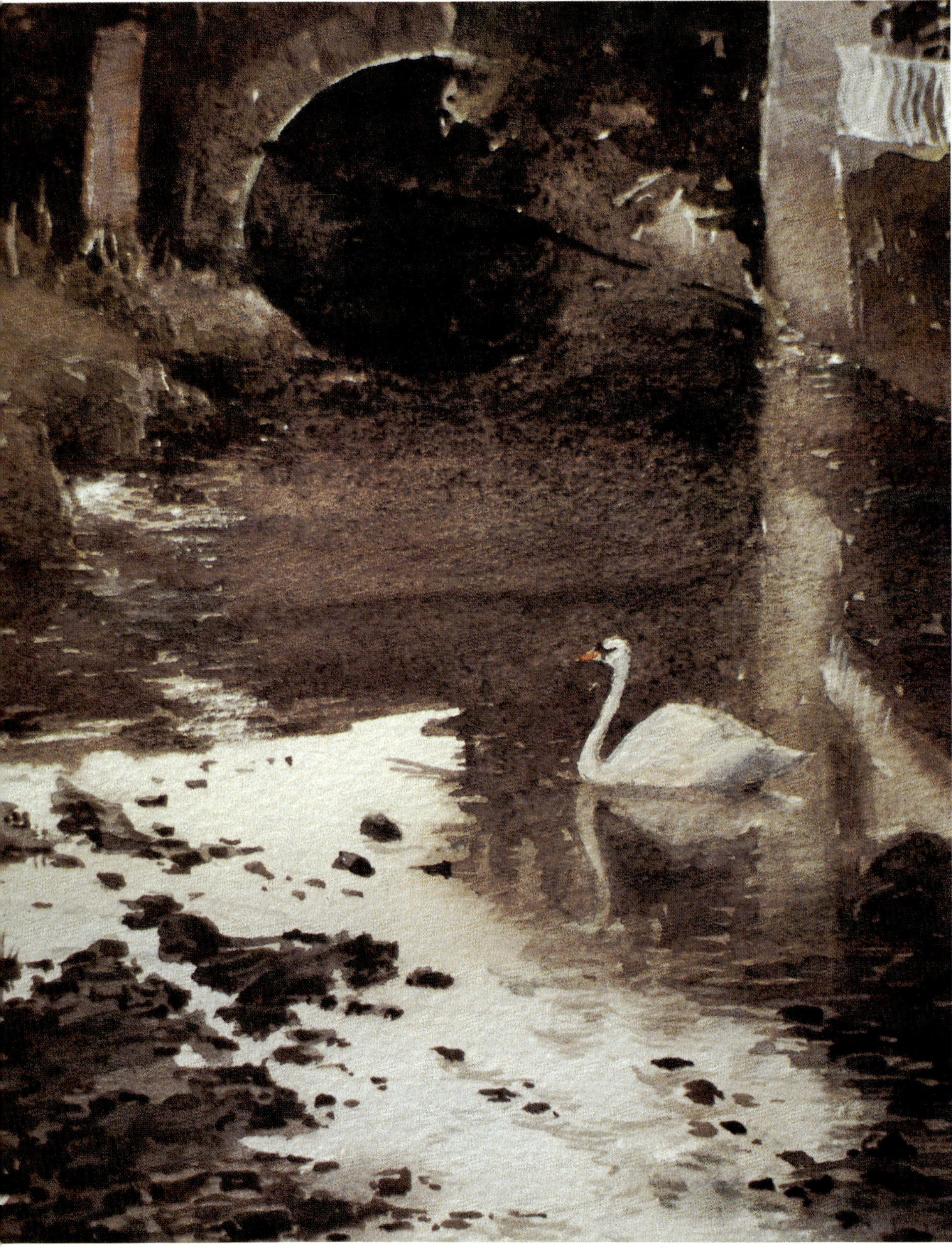

Lonely swan. *The wall on the right and the bridge form the boundary to our garden. This is a very private place, a haven for birds and for many years a favoured nesting place for our swan couple.*

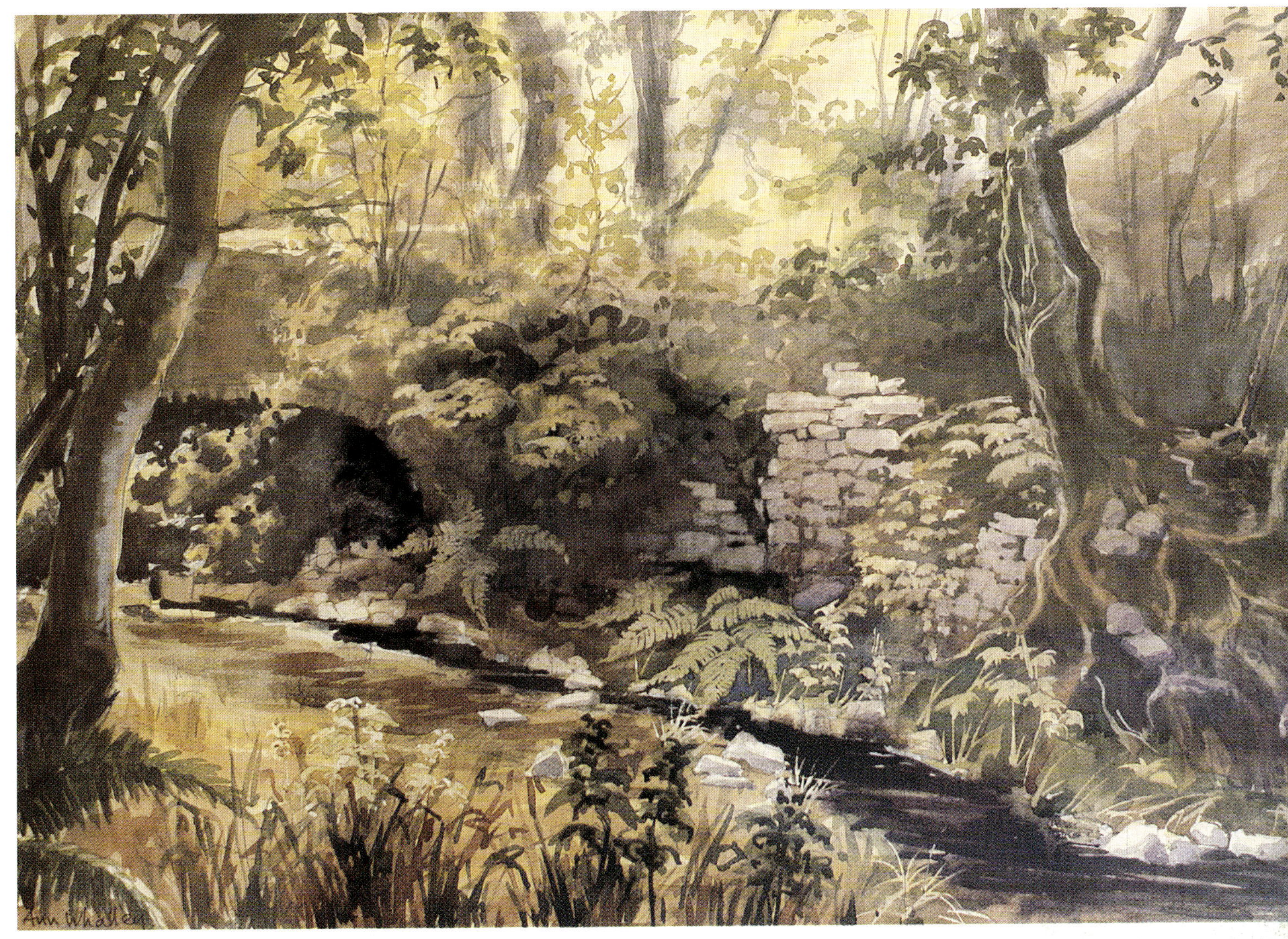

Old mill grounds. *There was once a paper mill here, driven by the 'race' taken off the Cleddau, but it has been a ruin for many decades.*

GOUACHE

A similar effect may be gained in reverse, as it were, by dragging thick white gouache across previously painted, dry, dark areas. Don't be tentative. Have enough paint on a large brush to complete the stroke, carry it out, and then leave it alone. Very fine slivers of light may be best achieved by scraping out with a sharp blade right at the end.

While all these techniques are useful aids, keep their use to a minimum and only where they will have the greatest effect. Make inventions of your own, and experiment and practise all the time to enlarge your repertoire. Relax and become fluent with the techniques, using them not for their own sake but as the means of enhancing your own expression of feeling in your work.

THE ABSTRACT IN ART

It might be appropriate at this point to say a brief word about the concept of the abstract in art. I must emphasize that this refers to what the term 'abstract' means to me, as I do not claim to offer an absolute definition.

I maintain that there can be no such thing as non-abstract art – to say so is to negate the meaning of art. If its purpose were merely to reproduce the world exactly as it is, what would be the point of it? Quite apart from the sheer impossibility of such an undertaking, exact reproduction allows for no intellectual or emotional content, no individualism, no imagination, no reflection of beliefs – all the elements which give art its value.

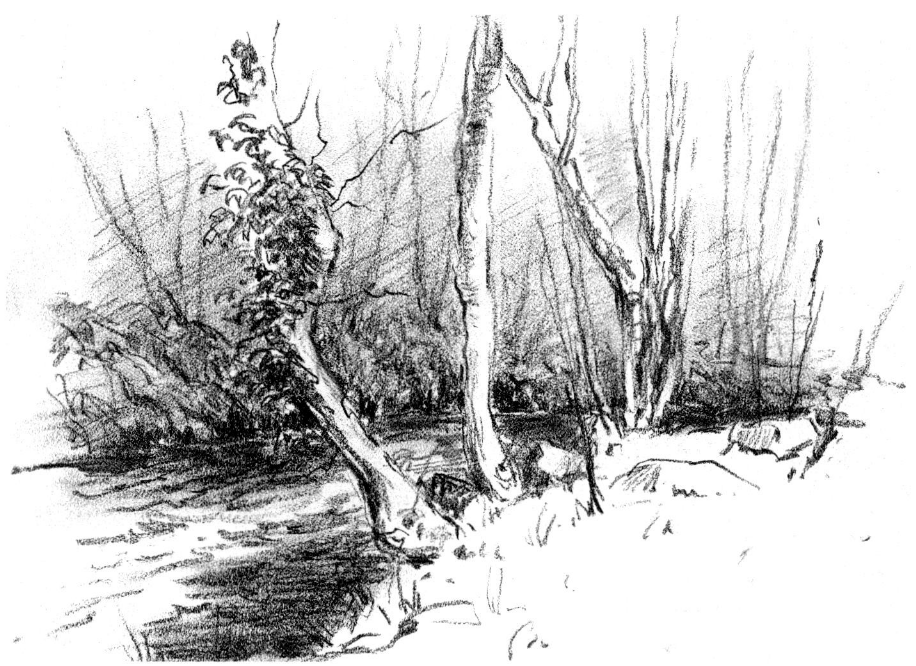

To me, the purpose of art lies in the pursuit of an understanding of our world and ourselves through visual interpretation, and if you accept this, then exact reproduction becomes not only impossible but pointless. In this sense *all* art is abstract, and only the degree and style of the abstraction varies. My dictionary defines the word abstract as 'non-representational in purpose, the essence, an exercise of the intellect, a figment of the mind', and that, I feel, says it all.

(Left) **Tree trunks.**

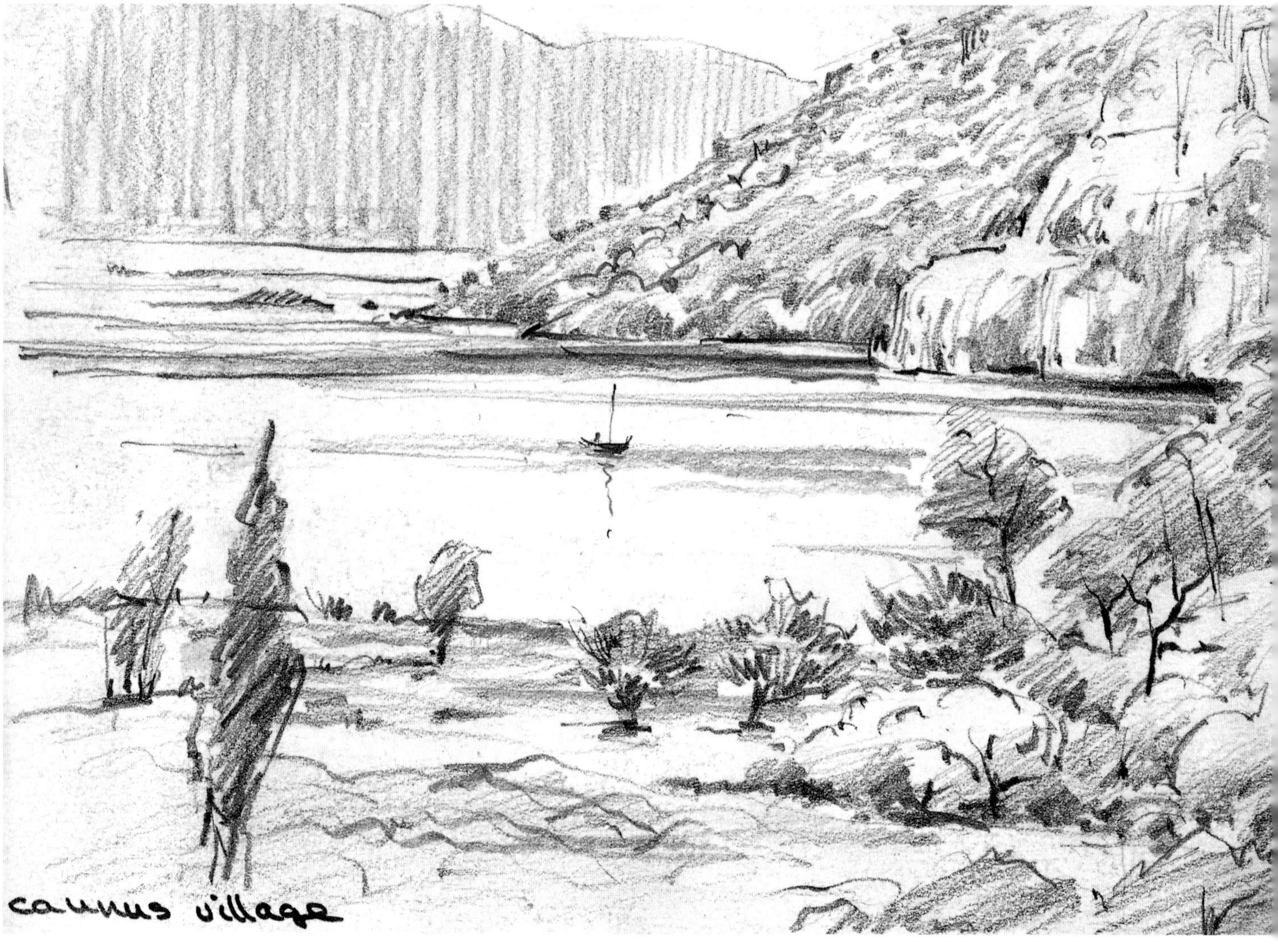

caunus village

The abstract affects us even before we pick up a pencil. As we first begin to assess the potential of a scene, we are mentally making adjustments, emphasizing a shape here, modifying a colour there, or deciding to eliminate something entirely. This is something no-one can do for you, and the degree to which you choose to depart from reality sets your work apart from that of others and defines your own style.

Prove this to yourself by taking what you would consider a very 'realistic' painting and then comparing it to the real thing (failing that, use a photograph) and see just how far the painting departs from the actual – and how much more interesting it is as a result. While it is vital to observe and record accurately and to use nature as source material at all times, this is never enough in itself.

Caunus village, southern Turkey.

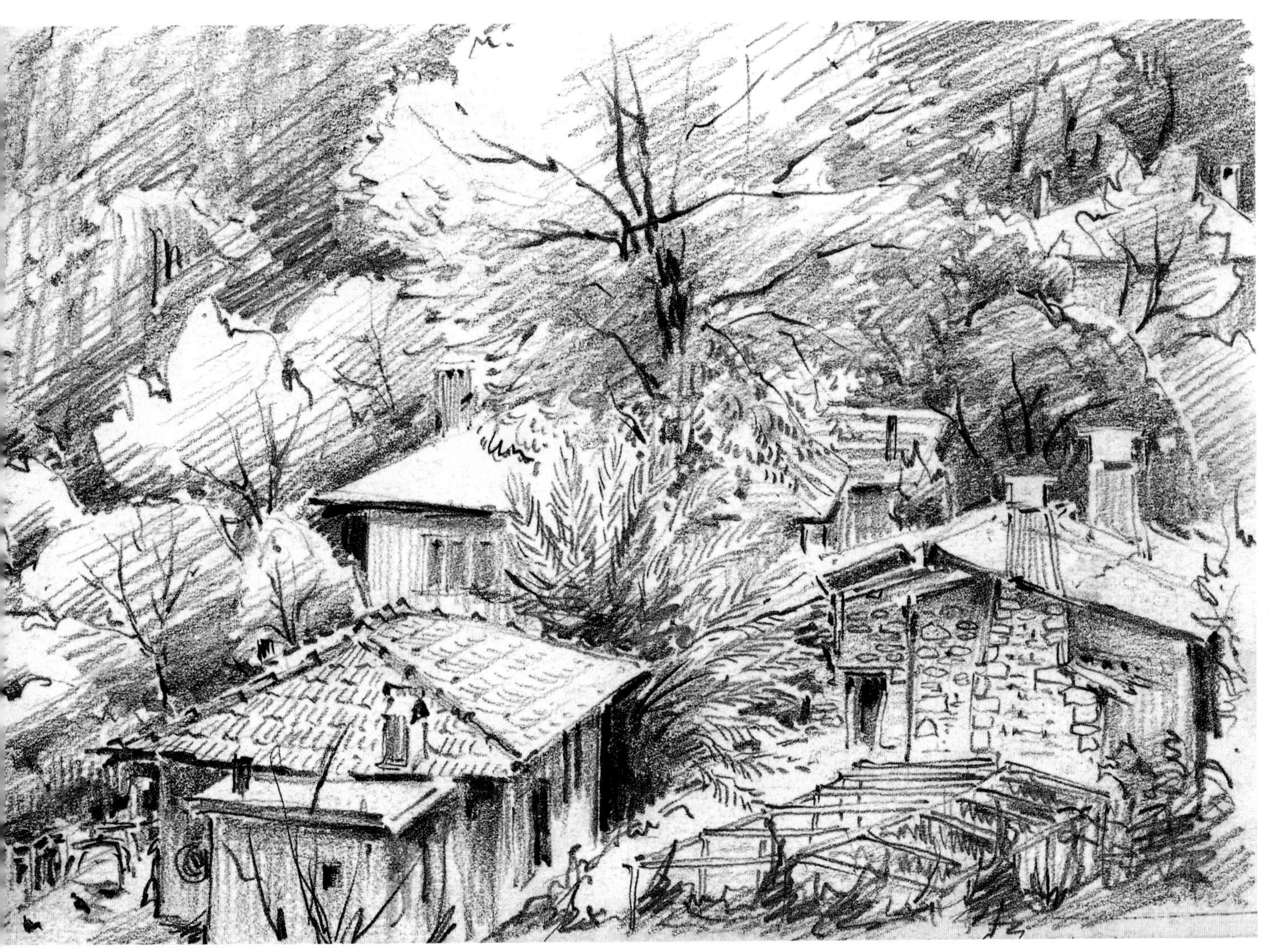

CONCLUSION

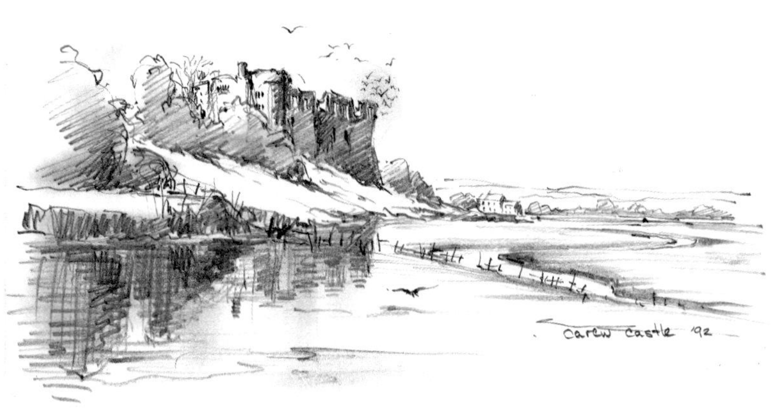

Ending a book is almost as hard as beginning – rather similar to deciding when a painting is really finished. I hope that this book has been enjoyable and of value to you, stimulating some new thinking and strengthening your resolve to see the world anew every day. I believe that from this will grow that personal inner vision which lends even the most familiar scene a touch of magic.

How does one become an artist, or, for that matter, why? I don't really know the answer to that question – it just seems to happen. It can't be because painting is easy or even vastly profitable; the best reason I can offer is the sheer enjoyment that it brings. How good one becomes depends largely on how hard one is prepared to work. I know a number of very talented people who, sadly, will never amount to much as artists simply because they are not prepared to put in the effort; and, conversely, some of my students who can be said to have started way down the artistic ladder have, by their dedication, become very good painters.

Painting is a lonely and often selfish business. You must be stubborn enough to do only what *you* think is right, uninfluenced by what anyone else may say. I believe that one should never paint only to sell, as that road leads to total loss of integrity. Determine your goals and set them high, and then put all you have into reaching them.

Having accepted the need for self-confidence, I don't think it is contradictory to say that, if I have learned anything over the years, it is the importance of retaining a sense of humility. It is a wonderful feeling when an exhibition goes well, and people say nice things and buy the paintings, but, alas, it doesn't last. Back in the studio and faced with the next painting, it is suddenly only too clear that nothing has changed, and that you are still the same learner about to start all over again!

Everyone reading this book must at some time have experienced that shining moment when all goes right; when a seemingly external force takes over and, almost despite yourself, the painting takes shape. Somehow the picture seems to be painting itself with you merely holding the brush. And later, as you gaze at what you did, you can only wonder at the result and the stranger within who was responsible. It doesn't happen very often – about three times in ten years for me – but it is for these brief golden moments that artists live, and for them we are willing to endure rage, frustration and repeated failure.

Hanging trees over Lake Orta.

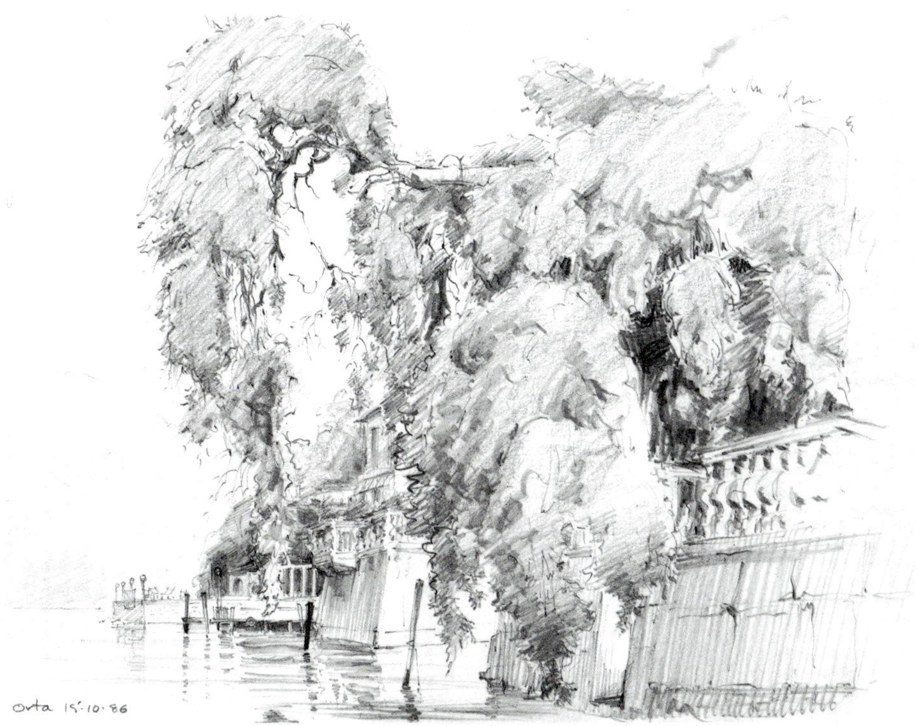

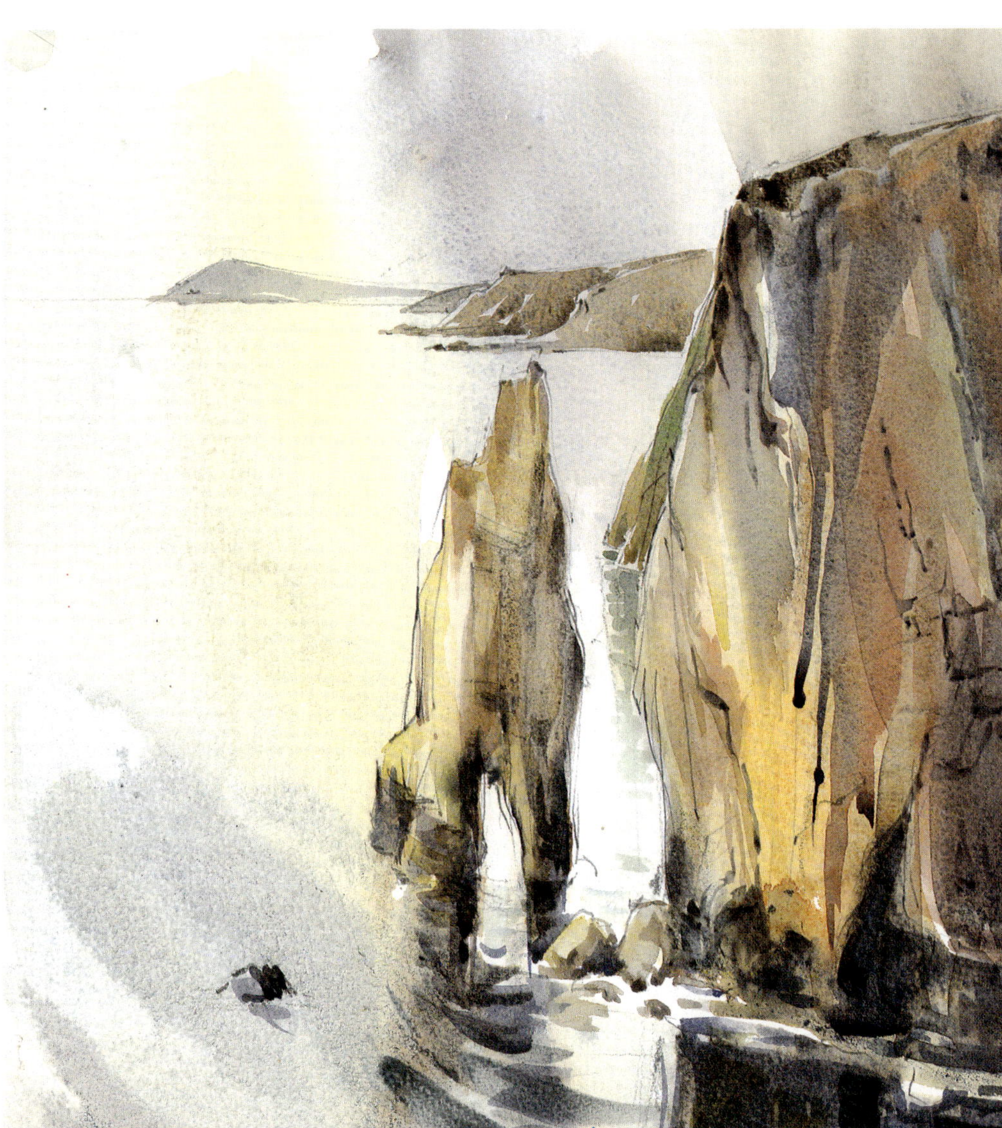

North Pembrokeshire coast – rock arch. *This was painted very wet, using inks as well as watercolour, with the colour allowed to run and drip.*

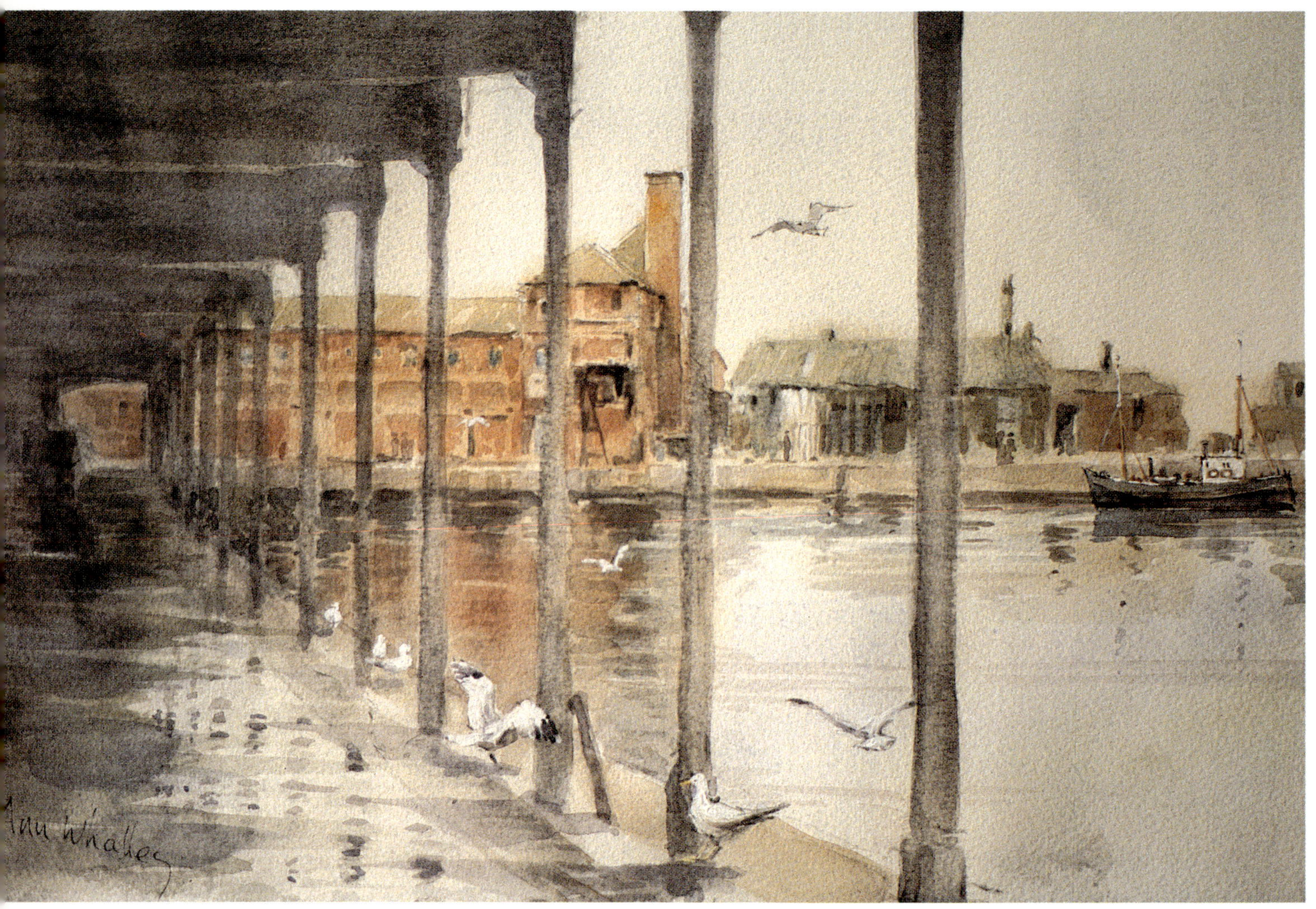

The old fish quay, Milford Docks.

Moments such as this certainly never occur out of the blue, on a day when you haven't picked up a pencil for a week. Anyone who tells you that painting is all due to 'inspiration' is talking nonsense. Inspiration is the occasional reward for years of dedicated slog, so when it happens to you, rejoice: you deserve it.

To return to more mundane matters, let us suppose that all has not gone perfectly and a moment of disillusion has set in. Luckily there are a number of techniques to rectify an apparent disaster, such as lifting and sponging, glazing, changing tonal or colour values, re-drawing, or the judicious use of other media such as inks, pastel, body colour and so on.

Most of these techniques have already been discussed, and I hope you will at least give them a try in your work. Much reclamation is possible merely by removing a little of the pigment in areas where the colour has become darker and deader than intended. Clean water and a large brush easily lifts the excess and leaves one free to try again. There are times when the only thing to do is to put the work in the bath and run the shower over it. The faint impression left behind is often an excellent starting point for another try.

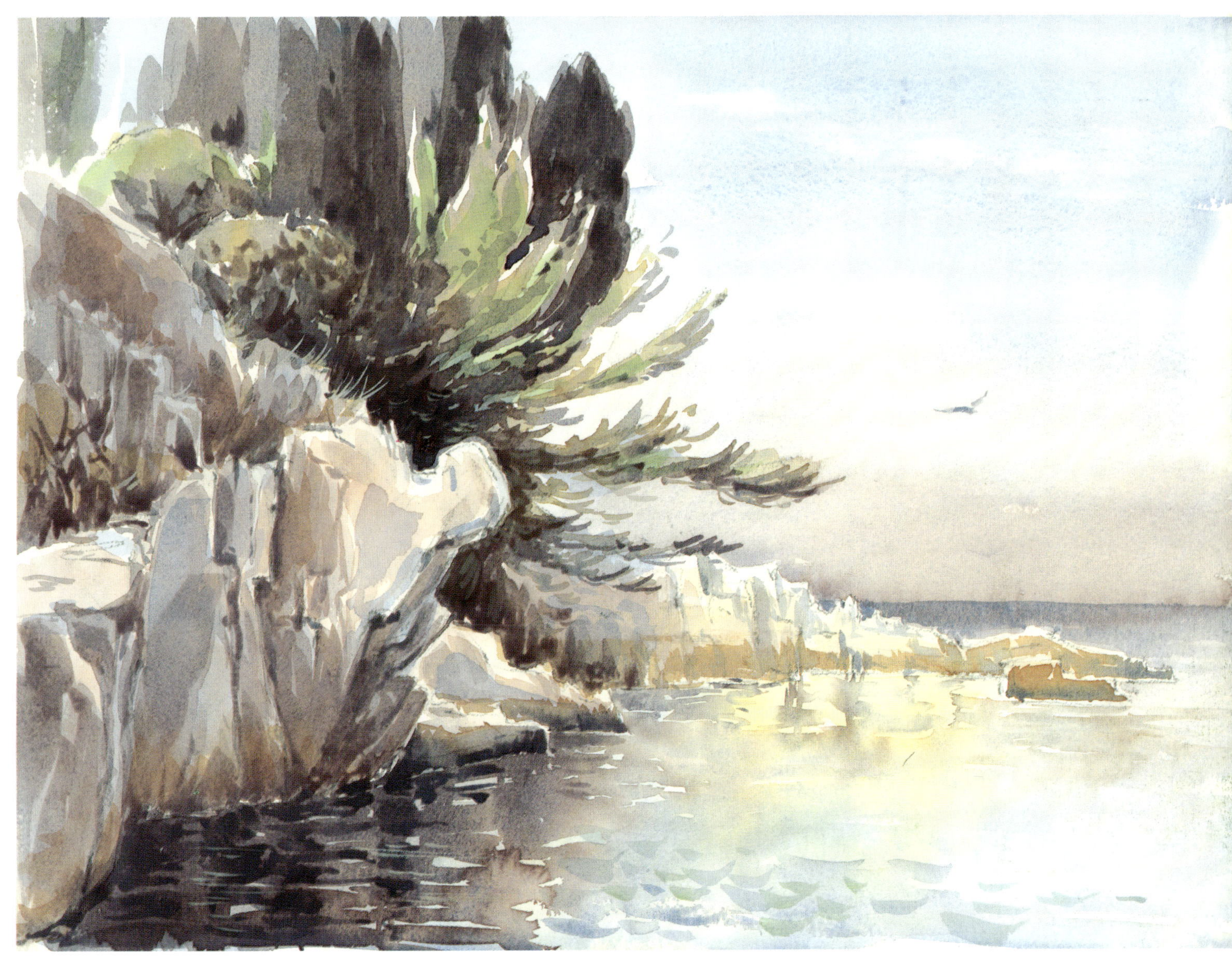

Avoid the pernicious habit of dabbing with tissues, as this always leaves a dirty image and destroys the surface of the paper.

The dark areas should not be neglected, but also made to be of interest, rather than leaving them as dingy, opaque blots. Having lifted out some of the pigment (the paint will probably have been too thickly applied), wash in some cool colour, such as pure blue or lavender, and you will be able to suggest shadow without having to over-emphasize the tone. Indeed, the shadowed side of an object does not necessarily have to be a darker tone than the light; placing a cool colour next to a warm one of similar tone will automatically suggest a shadow, with no loss of transparency.

Coastline near Rovinj. *I completed this painting at home from a drawing that I had made on the spot, but the memory of the pinky-gold limestone rock was clear in my memory.*

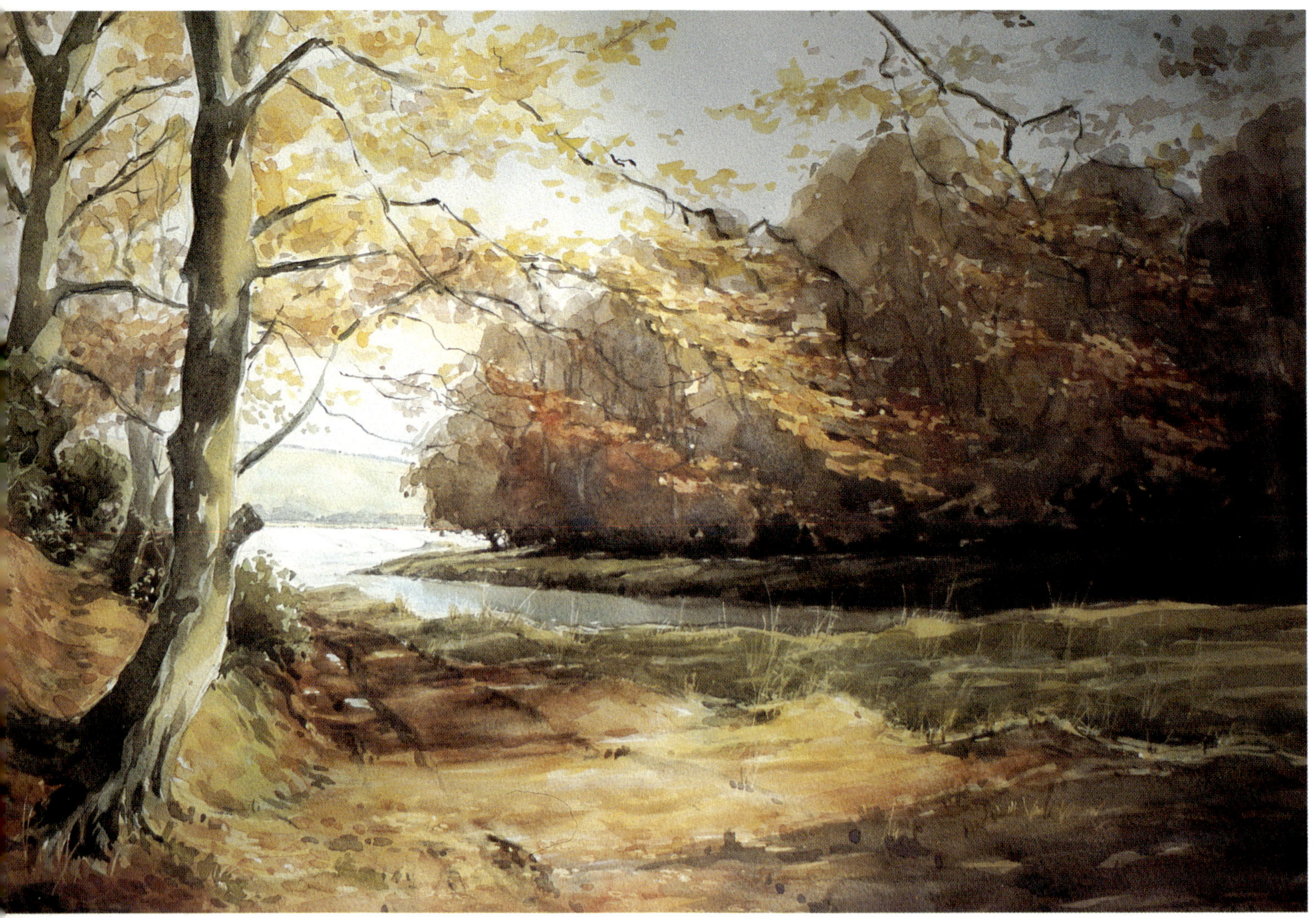

Fernhill Pill in autumn.

Inks are so wonderful to use that it seems a pity not to include them. Their transparency and purity of colour makes them especially effective as glazes, and they can breathe life into tired, over-worked colours. The textural phenomenon peculiar to their use with very wet watercolour offers many exciting possibilities for enlivening featureless spaces.

I try hard to be positive in my thinking when beset by difficulties (most of them, depressingly, of my own making) and strive to cast my mind back to that first moment of excitement which initiated the whole project. What caught my eye? What special quality was present that singled it out? Keep the intention simple and direct, and stop when you have fulfilled the purpose. Be of good heart, and remember that one learns far more from failures than from successes, which, in any case, cannot ever be repeated. Always strive to take another step into the unknown, and never be tempted to go on turning out 'safe' pictures just because you have sold some in the past.

Do take every opportunity to look at other artists' work, even the work of painters you do not particularly admire. Study their methods and their mental processes: what motivated them

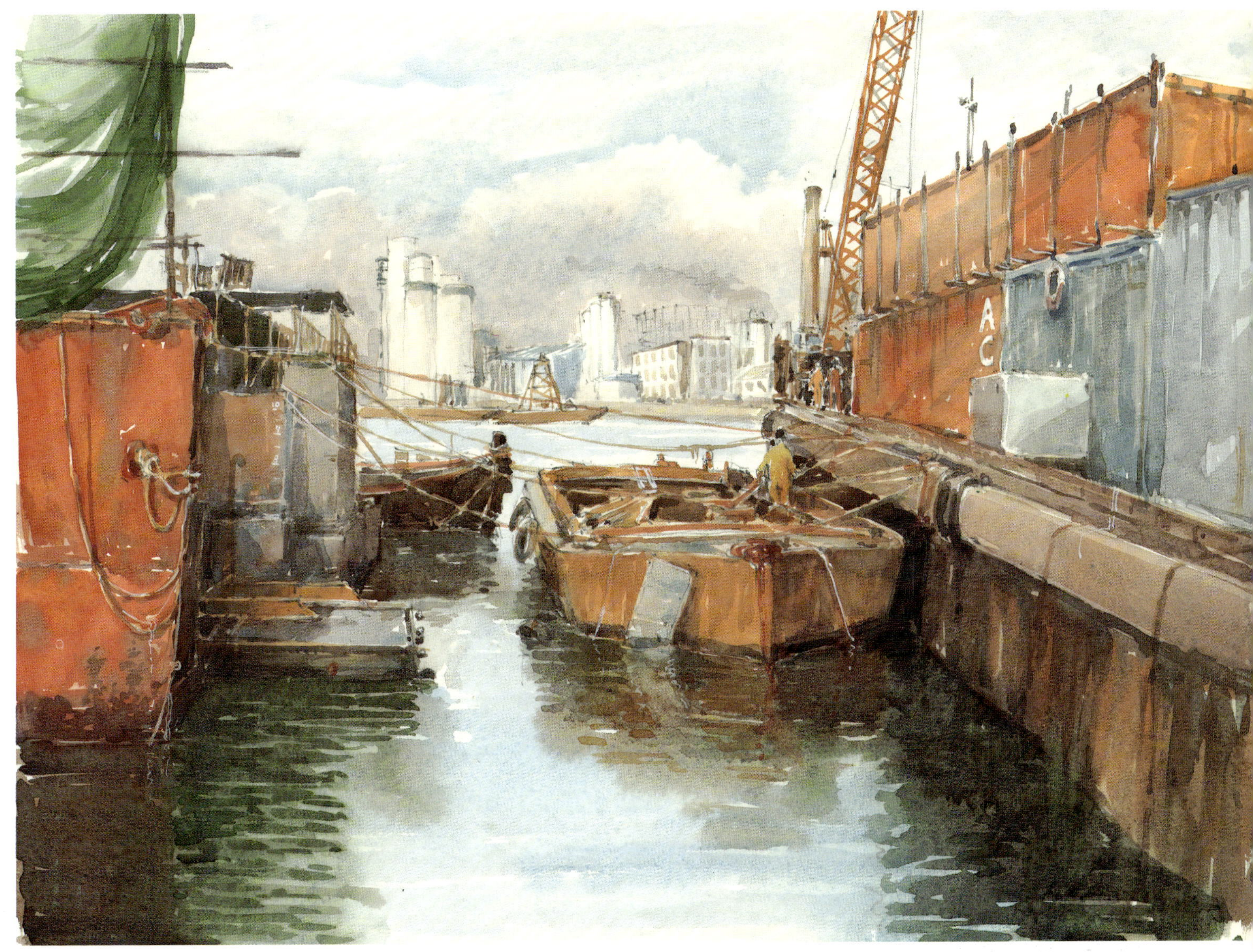

and what are they trying to convey? We are all, great or small, struggling with the same problems, and there are as many solutions. Unfortunately some artists solve them more successfully than others. An honest approach will always shine through a painting, and has to do with direct observation allied with personal interpretation, not borrowed ideas.

When students ask me how to draw a tree, I have to say that I don't know. I know how *I* draw a tree, but what good is that to someone else? I can only advise going out and looking at a tree, and then drawing what they see. I once had a student who came with my group to Symi in Greece, and she had achieved some local recognition for her work at home. One day we all went out to look at the trees on Symi (cyprus and eucalyptus, mainly, plus a lot of olives) and after a while I went to see how she was getting on. To my surprise I found that her trees bore no resemblance to those in front of her. When I asked if this was how she really saw them, she said, 'but I always do my trees like this'! There was no answer to that. Of course,

London Docks.

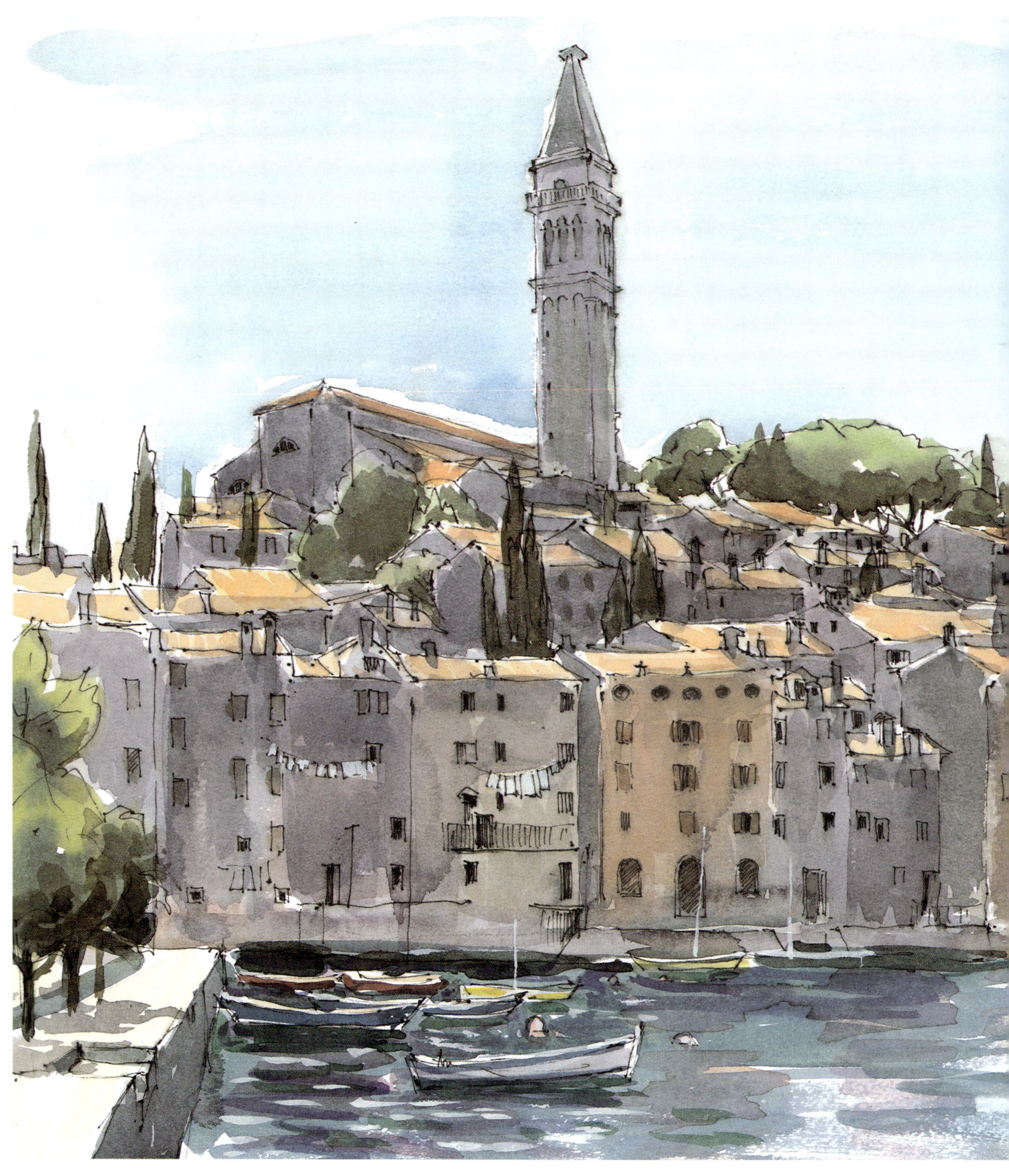

that was a rather extreme case, but it is all too easy to fall back on habit, and to stop 'seeing' the world for the unique place it is.

Always set your ambitions beyond your capabilities, and then strive to catch them up. Your aim must be to develop not a method to paint, but a way to think. The viewer should be interested in what you have to say rather than in the skills you show, while technical expertise should never be paraded for its own sake, but used as a means to an end. A good painting transcends its medium, whatever it may be, to exist as a work of art and not merely a piece of clever work. Give every painting a purpose, and let it grow so that the result comes from your unique vision of the world. Ability varies from person to person, but real integrity shines through like a bright flame.

My life as a painter is a privileged one, and I am grateful that I am able to earn a living in this way. As artists, wherever we are and whatever the conditions, we can ply our trade, be moved and excited by what we see, and have in our fingers an instant means of communication with all the peoples of the world. What more could anyone wish for in this life, but beauty, love and work! So here's to painting and long may I live to continue; and here's to you too, and may painting fill your life with joy as it has done mine.

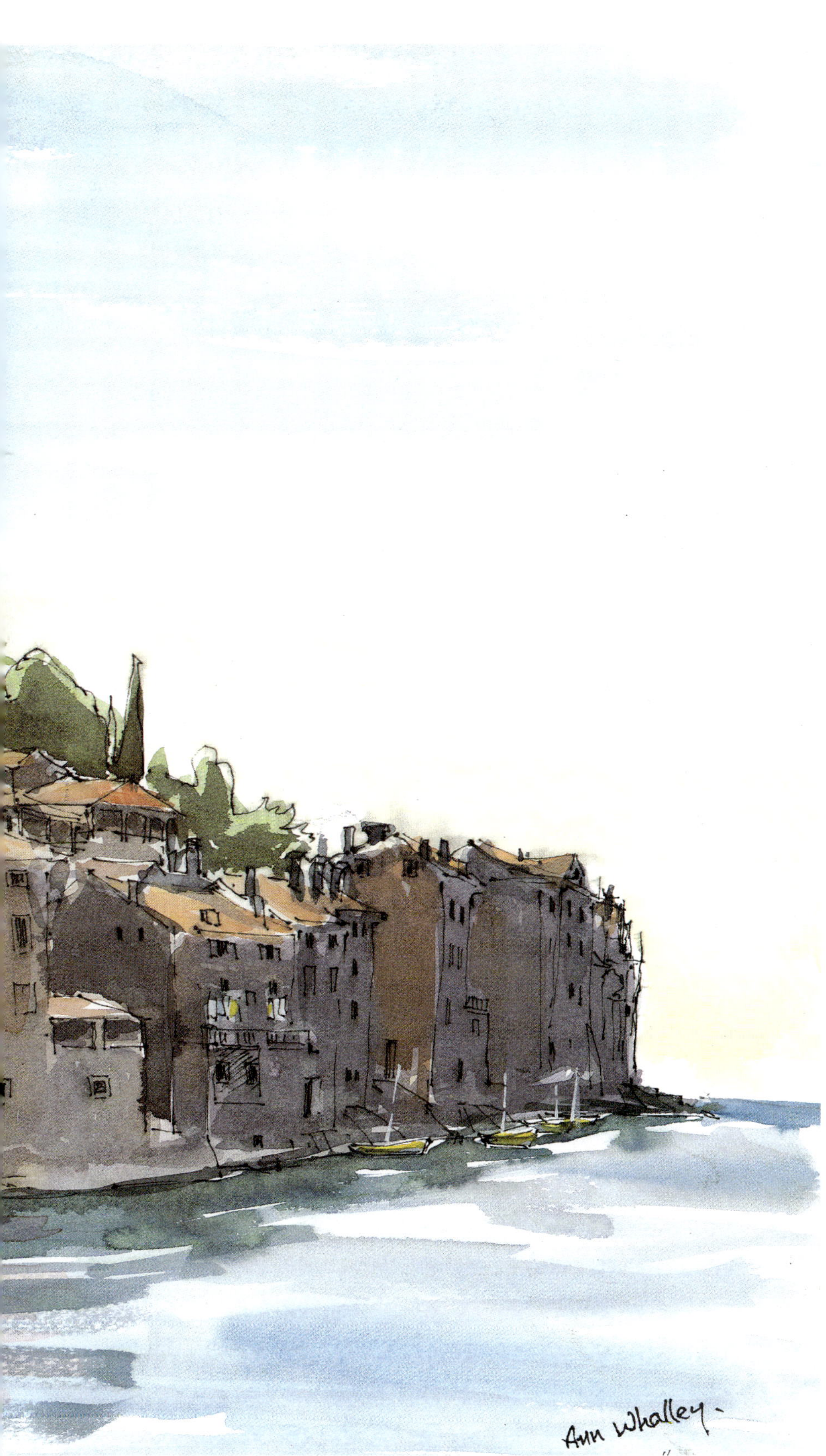

Waterfront, Rovinj.